THE MINDFUL MUSICIAN

ConGratulations
nate ♡
on making it
thru L.H.S. ♡

Bunches of love,
From

mimi & Papa

2021

THE MINDFUL MUSICIAN

Mental Skills for Peak Performance

Vanessa Cornett

OXFORD
UNIVERSITY PRESS

OXFORD
UNIVERSITY PRESS

Oxford University Press is a department of the University of Oxford. It furthers
the University's objective of excellence in research, scholarship, and education
by publishing worldwide. Oxford is a registered trade mark of Oxford University
Press in the UK and certain other countries.

Published in the United States of America by Oxford University Press
198 Madison Avenue, New York, NY 10016, United States of America.

© Oxford University Press 2019

CIP data is on file at the Library of Congress
ISBN 978–0–19–086461–3 (pbk.)
ISBN 978–0–19–086460–6 (hbk.)

Linda Booth Cornett
(1944–2004)

This book is dedicated to my wildly creative mother. It is my hope that
I inherited—or at the very least, modeled—some of her open-mindedness,
love of books, passion for writing, West Virginian pride, offbeat sense of
humor, and obsession with human consciousness and other intangible
realities. She often said, "There is more to life than what we see." In crafting
a book on mindful awareness, I unwittingly immersed myself in something
that can be experienced but not seen, and I learned to perceive a more lucid
reality by directing my attention inward. This book is a tribute to yet another
invisible force, Linda's quiet wisdom.

CONTENTS

PREFACE

> I shall be telling this with a sigh
> Somewhere ages and ages hence:
> Two roads diverged in a wood, and I –
> I took the one less traveled by,
> And that has made all the difference.
>
> —Robert Frost

I often repeat to myself the last three lines of Frost's famous poem, "The Road Not Taken." I love how those words unfurl, with their hypnotic rhythm and slow duple meter. More than anything, I like how they remind me of the very nature of mindfulness.

Our modern culture rewards and celebrates a chronic cycle of striving, achieving, taking on more, and staying busy. Unless we are fully aware of this accepted pattern of existence, we may continue to work faster, try harder, and add ever more stimulation to our already overenriched lives. While this path can feel engaging and energizing in the moment, it can also become a conditioned way of surviving and an unnecessary source of stress and fatigue. We may lose ourselves in what we do, forgetting our authenticity. We may begin to identify with our external accomplishments rather than our own quiet inner nature. Artistic performers who use their bodies, minds, and deepest emotions to bring music to others can experience this struggle even more intensely.

For most readers, the practice of mindfulness will be the road less traveled. A counterculture, it gently defies and heals the social norm of autopilot, multitasking, gadget reliance, and media addiction. It replaces thinking with experiencing, trying with allowing, and doing with being. For musicians, it offers the cultivation of quiet awareness, which in turn creates more space for artistic self-expression. It is my pleasure to explore these ideas and travel this road with you. Like me, you may find that it indeed makes all the difference.

ACKNOWLEDGMENTS

The Mindful Musician was made possible through the enduring support of my students, clients, and colleagues. I appreciate the many musicians, particularly my undergraduate piano majors at the University of St. Thomas, who practiced various mindfulness activities and provided valuable feedback over the years. I am especially grateful to Sophia Hausman, Belinda Huang, Joshua Bestgen, and Erik Gerhardt, who read an early draft of the manuscript and offered their student perspectives and wisdom.

Many professionals contributed their time and expertise in reviewing this book in its various stages. These include Salam Murtada, Kristine Hurst-Wajszczuk, Linda Cockey, and Barbara Lister-Sink. I am particularly indebted to Jeanne DeFoe, who not only evaluated a draft of this book from her judicious and enlightened perspective, but who continues to be my most beloved piano teacher and lifelong mentor. She was the first musician to teach me to listen with my heart as well as with my ears.

I completed much of the valuable research for this book during a sabbatical from the University of St. Thomas. I would like to acknowledge members of the College of Arts and Sciences, Center for Faculty Development, Center for Writing, Wellness Center, and Project for Mindfulness and Contemplation for their financial, logistical, or moral support of this project. I am especially thankful for my mindfulness conspirator at St. Thomas, William Brendel, for his wisdom and friendship. A number of other professionals offered their fresh viewpoints over the years; these include Justin and Carlin Anderson, Henry Emmons, Barbara Nordstrom-Loeb, Merra Young, Julie Jaffee Nagel, Jessica Johnson, Paola Savvidou, Mary Ann Spears, Angela Kasper Broeker, Tom Bushlack, Suzanne Schons, Sarah Schmalenberger, Craig Eliason, Erika Scheurer, and Marvin Belzer.

I am indebted to many at Oxford University Press, including Suzanne Ryan, editor-in-chief of humanities and executive editor for music books, Victoria Dixon, editorial assistant, and Victoria Danahy, copyeditor, for their assistance and expertise in preparing this manuscript for publication.

Finally, this book would never have transpired without the relentless support of my husband, Salam Murtada. He sparked the research that began many years ago and that ultimately brought me here.

I use pseudonyms for all names except for my husband.

ABOUT THE COMPANION WEBSITE

www.oup.com/us/themindfulmusician

We have created a website to accompany *The Mindful Musician: Mental Skills for Peak Performance*. This website includes audio files of guided breathing, relaxation, and creative imagery exercises, as well as a number of downloadable assessments, forms, and templates for many of the activities presented in this book. The reader is encouraged to consult this resource as needed. Materials available online are indicated in the text with this symbol ⊕.

THE MINDFUL MUSICIAN

1 THE MINDFUL MUSICIAN

This book begins with a true story.

Once upon a time, I had the opportunity to attend the Van Cliburn International Piano Competition for Outstanding Amateurs in Fort Worth, Texas. This quadrennial event attracted just under 100 adult competitors from six countries and received much attention from the media because of the reputation of the founder himself, Van Cliburn. It featured doctors, attorneys, computer scientists, and retired homemakers who performed at an incredibly high level. I traveled to Fort Worth because my husband was competing in the event, but I was also interested to find out what motivated the other competitors to pursue their interests in music. I learned a great deal. For example, I discovered that many of them were veteran participants in regional, national, or international competitions for outstanding amateurs. They regularly traveled to these events in order to network and socialize with like-minded adult musicians. I also learned that a surprising number of them took prescription medications to ease their anxiety or just help them "get through" what should have been the exhilarating opportunity of a lifetime. But I learned even more by watching my spouse experience his own personal transformation during the course of this event. At the time, I didn't realize that my experiences there would completely alter the course of my career, including my professional research agenda and my entire philosophy of music teaching.

My husband Salam was an engineer by day and a superb musician by night. Although he had coached with some of the best teachers in the United States, he was a nervous and high-strung musician who experienced extreme anxiety, self-doubt, and even physical illness before each major performance. His description of a concert performance ranged from mild dread to "mental torture," but his love of music compelled him to follow his passion. In the weeks preceding the competition, he practiced the piano daily, took regular piano lessons with an outstanding teacher in the community, and con-scientiously worked to refine his own interpretation of the repertoire. In addition, he and I worked together to help him improve his perfor-mance skills, particularly his level of comfort performing in public.

Although I was more or less flying by the seat of my pants, I devised an impromptu mental training program for Salam to follow. I was keenly aware of his superlative musical talent and performance ability, and I wanted him to be able to demonstrate that ability in front of a discerning international audience. I hoped to find a means by which he could focus his mind and use the excess adrenaline in his body to his advantage, the way top Olympic athletes do. In fact, I collected a number of workbooks and manuals used by athletic coaches to see if I could adapt some of the ideas for musicians. My motivation was based on sheer curiosity. It was a personal experiment of sorts.

As Salam prepared for the competition, he kept a written record of his motivations, reflections, and personal goals. We embarked on an ex-temporaneous curriculum of guided visualizations, self-assessments, mindfulness exercises, and preparatory performances. This experi-ment kept me on my toes; it was a lot of fun, and I figured that, at the very least, it couldn't hurt. I expected that Salam might play better than usual at the competition, simply because he had worked so diligently to address the mental component of performance. What I didn't expect was the dramatic transformation that I observed from my seat in the audience. The man who walked across the stage with uncharacteristic ease and confidence was a man I barely recognized as my husband. His smile was warm and sincere as he greeted a thousand applauding ticket holders, which included members of the international media. As he began to play, I was stunned to hear the change in his music. His technique seemed so natural, his musicianship so compelling, that if I were not watching him I might have thought I were listening to a pro-fessional concert pianist. Afterward, the self-described "basket case" who normally agonized over every missed note was grinning, genu-inely pleased with the experience. In fact, that performance garnered the attention of many critics in attendance, and subsequently Salam was interviewed by *The London Times* and the *Fort Worth Star-Telegram*, and was featured on BBC Radio. He had demonstrated a friendly command not only of the instrument, but of his own sensitive mind. I realized that all of us, regardless of our age, experience, or level of ability, are worthy of our own similar victories on stage. This was a success story that every musician deserves to experience on a regular basis, so that we can perform with confidence and joy, and we may all live happily ever after.

The End.

No, wait! That's not the end at all. In fact, it was just the beginning. Because of that extraordinary experience at the Van Cliburn, I have spent many years of my life coaching professional and preprofessional musicians who struggle with anxiety and other inner challenges related to performing in public. That journey, however, has been a very slow and arduous one. I am a performing musician as well, and I have experienced countless episodes of preperformance jitters and smoldering self-doubt. Somehow, though, I always found a way to cope with these issues. Many instructors will acknowledge that we can't possibly be masters of everything, and I discovered a significant weakness in my abilities as a teacher. I realized that I was not effective at helping my students manage their performance stress.

My early attempts to support my own nervous students led me to pursue further education in neuroscience research, cognitive psychology, and various mindfulness practices. I spent a sabbatical year away from my university working with sport psychologists, meditation teachers, counseling psychologists, and various medical professionals. I pursued certifications in meditation and hypnotherapy, and these disciplines have transformed my understanding of a musician's potentially powerful arsenal of mental resources. My passion now is to organize and present these skills for performers of all ages and levels of ability.

In the field of competitive sports, excellent coaches and trainers have understood the importance of performance psychology for many decades. To prepare for success in a competitive field, mental skills for peak performance are often embedded in the athletic training regimen from the very first year. Musicians, however, are less successful in their attempts to manage performance anxiety. In fact, music students who quit lessons frequently report a negative experience related to stage fright, and professional musicians who switch careers often cite performance stress as a primary reason. Books abound on the topic of performance anxiety management for public speakers and musicians, but the demand for these resources is considerably less among well-trained athletes. The truth is that there has never been any real curriculum related to psychological performance skills for musicians. The result? The vast majority of musicians, amateurs and professionals alike, lack the mental skills training necessary for comfort and confidence on stage.

If you are reading this book, chances are that you want to become a more successful performing musician or you know or teach someone who would benefit from mental skills training. Any human being, musician or nonmusician, can benefit from the material here, because it transcends the stage and spotlight. After a few years of working through these practices, I began to realize that these are skills for *life* as much as they are for music. I acknowledge that I have just made a pretty lofty assertion, so I will let you read and decide for yourself. I will offer that each of the activities presented in this book has one thing in common: They are all united by the philosophy of mindfulness, which is intimately related to awareness. And, at least in my opinion, any component of life experience that brings greater awareness to that life experience is worth pursuing.

The Meaning of Mindfulness

You are the sky. Everything else—it's just the weather.—Pema Chödrön

Awareness is the most valuable resource we possess as humans. Through awareness, we experience our individual realities and direct our consciousness at will. Whether we feel joy or sorrow, whether our current situation is peaceful or chaotic, awareness always abides in the background with quiet presence. It is the very foundation of our perceived experience.

The nature of human consciousness may seem an exceptionally abstract and fathomless topic to consider, but doesn't music share these same qualities? We use music to express the ineffable, to connect with others in ways we can't explain, and to explore our most deeply personal experiences. When we perform music, we are engaging in a form of contemplation that requires our attention to the present moment. We are compelled to find a paradoxical balance between control and surrender, tension and relaxation, accuracy and freedom.

Mindfulness, in its simplest form, is moment-to-moment awareness. It involves paying attention to *what is*, particularly to the everyday thoughts and events that one normally might not notice. This is a strangely difficult concept to grasp, particularly in a society in which people are encouraged to juggle multiple responsibilities at once. If you think about the proliferation of personal computers, handheld gadgets, social media platforms, and various iThings, you may realize how often we spend our waking moments absorbed in mental tasks or virtual realities rather than in observing our own surroundings. Functioning on autopilot has now become the norm rather than the exception in our culture; this makes it an even greater challenge to focus the mind for an extended period of time. Learning to offset this sort of distracted mental conditioning is essential for creative artists.

Focusing awareness is within our control, but requires regular practice. As an example, you might hold your hand out in front of you, placing it in between this page and your line of vision. If you gaze at your hand, you will notice that the words on the page become blurry or indistinct. If you shift your attention back to this book, the words come into focus while your hand becomes fuzzy in the foreground. Notice that your ability to shift your focus back and forth is completely within your control, and, regardless of how you choose to direct your gaze, your target automatically comes into focus. In other words, you don't consciously have to remember to focus on a chosen object, because all you have to do is gently direct your attention toward it. The same is true of mental awareness. As you read, you can focus a part of your awareness on your physical body: how you are positioned in your seat; the sensations in your hands, arms, or neck; or maybe the sounds and images picked up by your senses. You may not have been aware of these before, until you chose to notice them. Importantly, you can't give these sensations your *full* attention unless you stop reading and focus exclusively upon them. So, you can be completely unaware of your physical body as you read this, or you can split your attention between this book and your awareness of your body, or you can put down this book and give your physical body your full attention. You can allow your attention to wander aimlessly on its own sort of autopilot, or you can consciously choose to focus it. The act of pure observation is frequently rooted in the here and now.

Mindful awareness is one of the many varied forms of contemplative practice. People often think of mindfulness practice as a form of stillness, involving quieting or centering the mind, or sitting down to meditate with the eyes closed. This can be true, but it is only a very small component of contemplative experience. Mindfulness is often awareness in action.

Journaling is one example of a contemplative practice that combines the gentle focus of awareness with original creation. Contemplative walking, running, dancing, yoga, or pilgrimage can all be forms of mindfulness in motion. One can engage in mindful contemplation of an artwork, a passage of literature or scripture, or a piece of music. Mindful music making is not limited to the practice or performance of existing music; it may involve improvising, composing, or deep listening.

People engage in introspective practices for many different reasons. They may seek fresh experiences, more imaginative ways of thinking, greater self-understanding, transformation, peace of mind, or self-compassion. Many approach mindfulness practice as a way to improve their physical health, lower their blood pressure, and learn relaxation techniques. Others are interested in the psychological benefits of contemplation, such as improved focus and concentration, decreased stress and anxiety, and an enriched sense of well-being. Mindfulness is a holistic practice that benefits every part of our experience. Because of this, many people embrace these disciplines with the desire to experience or improve the overall sense of wholeness in their lives.

How can the practice of mindfulness benefit a performing musician? Successful musicians are already experts at directing their attention when they practice and perform, although many of them are interested in improving this ability. The deliberate practice of awareness can yield benefits far beyond the ability to learn music, however. It can lead to greater body awareness, which can lead to improved technique and reduced chance of overuse or injury. It can help improve the ability to remain focused on stage or to quickly refocus after a mistake or distraction. With mindfulness, we can learn to deal with critical self-talk or ignore unhelpful mental chatter. We can develop a sense of freedom and acceptance as we learn to trust our own abilities. Mindfulness is one of the most consistently effective tools with which to manage stress and performance anxiety, and—even more important—to develop compassionate resilience. We will discuss mental skills in more detail later on in this chapter and throughout the rest of this book.

As you work through this book, you will notice that some of the chapters seem to engage directly with the practice of contemplation, but that others seem to focus more on behaviors and habits instead. My goal is to approach mindfulness, in the context of performance preparation for musicians, from a truly integrated perspective. When we are *truly aware*, we are conscious of every part of our practice, from goal-setting to creative imagery to identifying and changing unhealthy thought patterns. Although Chapter 7 focuses exclusively on mindfulness as a formal practice for musicians, every chapter seeks to develop the reader's awareness in various ways. Some forms of mindfulness require that we consciously *direct* our thinking, and other practices require that we consciously *observe* our thinking. Directing our thoughts means making very deliberate choices about our ideas and behaviors. This may include careful forethought, split-second decision making, or actions toward a specific goal. Observing our thoughts often involves a sense of allowing, rather than guiding. It may or may not embody feelings of objective curiosity, or even a subtle sense of detachment from the self. The distinction between directing and observing our thinking is an important one, which will hopefully become clearer as you read. The musician who has mastered both skills holds the most powerful ticket to performance success.

A Diverse Cast of Characters

We all live with the objective of being happy; our lives are all different and yet the same.—Anne Frank

Musicians are a widely varied group of people. They range from the most introverted to the most extroverted people you would ever want to meet, with vastly different personalities, preferences, artistic processes, creative potential, and levels of determination. The challenges that performers face on stage, however, are somewhat universal. I have compiled a short list of scenarios or personality types from the many students and performing artists I have worked with, including myself. Do you recognize a part of yourself in any of these examples? Or, if not, what did I leave out?

· *Amy* is a conscientious musician who practices regularly and experiences steady improvement. She performs well when she is by herself, but if someone else so much as walks into the room while she is practicing, she immediately freezes up. She makes mistakes in even the simplest passages and often feels frustrated and impatient with herself.
· *Bill* is able to focus intensely for a long period of time, which makes his practice sessions productive and positive. When he performs on stage in front of an audience, however, his mind seems to go blank.

Sometimes his instrument or music looks strangely unfamiliar, as if he has never seen it before.

- *Christine* is a confident and talented musician, but comes across as extremely flaky and disorganized to other people. She often forgets her music, puts off practicing, and comes late and breathless to rehearsals. At times it almost seems as if she thrives on procrastination and chaos. She doesn't like this aspect of her personality, because she feels like she is sabotaging her own success, but nothing seems to change.

- *Dave* can't seem to stop the negative voice in his own mind from criticizing everything he does during a practice or performance session. If he listens closely, he can almost hear this inner voice. It is as if his brain creates a constantly running mental commentary that accompanies everything he does, pointing out flaws, mistakes, and disappointments.

- *Erika* psyches herself out before every performance, overthinking her music and trying to remember how each of her songs begins. She frequently convinces herself that she doesn't really know every note or word of the music, and then she worries that she's not ready. Even when things are going very well, she often sings with a feeling of uncertainty or mistrust.

- *Felipe* never plays well enough to please himself, no matter what anyone else tells him. Even after a recent competition in which he happened to win first prize, he could think only about all the mistakes he made and how he should have done some things differently. Not even his closest friends or most respected mentors can cheer him up or convince him of his successes.

- *Gwen* isn't an extremely nervous performer, but any time she plays the piano in front of people, her body suddenly tenses up. She has a hard time relaxing her shoulders and neck, and sometimes she feels like she can't breathe. Often, her hands shake visibly on the keyboard, even if she is feeling confident on the inside. One time her entire leg shook on the pedal, which caused her even more embarrassment.

- *Harry* doesn't want people to know how secretly superstitious he is about performing. He carries a lucky charm in his guitar case and often wears a shirt of one particular color when he has a concert. He tries to get the same amount of sleep, eat the same food for dinner, and warm up for the same amount of time before each performance.

If he skips a step or varies his routine, he feels as if his performance will fall apart.

- *Izzy* always worries about what one critical audience member will think about her performance or appearance. Days before a performance, she will imagine that one judgmental person, the one she knows will be in attendance, and this image clouds the spontaneity of her practice sessions. She often daydreams that she is viewing herself through the eyes and ears of the other person, trying to predict their reactions, opinions, or specific criticisms.

- *Jake* is a fine performer until he makes his first mistake. He tries hard to offer a flawless performance, but he silently dreads hitting a wrong note or missing an entrance, because once that happens, other mistakes begin to follow and multiply, like a steady stream of errors.

- *Kara* is a dedicated musician who is extremely distracted in the practice room. After about 5 or 10 minutes of practice, she thinks of something important that she needs to do. It is difficult for her to refocus until she sends the email or text message that seems to be nagging her. Although it slows her progress and affects her ability to concentrate, she feels compelled to alternate minutes of practice with minutes of checking her smartphone. Some days she is able to keep her phone out of sight, but sometimes she props it up on her music stand in order to keep track of her incoming messages.

- *Lenny* begins to experience performance anxiety several weeks before his actual performance. Every day he worries about what could go wrong, and he often has trouble sleeping. Sometimes he develops embarrassing stomach problems, even when the concert is several days away. He doesn't know how to get a handle on his feelings or physical symptoms.

- *Maddie* is an outstanding musician and performer. She deliberately overpractices her music, making sure she is always more than well prepared for a performance. Her greatest fear is that someone in the audience will eventually recognize that she is an imposter, not as talented or accomplished as other people generally believe her to be. Because of that, her daily life is shadowed by a low-level but constant state of nervousness and guilt.

This list of scenarios could go on and on, but the stories are all strangely recognizable. The real musicians who inspired these fictitious characters are the same ones who inspired me to write this book. Clearly, adequate talent and preparation are not enough if musicians don't develop the mind-fulness skills that can positively influence their own mental processes. It doesn't matter if you perform classical music in Alice Tully Hall or hardcore punk in your grandpappy's basement, because all musicians have one thing in common: They all seek gratifying and successful perfor-mance experiences. Some people call these peak performances or optimal experiences. But what does that really mean?

Peak Performance Experiences

The optimal state of inner experience is one in which there is order in consciousness.—Mihalyi Csikszentmihalyi

Musicians and athletes often strive for peak performances. Those elu-sive experiences, although uncommon, are indeed possible. If you were somehow to recall all of your musical performance experiences, and if you were to categorize each one as a peak experience (best of the best; as close to perfection as possible), an optimal experience (excellent, desirable, sat-isfactory), or a suboptimal or negative performance (fair to poor), chances are that you would wind up with very few peak experiences. If you think about it, those "best of the best" performances are rare. If they weren't, athletes would break their own world records every week, and each music recital would be better than the one before, and that's just not how it happens. I don't mean to suggest that we shouldn't have high expecta-tions or strive for excellence. As the title of this book implies, I believe it is healthy and advantageous to aim for peak performances, because that is what drives us to grow and flourish as creative artists. A healthy balance is one for which we aim high, but can also be satisfied with successful-yet-imperfect performances. If we always *expect* perfection, we will often be disappointed. An optimal performance experience, one that we might label as satisfactory, excellent, even outstanding, is a healthy and realistic goal to achieve.

The previous scenarios describe a variety of unfavorable practice or per-formance experiences that most of us have faced at one time or another. Think back to one of your own disappointing performances in the past. Are you able to recall the specific qualities of that negative experience? The attributes of a disappointing performance might include physical ten-sion, technical flaws, lack of confidence, general discomfort on stage, lack of focus, or excessive self-criticism. Some performers experience cold or trembling hands, a dry mouth, or other distracting physical manifestations of stress. Others tend to second-guess their own abilities as performers or dread the possibility of freezing up on stage. We often focus on these negative characteristics, because they may be the experiences we fear the most. But what if we did the exact opposite, and contemplated the qualities of an optimal performance experience? We would then be on the road to a healthier psychology of performance.

The following are a few characteristics of an optimal performance experience; perhaps you can add to this list. A desirable performance might include a feeling of physical ease, technical security, confidence, fearlessness, comfort, expressiveness, mastery, energy, enthusiasm, quiet awareness, joy, even a sense of spiritual connection. A musician might experience a communicative bond between herself and the music or herself and the audience. There may be a quiet sense of control that does not expand into the realm of hypervigilance. Perhaps an artist knows his music so well that he can let go and not think about how to perform each note or phrase. In this place of awareness, he can focus on the expression and the feel of the music from an almost altered state of perception. Some performers describe this experience as being in the zone. Although it is difficult to describe exactly what or where that zone is, many believe it to be a flow state of consciousness.

I once asked a dancer what it felt like to be in a flow state. Here is roughly what she said to me: "For me, time stands still. The past and future sort of melt away, and I'm only aware of each moment by moment. Sometimes I don't notice my physical body, and sometimes it feels as if I don't have a body at all. My movements seem to be involuntary. I feel a sense of surrender, as if I am relinquishing control of anything. Everything just sort of dissolves, and merges with the movements of the dance." Many people have had the experience of being fully absorbed in an activity, with a positive, energized sense of focus. You don't have to perform music to achieve a flow state, because it can also happen when you are playing chess, building or creating something new, playing tennis, solving a puzzle, playing a computer game, practicing a martial art, or anything that requires a certain level of proficiency, focused attention, and immersion.

The challenge with flow states, or with optimal performance experiences in general, is that many musicians feel they are unable to access these experiences deliberately. If we don't know exactly where the zone is, how can we get there? How can we consciously work toward positive musical experiences and take ownership of those experiences? A mindful approach to performance and practice, especially when directed toward the development of mental skills, can give any musician a more confident and creative edge. This can, in turn, lead to a greater sense of perceived happiness and well-being. To understand how mindfulness works, it is helpful to consider what *well-being* means in the context of being a performing musician.

Musician Wellness

The part can never be well unless the whole is well.—Plato

In Chapter 3 we will discuss several of the mental challenges that performing musicians face. Over the past couple of decades, the topic of musician health and wellness has become an important area of interest for musicians, academics, medical professionals, and research psychologists. The importance of musician wellness is emphasized now more than ever before, and yet there is still much that we don't understand.

What does "wellness" mean, anyway? This term is almost as ubiquitous as glittery nail polish and bacon-infested foodstuffs. Far from being a fad, though, wellness generally refers to the quality or state of being healthy, especially (and this part is important) as the result of deliberate effort. In other words, wellness is proactive in that it encourages the prevention of problems and illnesses, rather than relying only on treatment after something goes wrong. The quality of deliberate effort assumes that you are interested in your own health and happiness and that you will go out of your way, if necessary, to improve the quality of at least one component of your lifestyle. Musicians are well acquainted with the concept of deliberate effort, since it is at the very core of every practice session, rehearsal, score study, or splendid new book purchase.

An important aspect of wellness is the idea of integration or wholeness. Think about the many areas of life that contribute to your perception of your own well-being. Your physical and mental health, financial situation, personal relationships and social life, occupation, even your engagement in intellectual pursuits, all play an essential role in the quality of your life. If one area is compromised, it affects other areas of your life as well. For example, if you accidentally injure yourself on the morning of an important concert, that would certainly affect your physical health and possibly your ability to perform. But it would also affect you psychologically, because you would most likely worry about the upcoming concert or your ability to play well. Perhaps you would be in a panic to find a substitute musician for the event. It might affect your financial well-being if your injury required a trip to the emergency room, and it might disrupt your sense of connectedness if you are obliged to cancel important commitments with your family or friends. We are truly interconnected beings.

A musician's physical health may include any number of factors related to injury prevention and recovery, vocal health, hearing conservation, or physical perception and coordination in general. Musicians often put themselves at risk of injuries or disorders involving the muscular system, nervous system, or skeletal system. These disorders can stem from overuse or misuse of the body, illness, trauma, prior injury, or genetic conditions. Even a musician's unique anatomy or genes can contribute to injury risk. For example, pianists with small hands or hypermobile joints are at greater risk of injury than their large-handed or non-double-jointed colleagues. Height, lung capacity, even gender can put other musicians at a disadvantage, depending on the instrument. Regardless of the challenges we are born with, all musicians share the time-intensive, physically demanding tasks of practicing and performing. Many of us are placed in situations that require us to sit or stand in a specific position, sometimes an unnatural or nonneutral position for the body, for an extended period of time. Often, especially for professional musicians, there are few, if any, days off for rest. Overuse or misuse of the body can lead to muscle pain, tendinitis, carpal tunnel syndrome, vocal nodules, or a whole host of other injuries. Despite the symptoms of pain, stiffness, aching, burning, or cramping, some musicians choose to "play through the pain," an extremely maladaptive practice that can cause potentially career-ending physical trauma. Fortunately, most of us have the ability to prevent such circumstances from happening. Mindfulness is at the very core of well-being.

Musician wellness requires keen awareness of your practice and performance habits, and knowledge of the characteristics and limits of your physical body. Regardless of your instrument or voice type, adequate warm-up time is essential to healthy music making. Healthy biomechanics, a fancy way of describing how we move, includes an understanding of good alignment and posture at your instrument in addition to a well-coordinated physical technique. During a rehearsal or performance, fatigue may gradually affect the quality of your physical alignment and technique. Mindful musicians will take frequent breaks during practice, set a reasonable time limit for practice or performance, avoid excessive repetition of virtuosic passages in a single practice session, and know when the level of music is too difficult for them to master healthfully. Singers are advised to drink water frequently to keep the vocal folds hydrated, limit their intake of caffeine and alcohol, refrain from smoking, humidify dry surroundings when practical, and rest the voice during illness. Because of the holistic nature of well-being, self-care is an essential part of good performance psychology.

Speaking of self-care, every musician should understand the facts about noise-induced hearing loss, which is both irreversible and preventable. The louder the sound, the shorter the amount of time it takes for permanent hearing loss to begin. Most scientists agree that prolonged exposure to noise or music levels over 85 decibels can lead to lasting hearing loss. What does this mean? A noisy restaurant or loud traffic on a busy city street are both examples of sounds that register somewhere between 80 and 85 decibels. At this level, an employee may legally work a typical eight-hour workday without using hearing protection. At higher levels, hearing protection is required in the United States under certain conditions. A typical blender or hair dryer registers about 90 decibels, where noise-induced hearing loss can occur if the exposure is for longer than an hour. A live rock music concert can be louder than 100 decibels, but so can music streamed through a personal music listening device, if that device is used with headphones or earbuds at a high volume.

While the average solo practice session rarely poses an auditory health risk, musicians should be aware that ensemble rehearsals, band concerts, amplified music recordings, and mp3 players often register noise levels higher than 85 decibels. Serious performers are wise to invest in good custom earplugs designed for musicians. Again, our physical health affects our mental health, and our mental health affects all aspects of our lives. Both perspectives of wellness are extremely important components of being a healthy musician, and this book emphasizes the often-overlooked psychological side of performing.

Mental wellness includes the very broad concepts of rational thinking and decision making, the ability to adjust and cope with change or stress, and perceived psychological well-being. Mental health is an incredibly complex subject to consider, because our minds, experiences, and life circumstances are equally complex. The factors that lead to mental well-being involve aspects of our lives that are both within and out of our control. These include relationships with loved ones, our work or school environment, socioeconomic issues, biological factors, family history, life experiences, and our individual personalities. For many people, mental wellness may include understanding and expressing their emotions. For some, it may involve developing a greater sense of self-confidence, self-worth, or a more lighthearted sense of humor. Some may want to learn how to relax for improved life balance or how to take time away from work and practice without feeling guilty. Some may wish to explore issues related to their social, gender, spiritual, or cultural identities. The list is endless, if you consider how many factors contribute to our perceived mental health: optimism, compassion, realistic beliefs and expectations, feeling appreciated, and feeling in control of life's unexpected events.

While it is true that wellness is often recognized as the result of deliberate effort, it is important to acknowledge that not all psychological challenges can be solved by deliberate effort alone. I do not claim to be a mental health professional, and this book should not be viewed as a substitute for professional medical or psychological care. Throughout this book, I encourage you to consider two processes of personal growth that can lead to improved mental health: (1) developing a keen awareness of how you think, while learning to direct your thoughts in a way that leads to happiness and well-being; and (2) cultivating the ability to detach from those thoughts as a friendly and compassionate observer of your reality.

Mental Skills for Performers

The brain is wider than the sky.—Emily Dickinson

Think about all the components of artistic performance that rely most heavily on the refined mental skills of the musician. Difficult technical passages are often made more manageable by thinking about them differently. Effective memorization of music requires a number of mental and sensory techniques. For the majority of performers, the capacity to manage stress and anxiety and the ability to avoid distractions while remaining alert and positive can make or break a performance. On stage and off, the mind is every performer's greatest asset. As Plutarch wrote, "What we achieve inwardly will change outer reality."

Mental skills are internal, unseen by others, and related to how a musician is directing her mind before, during, and after music making. Every musical skill, including physical technique, relies on some aspect of psychology or of how we think about our playing or singing. Some musicians even go as far as to say that *all* technique comes first from the mind. Although that is an interesting topic to consider, this book is focused on those components of performing that are exclusively psychological, even though the results may manifest physically. If you were to include a component of mental skills training as part of your regular practice routine, alongside technical etudes and other practical skills, you would develop the mind and body both consciously and simultaneously. Someday we might even discover that an optimal, fearless performance is simply the happy by-product of outstanding mental skills.

Mental abilities are as diverse as they are comprehensive. For example, a live performance necessitates certain skills to be used in the heat of the moment, no matter what happens. These may include quickly accessible skills related to the deliberate direction of attention, refocusing after a distraction, and positive self-talk even in the event of a mistake. Other tools are used as a way of achieving short-term goals, such as those involved in preparing for a future performance. These include the use of mental practice, imagery, and productive self-coaching in the practice room. Broader and more long-term skills, which can be directed toward the whole of life experience, may involve organization, goal-setting, commitment, motivation, and cultivating a healthy lifestyle. All of these skills—whether focused in the moment, in the short term, or in the long term—require plenty of advance preparation, as well as a great deal of awareness, time, and dedication. In that sense, they are all long-term skills because we must practice them with the same commitment that we would prepare a demanding program of music. If we practice our music daily, why wouldn't we practice mental skills daily?

Regardless of the mental skills you would like to develop, reading about them will not be enough. You would never become a world-class blackjack champion, Olympic swimmer, or great jazz drummer simply by reading books about these activities. Similarly, just thinking about practicing a solo will not give you the proficiency to perform it well at a job audition. As important as our thoughts and dreams are, it is our behaviors and actions that determine our successes. To paraphrase an old Irish proverb, you will never plough a field if you turn it over only in your mind. Of course, there is no way that this or any book can cover all topics related to mental skill development in the comprehensive detail they deserve and in a way that is relevant to all situations and personalities. Understanding some of these skills can give you an excellent start, though, and can lead you to a healthier and more organized way of thinking about practicing and performing. This, in turn, can help anyone become a whole and balanced musician.

According to Miguel Cervantes, "To be prepared is half the victory." The greater the internal resources, the more powerful tools you will have at your disposal as a performer. The artist Paul Klee once said, "And now an altogether revolutionary discovery: to adapt oneself to the contents of the paintbox is more important than nature and its study. I must someday be able to improvise freely on the chromatic keyboard of the rows of watercolor cups." I love the image of an artist improvising with a brush on a chromatic keyboard of watercolors. Think for a moment about an artist who strives to adapt himself to the contents of his paintbox. What mental skills would you include in your paintbox?

Performance Skills Self-Assessment

Being entirely honest with oneself is a good exercise.—Sigmund Freud

All of this information may sound interesting, overwhelming, or a combination of both. It may feel like a daunting task to decide which performance skills to develop or, more realistically, which skills to prioritize first. At the very outset, it will be essential to determine which areas of practice and performance are propelling you toward success and which areas are holding you back. All performing artists possess strengths and weaknesses related to creating, practicing, or performing music, even though many high achievers prefer to focus on their weaknesses without celebrating what they already do well. The following self-assessment is designed to help musicians of all levels establish a personal context before embarking on this journey.

Based on your own personal background, rank each item below according to how often you experience or agree with the statement at this time. Try to be as objective as possible. You may prefer to evaluate your strengths and weaknesses periodically, over the course of several months or years. As your performance experience evolves, your scores will change.

You will find a copy of this assessment on the companion website (🌐 item 1.1).

Passion and Commitment

	Never	Rarely	Half the Time	Usually	Always
I find enjoyment in practicing music.	1	2	3	4	5
I find enjoyment in performing for others.	1	2	3	4	5
I feel passionate about my choice to be a musician.	1	2	3	4	5
I have a clear sense of purpose as a musician.	1	2	3	4	5
I am committed to being the best performer I can be.	1	2	3	4	5
I feel motivated to improve my skills.	1	2	3	4	5

Life Balance and Self-Care

	Never	Rarely	Half the Time	Usually	Always
I get enough sleep most nights.	1	2	3	4	5
I eat balanced, healthy meals at least once a day.	1	2	3	4	5
I find time to be physically active every day.	1	2	3	4	5
I am able to make time for my hobbies and other leisure activities.	1	2	3	4	5
I find adequate time to spend with my family and friends.	1	2	3	4	5
I am able to relax periodically without guilt for not working or practicing.	1	2	3	4	5
I warm up my body before each practice or performance.	1	2	3	4	5
I gently stretch after each practice or performance.	1	2	3	4	5

Life Balance and Self-Care

	Never	Rarely	Half the Time	Usually	Always
I remember to take breaks during long practice and rehearsal sessions.	1	2	3	4	5
I always stop playing or singing if I feel pain.	1	2	3	4	5
I protect my hearing when necessary using earplugs designed for musicians.	1	2	3	4	5
I seek help when experiencing physical pain or psychological distress.	1	2	3	4	5

Organizational Skills

	Never	Rarely	Half the Time	Usually	Always
I tend to manage my time well.	1	2	3	4	5
I document my musical progress in writing.	1	2	3	4	5
I am usually well prepared.	1	2	3	4	5
My life is not too chaotic.	1	2	3	4	5
I often set realistic long-term goals for my musical improvement.	1	2	3	4	5
I set specific goals before I begin a practice or rehearsal session.	1	2	3	4	5
I am able to achieve the musical goals I set for myself.	1	2	3	4	5
When I repeat passages of music in practice, I identify a specific goal for each repetition.	1	2	3	4	5
I listen to recordings of my performances to assess my achievements and my areas for improvement.	1	2	3	4	5

Organizational Skills

	Never	Rarely	Half the Time	Usually	Always
I have an organized practice routine that boosts my confidence.	1	2	3	4	5

Anxiety Management

	Never	Rarely	Half the Time	Usually	Always
I tend to manage life stresses well.	1	2	3	4	5
I am aware of the hidden signs of anxiety.	1	2	3	4	5
Before I perform, I feel excited but not too anxious.	1	2	3	4	5
When I feel nervous on stage, I find a way to cope successfully.	1	2	3	4	5
I am able to interpret my adrenaline as excitement instead of fear.	1	2	3	4	5
I can perform without distracting physical symptoms of anxiety.	1	2	3	4	5
I am able to keep my mind from questioning my own abilities.	1	2	3	4	5
I can express my feelings through music even when I'm nervous.	1	2	3	4	5
I feel somewhat at ease in front of an audience.	1	2	3	4	5
I am able to manage my performance stress.	1	2	3	4	5

Attention and Cognition

	Never	Rarely	Half the Time	Usually	Always
I can practice or perform without distracting thoughts.	1	2	3	4	5
I know when my thoughts are healthy or unhealthy.	1	2	3	4	5
I can identify my emotional triggers.	1	2	3	4	5
I am able to stay focused without my mind wandering.	1	2	3	4	5
I am able to pay attention to whatever I am doing.	1	2	3	4	5
I am able to refocus quickly when I get distracted.	1	2	3	4	5
I turn off or ignore my cell phone when I practice.	1	2	3	4	5

Adversity Management

	Never	Rarely	Half the Time	Usually	Always
I have an optimistic mindset about practicing.	1	2	3	4	5
I feel generally positive when I perform.	1	2	3	4	5
In performance, I can resist the urge to pause or fix my mistakes.	1	2	3	4	5
I am able to recover quickly after a mistake and move on.	1	2	3	4	5
I do not beat myself up after a bad performance.	1	2	3	4	5
I can handle the criticisms of others.	1	2	3	4	5
I know what I can and cannot control about each performance.	1	2	3	4	5

Relaxation

	Never	Rarely	Half the Time	Usually	Always
I am aware of my body when I practice.	1	2	3	4	5
I can sense when I am physically out of alignment.	1	2	3	4	5
I can easily detect excess tension in my body.	1	2	3	4	5
I feel physically comfortable when I practice or perform.	1	2	3	4	5
I practice breathing exercises regularly.	1	2	3	4	5
I am able to regulate my stress levels with my breathing.	1	2	3	4	5
I am able to consciously release tense muscles.	1	2	3	4	5
I practice yoga or engage in mindful stretching or progressive relaxation exercises.	1	2	3	4	5
I know how to relax my body and mind when I am under pressure.	1	2	3	4	5

Imagery

	Never	Rarely	Half the Time	Usually	Always
I am able to envision my own successes.	1	2	3	4	5
I regularly imagine myself performing well.	1	2	3	4	5
I am aware of the images that come into my mind.	1	2	3	4	5
I can deliberately guide my daydreams if I wish.	1	2	3	4	5
I can mentally recreate positive feelings and emotions.	1	2	3	4	5

Imagery

	Never	Rarely	Half the Time	Usually	Always
I can hear my music in my mind before I play.	1	2	3	4	5
I am able to visualize or remember notated music in my mind.	1	2	3	4	5
I am able to imagine what it feels like to sing or play my instrument.	1	2	3	4	5
I systematically use mental practice techniques.	1	2	3	4	5
I know how to use creative imagery to enhance my performances.	1	2	3	4	5

Mindfulness

	Never	Rarely	Half the Time	Usually	Always
I am able to stay focused in the present moment.	1	2	3	4	5
I become completely absorbed when I perform.	1	2	3	4	5
I am aware of my thoughts and feelings.	1	2	3	4	5
I am a good listener to others.	1	2	3	4	5
I have the ability to quiet or center my mind when needed.	1	2	3	4	5
I am able to assess my musical performances with balanced objectivity.	1	2	3	4	5
I can perform without self-judgment.	1	2	3	4	5
I am able to trust myself and let go on stage.	1	2	3	4	5

Mindfulness

	Never	Rarely	Half the Time	Usually	Always
I am able to accept what happens.	1	2	3	4	5
I can handle conflicts with empathy and objectivity.	1	2	3	4	5
I often experience a sense of quiet serenity.	1	2	3	4	5
I treat myself with kindness and compassion.	1	2	3	4	5

Self-Coaching

	Never	Rarely	Half the Time	Usually	Always
I feel mentally prepared before each performance.	1	2	3	4	5
When I perform, I am usually able to do my best.	1	2	3	4	5
I can keep myself motivated when I need to.	1	2	3	4	5
I practice positive self-talk.	1	2	3	4	5
I feel confident in my abilities as a musician.	1	2	3	4	5
I regularly practice mental skills for peak performance.	1	2	3	4	5

Look back over your scores, and make a note of any themes you detect in your answers, or any skills which you would especially like to address or improve. This will help focus your attention in a very personal way as you work through this book. I will be with you every step of the way!

Let us step into the night and pursue that flighty temptress, adventure.
—Albus Dumbledore

HABITS OF SUCCESSFUL PERFORMERS

A good lather is half the shave.—William Hone

The Whole Musician

I have a body and I am more than my body.
I have emotions and I am more than my emotions.
I have a mind and I am more than my mind.—Kabbalah saying

You are more than any one part of you that sings or plays your instrument. And, of course, you know that. Musicians can learn to approach their craft with an understanding of how the body and mind work together to create artistic performance experiences.

A complex living system, your entire being consists of diverse interacting components. Your physical body, for example, includes the muscles that allow you to play an instrument, sing, and express yourself in a variety of ways, but it is more than that. It includes an intricate nervous system that communicates with these muscles, as well as other systems responsible for respiration, blood circulation, and the digestion of food that fuels the body. If imbalance occurs in any one of these areas—for example, if you pull a muscle, are poorly nourished, or experience allergies—the physical body will not work as well as it is designed to.

The mind is perhaps the most complex system of all. The brain is certainly an important part of cognition, and we will explore some of the ways in which that fascinating three-pound loaf of gray matter helps us learn and perform music later on in this chapter. We must also consider that even though the terms are sometimes used interchangeably, the brain and the mind are not exactly the same. While the brain is visible and tangible, the mind cannot be objectively observed or measured. Most important, the mind plays a preeminent role in creating our perceptions of reality. It helps us interpret our experiences in the world around us by creating thoughts and forming beliefs, either consciously or unconsciously. It is the root of our personalities, preferences, and emotional responses to the events that occur in our lives. Because of our minds, we can also experience gratitude, connectedness, peace, and emotional well-being.

To complicate matters even more, the mind isn't the only part of us that perceives our surroundings and learns new things. Research in the area of embodied cognition suggests that, in essence, we think with our bodies as well as with our minds. In other words, intelligence is a much broader experience, one that includes aspects of the motor system related to perception and movement. Many musicians have had the experience of learning a piece kinesthetically or recalling it through "muscle memory." The father of modern philosophy, René Descartes originally believed that the body and the mind are separate but interacting entities. He coined the famous phrase *cogito ergo sum*, "I think, therefore I am." In recent years, however, Arizona State University's Laboratory for Embodied Cognition reinterpreted Descartes to form their motto, *ago ergo cogito*, or "I act, therefore I think." Could both perspectives be true?

It may be easier to think about these concepts in musical terms, since music is also a holistic system of interacting parts. If you think about a tune you love, you cannot really separate the pitches, either the melodies or the harmonic progressions, from the rhythm and meter. If you do, the piece of music becomes unintelligible or unrecognizable. If you were to remove even one part of one component, say, half the pitches of the scale, the music would still fall apart. The same is true of yourself as a performing musician, since creating music requires a delicate interaction among physicality, thought, emotion, and (for some), deeper spiritual experience. Therefore, although this book focuses primarily on the most overlooked component of musical performance, the mind, you will discover that many of the discussions and activities involve the physical body, the emotions, or a sense of transcendental awareness. Mindfulness of an abstract yet simple truth, that everything you think and do affects every other part of your being, can profoundly alter your perspective of yourself as a person and as a musician.

Practicing With Awareness of Mind

Sitting on your shoulders is the most complicated object in the known universe.—Michio Kaku

The brain is a magnificent piece of anatomy. We can train the brain to develop new mental skills until very late in life. Through repetition, we can consciously build up neural connections that help us learn and form new habits. We can also break down neural connections through neglect or distraction. Since this fluid, plastic quality allows the brain to respond to both our conscious and unconscious efforts, it can be continually "rewired" throughout life. Neuroscientists are fond of saying, "Nerves that fire together wire together."

I like to contemplate that idea by imagining that I am breaking a path in the deep snow after a winter storm. Perhaps the snow is up to my knees, and I need to hike to a little shop to score some emergency hot chocolate. The first time I walk through the snow, the process requires great effort. Since there is no available path to follow, I must create my own with each deep footstep. When I return from the store, the walking becomes a little bit easier because of my previous tracks; I can simply step in each snowy depression that I originally made. If I were to return to the store later that day (say, because I forgot to buy marshmallows), the process would be even easier because of the gradual path created by my repeated footsteps. Eventually, assuming that I hiked obsessively to the little store and back, with no additional snowfall, I would create a solid walkway. My journey to the store would become so effortless that I could do it quickly and with very little exertion. I *could* walk a different route to a different store if I wanted to, but it would take much more effort to break a new path in the snow.

This is analogous to the brain's process of building up habits through repeated neural connections. When you are learning a new passage of music, the process is like breaking that path through the snow. The first few attempts require significantly more effort than after you have mastered the passage. This is also why, if you learn a rhythm incorrectly or use a wrong fingering or articulation, it is so difficult and time consuming to correct the mistake and relearn the passage differently. You have to break a brand-new figurative path through the snow, when your brain prefers to take the original easy path. If you imagine an almost infinite number and variety of little tiny paths to little tiny hot chocolate stores in your brain, you can almost begin to conceive of the trillions of thoughts, habits, and beliefs that you have built up through time. The most empowering thing to remember is the extent to which you have conscious control over many of these neural connections. Often we allow our thoughts and behaviors to form without deliberate intent. How much influence would we have over our happiness and success if we paid more attention to how we were forming our own reality?

One time I knew a man who had been through a divorce and was just starting to get his life back together. He had a new job and a new girl-friend, and everything seemed to be going just fine. Eventually, though, he ended up seeing a therapist because of a crushing sense of despair he began to feel each day. He came to realize that although he usually felt fine in the morning and during the day, by the time he came home from work, he was in tears. He felt hopeless and lonely, even though he had two great kids and many close friends. There was absolutely no humor in my friend's suffering, but here's where the story gets sort of funny. In therapy, he discovered that one small driving habit was completely sabotaging his mental health. Can you guess what it was?

Well, my friend was a huge fan of country music, and it turns out that he had been listening to his favorite classic country music station on the way home from work. I don't know how many of the great old country songs you've heard, but the lyrics often involve gloom and despair. You know, "My wife she up and left me/my dog he ran away/my truck won't start, it broke my heart/I'm so alone, baybay." (And thus ends my career composing country song lyrics.) Unbeknown to my friend, these down-and-out songs were triggering a whole host of sad memories and regrets, even when he had started the day in the best possible mood. Even more fascinating is that he began to get depressed even when he forgot to turn on the radio in his car. That habit of becoming sad while driving home, that singular mental pathway through the snow, had become so thor-oughly learned that after a while he didn't need the music to initiate it! The good news is that he was tickled to discover the cause of his problem, and he was able to change that habit (and maybe his radio station) and get on with his life.

You might recall a similar habit of thought that you have had about your music or your experience as a performer. If, for example, a cer-tain passage of music makes you feel anxious when you practice it, it is possible that you may become nervous out of habit every time you approach that passage. Or, if the idea of performing on stage dredges up an old memory of a bad performance experience, that memory may come into your mind as a matter of routine. Or, if someone criticized the way you executed something in a particular piece, thoughts about that judgment may pop up every time you practice it. Sometimes we can practically hear the voices of our teachers, critics, and peers in our minds as we practice. These habitual thoughts, the ones that are particularly negative or unhelpful, can be confronted and changed. You can form new habits of thought by consciously directing your mind in a positive way. In those previous examples, you might consider writing out the more positive or optimistic thoughts at strategic places in the music.

In addition to noticing these thought patterns, you can adjust your practice habits as a mindful musician if you are aware of how the brain best learns and remembers music. For example, the more actively engaged your mind is in the practice session, the better you will learn and retain what you are studying. This is why mindless repetition is almost never a good use of your time. You can refresh the mind by stating, out loud, what your intention is for each repetition of a musical passage. Will you make it smoother, quicker, or more beautifully shaped? Will you improve your tone or listen more closely to your articulation? Talking out loud is a helpful way to keep yourself focused because it involves the multiple functions of thinking, saying, and hearing.

Another strategy to reengage the mind is to take short breaks every 20 or 30 minutes. When you resume your practice after a break, you will have created a new psychological unit of practice. Rather than a 2-hour marathon, for example, you could create four to six brain-friendly mini-segments of practice. Resting, stretching, or getting a sip of water in between bursts of concentrated practice is not only good for the mind, it helps reduce physical fatigue and overuse. Experts in injury prevention recommend a 5-minute break for every 25 minutes of practice, or a 10-minute break for every 50 minutes of practice.

It may be helpful to consider that the brain can focus intently on one task for only a limited amount of time. After that time, the brain no longer works as actively to encode new information. If you divide your practice time into manageable segments, or if you vary your repetitions to keep them fresh and new, you are more likely to remain focused. Since the mind loves variety and novelty, you will not learn as quickly or as thoroughly when you feel bored or distracted. Suppose you need to practice your scales, and you decide to play one problem scale 10 times perfectly in a row, because you got that idea from a good teacher. Perhaps the teacher suggested that if you make a mistake in the sequence, you must start over again from the beginning, so that by the end of your practice you will have played the scale correctly 10 times in a row. While there is nothing inherently wrong with this practice suggestion, assuming you avoid physical strain, things can begin to get monotonous if your focus is the same for each scale. An engaged mind prefers that you think of 10 different ways that you can play a correct and beautiful scale. You could vary the dynamics, the articulation, the color, or the shape of the scale as a phrase. You could also employ a *think–play–rest* cycle of practice (or even *speak–play–rest*), articulating a specific goal before each repetition. This would separate each repetition into its own little conscious unit. Because the scale is conceptually different each time, the brain stays more engrossed in the learning process. Those scales might also become more musical and artistic sounding.

We tend to remember best what we do at the beginning and ending of each practice segment. The French cabaret singer and actor Maurice Chevalier once said, "You must start well, and you must end well. What is in the middle is not so important because no one is listening then." Although the quote is meant to be humorous, there is some truth related to how and when we pay attention. When you begin to practice, once you are warmed up, consider starting with a new piece, a new technical study, or a recently learned concept, rather than reviewing an older piece or some well-worn etudes. It may be important that you practice the older piece and the etudes, but you could tackle those in the middle of the practice session, rather than at the beginning. While the mind is still fresh, it is often helpful to begin with something you have been working to memorize or master, even if it happens to be tucked away in the middle of a piece of music. In fact, *not* starting at the beginning of a piece of music is a practice technique that models this concept perfectly. If you think about it, the toughest spots are usually not at the beginning of a piece, yet the beginning seems to be what gets practiced the most. Why not begin your practice with the challenging solo, cadenza, or coda instead? And at the very end of your practice session or rehearsal, before you call it a day, why not go back and review those challenging concepts you began with?

Humans respond well to emotions and imagination. The more emotionally involved you are in a musical piece, the more deeply your mind may grasp it. Associating certain moods, characters, colors, or story narratives with different parts of a musical piece can help you absorb the music on multiple levels. (You will read some examples of this later on in this chapter.) For musicians who memorize their music, this process of association can help them internalize the piece faster and retain it longer. In fact, exploring more than one sensory approach in learning music is often a good idea. Musicians sometimes mistakenly believe that they should cater to their preferred sensory modality when learning anything. In truth, a multisensory approach better engages the brain when learning or memorizing music. For example, whether you consider yourself a visual learner or not, writing notes and visual cues in the score, using colored pencils or adhesive flags, and creating different imagined visual scenes or characters for different pieces can all enrich the learning process. Engaging visual, aural, kinesthetic, and analytical approaches in the practice room are all beneficial to musicians engaged in an abstract performing art.

Since we tend to remember beginnings and endings most vividly, closure can help a performer organize and retain recently learned information or skills. If you keep a practice notebook or journal, you can quickly summarize at the end of every rehearsal what you practiced, learned, or observed. (If you do not currently keep a practice journal, my hope is that you will be inspired to do so by the time you finish this chapter!) You can also jot down a brief reminder or two of where to pick up the next day. Not only does this help you synthesize the work you just completed, it allows you to establish new short-term goals for success.

Our bodies and minds are more sensitive to our environment than we may realize. For example, if you are hungry, tired, or dehydrated before you begin your practice, you may not learn or retain as much new information. If the temperature of your practice area is too cool or (especially) too warm, this can negatively affect your ability to focus. If you are not able to control the climate to within a few degrees of a comfortable performance temperature, 70 °F (21 °C) for most people, consider dressing in layers or come prepared in a different way. If your practice area is too dimly lit, it may be harder for you to pay attention. Although some musicians prefer indirect, low lighting for a cozy, artsy atmosphere, consider practicing brand-new material in a space that is more brightly lit. Also, be aware that the most important fuel for the brain, besides the 20% of your body's blood that it uses, is oxygen. Chapter 5 describes a variety of breathing techniques that relax the body, oxygenate the brain, and bring about a sense of well-being. Just know that stretching, breathing deeply, and laughing all energize the body and mind, and help you stay focused and productive.

Finally, it is important to remember that the brain enjoys a certain amount of stress. This might seem counterintuitive, but by "stress" I am referring to opportunities to perform, be challenged, and even to get a bit nervous. Healthy sources of stress, at least for most musicians, can include lessons and coaching appointments, group performance classes, auditions, concerts and gigs, and studio recording sessions. Slightly less intimidating sources of stress might include recording your own practice session, playing or singing a new piece for a friend or colleague, or performing music as a volunteer at a community center. If you don't introduce enough healthy pressure into your musical life, it may hinder your ability to stay motivated and practice effectively. This is why performance preparation is such an important part of practice. Too much stress, however, can become a negative factor. The pressure of performing a concert with inadequate time to prepare, for example, can inhibit your ability to learn the music efficiently. Life hassles, such as personal conflicts or other stressors, can also negatively affect your ability to concentrate on your music. Try to resolve any immediate nagging problems before you practice or perform, or find a creative way to solve these issues. Later on, we will explore a number of ways to detach from stressful situations and focus on the task at hand.

Getting Organized

A goal without a plan is just a wish.—Antoine de Saint-Exupéry

When I spoke to a number of sport psychologists to learn how they teach mental preparation techniques to their best athletes, I was surprised to discover how many of these "mental skills" were actually changes in behavior. In other words, many techniques and exercises were designed to transform habits and actions rather than methods of thinking. I observed that the most successful athletes, and the most effective coaches, were masters of documentation and organization. This discovery was incredibly motivating when I considered that anyone can develop these skills, including the most wildly disorganized performing artist.

I now believe that cultivating a personal system of organization is one of the best-kept secrets of artistic success. This may sound unconventional, since our culture tends to celebrate the stereotypically unmethodical *arteest* who thinks outside the box while creating impromptu musical masterpieces on crumpled-up cocktail napkins. It may also seem to contradict the idea of mindfulness, until one remembers that mindfulness is a deep form of conscious awareness. As I mentioned earlier, consistent performance success often depends upon good time management, goal-setting, and self-awareness. And the best way to cultivate self-awareness is to keep track of that which you are becoming aware! Unlike professional athletes, most musicians do not have professional coaches who motivate them and keep their goals and practice sessions organized each day. Consequently, we must learn to be our own coaches, and that requires some degree of structure and self-monitoring. Before we dive further into the various skills that lead to optimal performance, we must explore the concept of coordinating and tracking our goals, practice sessions, musical milestones, even our anxieties and other emotional states. The most important thing to remember at this point is that, for those aspiring to be outstanding and consistent performers, the art of structure may be the key that unlocks everything.

Now, before some of you freak out and offer compelling examples of your lack of managerial skills, remember that a system can take many forms, depending on the style and temperament of the artist. Remember, too, that organization is a learned skill. Some musicians are naturally systematic in their approach, sometimes to the point of obsessing over detailed to-do lists. Others can barely find a box of reeds in a wildly cluttered living environment. But if you have the discipline to learn the necessary scales, lyrics, rhythmic patterns, or fingerings necessary to hone your craft, you can learn to cultivate organizational skills in a way that resonates with your unique creative brain. The ancient Greek philosophers taught that to understand anything in the universe, a person must first "know thyself." There is no better way to know thyself and to know thy practice habits than to become aware of these and keep track of them in some way.

The first step is to find a method of documentation that suits your personal style. Many people prefer to keep a small notebook or journal. This should be an object that is reserved solely to track habits and behaviors related to your musical performance skills. Of course, this method works only if you keep the notebook or journal with you every time you practice, and it does require that you regularly *write* in said notebook or journal. For what it's worth, some studies suggest that we absorb handwritten notes and personal reflections more successfully than when we type them using a computer keyboard or touchscreen. Plus, it's easier to draw expressive symbols, doodles, flowcharts, or emoticons when appropriate. If you decide to go the traditional paper route, I suggest that you keep your notebook in your music bag, with your stack of music, or in your instrument case if possible. Remember that, like breaking a path through the snow, documenting your progress can easily become a habit that serves you well. It only requires that you direct your attention to it at least once a day.

The more technologically savvy musicians out there may wish to go the sleek digital route, which is also a perfectly good option. You can easily keep one or more electronic files on a laptop or tablet, if that bit of equipment is always with you when you practice. A file can be as simple as a word-processing document or spreadsheet or as elaborate as a multimedia project, depending on your preference. Or, you may prefer to make use of a smartphone app. Many of these are free or inexpensive and offer a variety of formats based on your personal preference (list makers, journal keepers, personal organizers, and so on). Sometimes the most helpful features of these apps are those that allow you to record audio or video, organize and share files, or set daily reminders, timers, or alarms. One benefit of electronic documentation is that you can easily upload images and internet links if you wish, or share your journey with others.

Some musicians like to make use of online platforms or social media, including personal blogs and file-sharing programs. You may enjoy snapping photos to create a visual diary of your experience or sharing some of your successes and questions with your friends. One initial mindfulness activity will be to decide how much of your musical journey you wish to disclose to others. Some musicians thrive when connected to a community of friends working toward a common goal, because the moral support can be motivating and invigorating. Others prefer to focus individually on personal planning and quiet reflection, at first.

I would only caution that you not use social media as your only form of organizing and documenting your musical adventures and progress. You will probably discover, especially as we explore the many psychological and emotional ramifications of being an artist, that you will want to have a means by which you can express yourself openly and authentically to you and you alone. When we share something online, we tend to tweak or filter it to make it more captivating to others. Often, though, we just need to practice candid self-honesty. The musical journey is intensely personal. If Socrates were alive today, he probably wouldn't say, "Know thyself, and then share most of thyself with thy public followers."

So, now that you have obtained your colorful Hello Kitty notebook, what exactly will you be documenting? That is a personal choice based on your own goals and your interest in the various activities presented in this book. The last two chapters of this book outline a series of detailed mental skills activities that you can begin right away, if you wish. I do recommend that you choose at least two of the more general activities subsequently listed and begin to keep track of these as you progress through this book. The more familiar you are with your personal habits and musical tendencies, the more meaningful some of this content may become. If you find yourself immediately gravitating to one or more of the following suggestions, begin there. Over time, you may wish to consider tracking many of these, even if for a short period. And incidentally, I don't recommend that you spend an inordinate amount of time writing lengthy reflective paragraphs, unless that is your personal preference. Abbreviated shorthand, quick checklists, bullet points, anything works as long as it makes sense to you.

Music Practice and Rehearsals

This may be the most immediately helpful activity for many readers, particularly those who have not documented their practice in the past. When tracking your practice habits, you might begin by documenting the date, time, and duration of each of your practice sessions, but you would hopefully not stop there. (Of course, if simply getting to your practice on a regular basis has been a challenge for you, this single act may be a huge step in the right direction.) It is helpful to keep a record of which musical pieces or activities you accomplished during each practice session. You might choose to jot down questions that come up, or problems or challenges that you noticed. Perhaps you like to keep track of metronome markings, personal accomplishments, or reminders of things to do next time. The following day, when you open your journal or app and read your previous entry, you will immediately place yourself in the best mindset to begin your practice. You don't need to waste time trying to remember what you did or what you need to do, because you can pick up right where you left off. You may discover that documenting *what* you do during your practice becomes more helpful than quantifying the number of minutes or hours you spend practicing.

If you are like the many musicians who find it difficult to carve out regular or adequate practice time for yourself, you may find it helpful to read the section on Time Management in Chapter 8 (pages 185–186). Since time and attention are our two greatest resources, time management can become the ultimate mindfulness practice for many performers.

Daily Practice Goals

Planning small goals for each practice session can help you become a master of time management. This skill is essential for those who have incredibly busy lives, very limited practice time, or a huge amount of music to learn. You may find it best, at the end of each rehearsal, lesson, or performance, to outline your practice goals for the next day right away. What you need to do, including what you struggled with or what you didn't get around to practicing, will be fresh in your mind at the end of your practice session. Alternatively, you may wish to spend the first 5 minutes of a new practice session, while your mind is fresh, looking through your music and your calendar, sorting out your goals based on the amount of time you have to practice that day. Or you might try to spread out your practice plan a few days at a time.

For more information, you may wish to read the short section on Organized Practice in Chapter 8 (page 184). If you still have trouble getting started, you will find a number of practice organization templates on the companion website (⊕ items 2.1–2.5).

Short-Term Goals

I define short-term goals as more or less weekly or biweekly goals, but you should interpret this concept any way you like. When setting goals, strive to be as realistic and specific as possible, and see if you can find a way to assess whether you actually accomplished your goal. For example, "I will improve my sight-reading" is not as specific and measurable as "I will sight-read one new solo every day." Like a good coach, you will want to place your goals somewhere where you will see them every day. You will also want to write these goals down, since studies suggest that you are much more likely to complete your goals if you write them down than if you simply think them to yourself. The point is to reflect thoughtfully on the goals that are most meaningful to you.

To read more about effective goal setting, including examples of how to set strong goals, check out the section on Goal-Setting in Chapter 8 (pages 181–183).

You will find a goal-setting worksheet on the companion website (⊕ item 2.6).

Long-Term Goals

More ambitious goals would be those that you want to accomplish in several months, during the course of an academic semester, or in a year. If you decide to set a 1-year goal, you may find it helpful to divide that large goal into three or four smaller landmark goals over the course of the year. In other words, a year may seem very far away, but 3 months feels more imminent. From an interesting psychological viewpoint, "12 weeks" away seems closer than "3 months" away!

Large, challenging goals become much less daunting when broken down into very small milestones. For example, suppose you want to learn to play a demanding piece of repertoire over the summer: J. S. Bach's famous Chaconne from the Partita No. 2 for solo violin. It may seem like climbing a musical Mount Everest in only 3 months. However, if you were to divide the number of measures in the piece (257 measures) by the total number of days in June, July, and August (92 days), you would see that you could master only three measures a day and still finish the entire piece with a couple of weeks to spare. Even though this approach doesn't take into account the many other factors involved in learning difficult music, it is one example of how we can break down seemingly unattainable goals into small manageable segments. Remember the old riddle: How do you eat an elephant? Answer: One bite at a time.

It can be easier to establish long-term goals when you have in mind a very clear vision of your artistic future. You may wish to explore some of the activities in the section on Passion, Purpose, and Core Values in Chapter 9 (pages 214–216) before deciding on a long-term objective. Articulating your personal mission in writing can help focus your attention on what matters most.

Personal Habits

Remember that everything you do affects the musician you are. Since musicians rely on their physical bodies to make music, it is helpful to be aware of physical habits. Athletes document their personal habits rigorously, because they are keenly aware that the quality of their health impacts their athletic performance. Consider choosing one area of your life to track daily, as a form of mindfulness practice: what you eat, what you drink, how many hours you sleep, how much exercise you get, how often you check your smartphone, how many cat videos you watch . . . the possibilities are endless. The idea is not to practice harsh self-criticism, but to engage in objective self-awareness.

For example, suppose you choose to document the number of caffeinated beverages you consume each day. Somewhere, in a notebook or smartphone app, you would document each drink in order to review your personal patterns and tendencies from week to week. You may realize that you feel less jittery when you stop drinking caffeine after noon. Perhaps you learn that you drink far more caffeine than you had previously assumed. Using this information as feedback, you can adjust your behavior *if you choose to do so*. Or you may simply observe your behaviors as a form of mindfulness. It is much simpler to adopt a mindset of objective awareness without adding a layer of scrutiny and criticism to each personal choice you make. You can choose to release the urge to scold or reward yourself and simply observe the habit. We tend to learn more about ourselves, and treat ourselves with greater compassion when we diminish the practice of self-criticism.

For more examples of documenting personal habits, see the section on Mindfulness of Personal Habits in Chapter 8 (pages 187–189).

Stressors and Solutions

This problem-solving activity acknowledges the external factors in your life that affect you as a musician. Life stressors, including fatigue, personal conflicts, health issues, financial challenges, and family responsibilities, can influence your ability to perform well. I don't mean to suggest that you should sit down and contemplate all the stressful situations in your life, because that is not a very helpful activity. If something is really distracting you, however, it might be a good idea to write it down before you practice. Afterward, ask yourself, "What part of this situation is out of my control?" and make note of that if it is beneficial. It doesn't help to feel burdened by circumstances over which you have no control. Next, ask yourself, "What part of this situation is within my control?" and make a note of those thoughts. Finally, ask yourself, "What steps can I take today or tomorrow?" and write down at least one idea, no matter how small. Maybe that one task is to make a quick phone call, set your alarm clock for 15 minutes earlier, or outline the main points of a difficult conversation you need to have with someone. You will probably be able to come up with a short-term plan toward a solution, and then set the problem aside temporarily so that you can focus on your music. The idea is to direct your attention toward the solution rather than toward the problem.

For examples of how this strategy might be used during a performance situation, see the section on Situational Control in Chapter 8 (pages 203–204).

Habits of Thought

In the next two chapters, we will explore the psychology of being a musician and the power our thoughts have over our emotions and behaviors. If you struggle with negative, impatient, or self-critical thoughts, it might be a good idea to begin to identify and document these a few times a day. This is helpful during a rehearsal or performance, and also works well in daily life. For example, when practicing something difficult, if you often find yourself thinking "I'll never get this right," write it down in your practice notebook and put it in quotes or draw a cartoon thought bubble around it. Find a way to indicate to yourself that this statement is nothing more than a thought. If you would prefer to think something different, you can restate the thought in writing so that it is helpful or more positive. Maybe "I'll never get this right" will become "I know I can do this!" If that seems a little too optimistic for your taste, you could try, "Not yet, but I'll get there," or "Getting better every day," or something like that. If you find yourself thinking reassuring or optimistic thoughts, be sure to write those down as well! You can consciously encourage your mind to ponder those thoughts that will help you become a happier musician.

Patterns of Emotion

Music requires a strong degree of emotional engagement and abstract communication. Some people are more successful at consciously observing their feelings when they are performing than when they are going about their daily lives. Identifying and documenting your moods and emotions every now and then can prove to be revealing and rewarding. The main difference between this activity and the previous one is that the goal is not to dispute an unwanted emotion. While it is often possible to redirect or rephrase our thoughts, it is unrealistic to hope to change our emotions at will.

Recognizing emotional patterns is far from a superficial activity. You may wish to read further about Emotional Mindfulness in Chapter 8 (pages 189–192). If you struggle to find the right word or phrase to describe what you are feeling, do what I do and draw emoticons or other symbols!

Distractions

One of the greatest challenges for any performing musician is to stay focused during a rehearsal and while on stage. If you notice that something, either an external situation or an internal thought, is distracting you during a practice session, stop and write it down. If your smartphone is commanding your attention, either audibly or psychologically, acknowledge that and see if you can eliminate the distraction. If you detect an interference during a musical performance, make a mental note of it and write it down afterward. The practice of identifying distractions is helpful, because it is the first step toward mindful refocusing. Acknowledging the distraction is often more effective than just trying to ignore it. You can then plan ahead: How will you better deal with this the next time it happens?

To further explore distractions during a musical performance, read the section on Dealing With Distractions in Chapter 8 (pages 202–203). Since distractions are unavoidable, it is unrealistic to try to dodge all of them. We can, however, learn to redirect our attention quickly and continue to perform with confidence.

Mini-Victories

I encourage musicians to devote a portion of their practice journals to recording mini-victories or moderate victories or even giant victories. As critical creative artists, we sometimes give ourselves imbalanced feedback, concentrating only on what needs to be improved. If you focus on the successes as well, even the small ones, you can train your mind to acknowledge every small step toward progress. A mini-victory could be somewhat general, such as improvising a great solo, having a good rehearsal, or accomplishing every task on your practice schedule. It could be more specific, such as reaching a tempo or memory goal, nailing a difficult technical passage, or developing a creative and compelling interpretation of a piece. Or, you could record more personal victories, such as remembering to write in your practice journal, drinking water instead of soda, or identifying a negative habit of thinking and reframing it in a positive way. You might even amuse yourself by exclaiming "hooray!" or "victory!" or "booyah!" when one occurs. When you feel frustrated or discouraged, rereading some of your mini-victories can cheer you up and remind you to focus on the small successes that are always around the corner.

If you are interested in starting an Achievement Log, check out this section in Chapter 9 (pages 230–232).

* * *

These are only a few of the many activities you can begin to experiment with in order to cultivate excellent mental performing skills. As you become accustomed to observing yourself objectively, you will find it easier to incorporate some of the other mindfulness exercises presented in later chapters.

Creative Mental Practice

Think ten times, play once.—Franz Liszt

Although this book is not really a book about mental practice, mental practice is an essential tool for any musician. So much of what we do when we perform is first and foremost a mental phenomenon. While this section will not walk you step-by-step through mental practice techniques specific to every instrument, it will hopefully spark your imagination so that you can begin to create your own mental practice activities. Here, I define mental practice as the deliberate, intense, silent practice of music. Mental practice involves a number of internal processes, usually (but not always) away from your instrument, with or without notated music. Studies have shown that just *imagining* that you are making music is as real to parts of your mind as if you were actually performing. You don't even need to move your body or wiggle your fingers when engaged in this sort of creative imagery. The most successful mental practice is vivid and methodical.

Some activities that don't technically fall within the category of mental practice can still be advantageous. Any time you think about or study your music in a constructive way, you are enhancing your mind's ability to learn and express that music artistically. Preparing your score is an excellent example. The time you spend with your music before you play or sing through it, regardless of the specific activity (translating the text, anticipating the challenges, analyzing the form, even adding rehearsal numbers), is a beneficial mental activity. When you "hear" your music in your head during the day or when you listen to a recording of you or someone else performing, your mind is still engaged in the process of encoding and interpreting that music.

Mental practice is a handy skill because you can still be productive when you are away from your instrument. When traveling, for example, you can make effective use of your time on a plane or subway. When you are sore or injured, mental practice can keep you from falling too far behind. It can be used as a second daily practice or as a way to solidify your memory. In a single rehearsal, you can alternate mental practice with physical practice to offset fatigue and interpret your music at a deeper level. The following sections give a few examples of how you can use mental or creative practice techniques to intensify your musical experiences. I'm certain you will be able to think of other innovative activities that are relevant to your experience.

Audiation

This fancy word simply describes the phenomenon of hearing music in the mind when no music is actually sounding. We do it all the time. In fact, chances are that you may frequently have a tune running through your head when you aren't listening to music. Audiation as a mental practice technique involves the conscious direction of attention for the purpose of learning or refining a piece of music. You can use this practice tool in a number of creative ways. To develop your technique and interpretation of notated music, for example, experiment with hearing a phrase of your music internally, before you actually play or sing it. You may or may not choose to look at the score. In your mind, imagine the phrase exactly as you want it to sound, with the best possible tone, articulation, contrasts, and character. With this aural model in mind, you can then perform the phrase. If you are able to compare your actual performance to the one you created mentally, you will be able to adjust your practice in order to become more closely aligned with your best imagined performance.

Audiation is also an excellent tool for improving your ability to read music at sight. You might, for example, sit with an unfamiliar piece of music for several minutes before you play it. Hear the notes and rhythms in your mind, imagining that you are performing it accurately. This requires highly developed aural skills, but even if you struggle to hear the correct notes in your mind, you can probably imagine the rhythm, or observe the contours of the melodies, the punctuation of the rests, or other important characteristics notated in the score. You may even be able to imagine your fingers moving around the keys or strings, or how the pitches might feel in your body if you were to sing them. You might breathe with the phrase that is unfolding in your mind, even though you don't make a sound.

If you are working to improve your improvisational skills, you can imagine a short, improvised phrase before you play or sing it. This important practice represents the opposite of what musicians often do, which is to listen as they improvise, and then react or adjust accordingly. With audiation, you are hearing your original creation in your mind first, and only then working to re-create your ideas. This practice expands your creative options, since your musical choices may not be limited to gestures that are physically natural on your instrument. A jazz or pop musician may prefer to experiment with imagining her own improvised melody while listening to a backing track of the rhythm and chord changes of a standard tune. We are bound only by the outer limits of our imagination.

Listen Back

Recording short segments of practice sessions, lessons, or ensemble rehearsals can be good for quality control and to help develop critical listening skills. Sadly, sometimes the music that we experience internally is not what we are producing externally, so it helps to listen back to be sure that we are communicating exactly what we intend. Musicians who record themselves on a portable device will often listen back while watching the music, marking notes in the score with a pencil. While the use of recordings can offer periodic reality checks, we should not rely on them to substitute for active listening. Hopefully, the occasional use of recordings can help a musician narrow the divide between what he hears while performing and what he hears as an objective listener.

My favorite way to use this mental practice technique is to listen back to the recording only a phrase at a time. First, hear the phrase in your mind exactly as you want it to sound. Then, press the play button and listen to how close you came to achieving your ideal sound. Stop the recording, make a few notes, and continue with the next phrase. Although my students have described this process as agonizing at first (often because of the discrepancy between what we want to sound like and what we actually sound like), it is possible to improve rapidly by practicing in this manner. After a while, you won't need the recording device very often.

Memorize With Meaning

Memorizing music is an outstanding way to hone your mental skills, even if you don't need to perform from memory. Through memorization, you can learn music more deeply and discover how your mind prefers to process music. Once you have mastered a piece, you can practice re-creating that music, away from the score or with your eyes closed, entirely in your mind. It can be beneficial to start with a phrase at a time, or a short section at a time, rather than trying to re-create an entire piece at once. Unlike audiation, memorization challenges you to imagine performing every detail of your music, in addition to hearing it in your mind. You could visualize the actual notes on the page, or imagine your body playing each note, internalizing each rhythmic and expressive nuance. If you get stuck and can't remember part of the music, that doesn't necessarily mean you don't know the piece. It only means that you aren't yet able to produce it mentally, without the kinesthetic benefit of actually performing. Mental memorization is a more advanced skill than simply playing from memory, so it should be a challenging and engaging activity.

I called this section "memorize with meaning" because we tend to internalize best what is personally significant. In other words, abstract notes on a staff mean very little to the creative mind. If a phrase has individual meaning behind it, however, the mind will grasp it more quickly and retain it for a longer period of time. We can create meaning by associating a specific feeling, personality, narrative, abstract thought, event, or musical purpose with each passage of music. The imaginative part of your mind, when engaged during mental practice, can generate a very vivid and realistic experience.

Developing Character

Mental practice can help any performer solve an interpretive dilemma, bring a specific passage to life, or develop a unique musical voice. When we are not distracted by the physical challenges of performing, we can imagine any possible interpretation, character, or mood in our music. In your mental practice, whether you are working phrase by phrase or section by section, experiment with hearing your music in a compelling and personal way. Since these events happen only in your mind, you can be wildly creative. It is a wonderfully abstract method of thinking in sound.

If your music were the soundtrack to a movie, for example, what would the movie be about? Would it be in bright technicolor, classic black and white, or animated as a cartoon? Might there be a specific plot or narrative? Can you imagine the characters, situations, or vivid emotions that might be hidden in each phrase? Or, if the music is deeply personal, are you able to tap into your own memories or experiences to bring your interpretation to life? If the music doesn't seem suitable as a movie soundtrack, perhaps you can imagine it as the accompaniment to a choreographed dance. In this example, what movements and gestures can you imagine from the dancers? How are they dressed? You may prefer to envision a more abstract form of music, such as a series of moving geometric structures, swirls of colors, or a painting or sculpture that has come to life. Perhaps you prefer a less visual approach and are able to evoke a series of kinesthetic experiences. These might include physical textures or sensations, even vivid emotions. The music may feel intensely personal, or it may seem as if you are interpreting it from a more detached perspective. Only you have access to these internal experiments.

Interpret Three Ways

I like to play this game to encourage creativity and outside-the-box thinking. Music can become stale after weeks of practice, especially if we perform it more or less the same way every time. We can also get locked into an interpretation if we never considered playing the music any other way. In this mental practice technique, you would take a phrase or section of a piece of music, and as you look at the score, you would imagine playing or singing the phrase three times in three different ways. What you change each time is completely up to you and would certainly depend on the stylistic parameters of the music. You can make subtle adjustments to the phrasing, tone, articulation, rhythmic energy, or other musical nuances. You can also experiment with altering the character, mood, or emotional energy of the passage. Once you are able to imagine the three interpretations vividly in your mind, you can re-create those in your practice.

I once had a student who was naturally very expressive and who seldom struggled with musical interpretation. The one notable exception was a portion of a Chopin waltz that she just couldn't seem to bring to life. She mentioned that she was having a hard time connecting with the piece and found that her mind often wandered while she was playing.

I asked her to come back the following week and to be prepared to perform that section of the Chopin in three different ways, with three different characters or moods, while maintaining the original style and tempo. When she returned a week later, she played that waltz with three very different interpretations, all very colorful and engaging, and we chose our favorite. I asked what she had been thinking about, assuming that she had explored the piece on some deeply philosophical level. Yet, she revealed that she had simply pretended that each had been performed by a different Disney princess. Surprisingly, she was able to portray some very striking differences in the personalities of those characters! I still smile when I think about her Rapunzel waltz.

Visualize the Technique

Mental practice can help solve technical challenges. Sometimes we just need to set the physical body aside so that the mind can become an active problem solver. If you are able to close your eyes and imagine yourself performing a short passage in vivid detail, this technique will not be very difficult. As you mentally practice a passage that has been giving you problems, you can imagine adopting a slightly different physical alignment, hand or arm position, quality of breath, or something else related to your particular instrument. You may prefer to focus on more abstract images or gestures that help you experience the passage differently. It may help to focus on tricky transitional passages and direct your visualization toward technical shifts or the spaces in between the notes. You may be surprised at how effective it can be to solve physical challenges first in the mind.

Creative Orchestration

It can be fun to imagine that a different instrument, or combination of instruments or voices, is performing your music. Mentally orchestrating your music can stimulate your imagination to consider different tone colors, characters, even subtle changes in articulation. You might even imagine how a famous conductor or bandleader might conduct the piece. This method of thinking outside the box can be helpful in considering new musical dimensions and nuances.

* * *

Mental practice should be somewhat exhausting. The sheer amount of psychological energy and focus required will often prevent you from practicing this way for very long stretches of time. A professional concert artist once told me he believed he could accomplish more in 1 hour on an airplane than he could sitting at the piano for 2 hours! Experiences vary, but mental practice should definitely be one tool in your arsenal of performance skills. Even the greatest athletes develop a system of practice that includes mental imagery along with physical skill improvement. While mental practice can never replace actual practice, it will certainly improve it and strengthen a variety of musical skills.

The mind is the most powerful force behind artistic music performance. We've only just begun to understand how the brain works to learn and memorize music, how organization and documentation can facilitate our successes, and how we can practice effectively using only our internal resources. Even more mystifying is the power of the mind to determine our experiences through our thoughts, beliefs, and emotions. The next two chapters will examine some of the psychological aspects of performing, including universal challenges such as performance anxiety, and will offer a number of techniques for adopting the mindful perspective of a skilled and successful performer.

3 MUSIC AND THE MIND

PERFORMANCE ANXIETY AND OTHER CHALLENGES

> *The Mind is its own place, and in itself can make a heaven of hell, a hell of heaven.*—John Milton

In the last chapter, we began to scratch the surface of a musician's remarkable mind. It is inspiring to think that your magnificent noggin contains one-hundred-billion brain cells and more possible neural connections than atoms in the universe. The human brain is incredibly adaptable, always changing, growing, and relearning throughout life. This is good news for us, since music performance requires a multitude of mental processes: attention, alertness, endurance, organization, motivation, analysis, memory, confidence, and a host of other abilities. This chapter addresses some of the many psychological roadblocks that musicians encounter on their artistic journeys. For countless musicians, these challenges include performance anxiety, emotional stress, self-criticism, and harmful patterns of thought. Luckily, the more we understand these issues, the better able we are to transcend them. We can approach mindfulness from the perspective of complete honesty.

The Performer and the Performance

> *All the world's a stage,*
> *And all the men and women merely players;*
> *They have their exits and their entrances,*
> *And one man in his time plays many parts.*
> —Jaques (Shakespeare, *As You Like It*)

What does it mean to perform? A musician will most often answer this question by describing an event such as a public concert or audition. We talk about performing music, but we also talk about performing an experiment, an act of kindness, even a miracle. The simple fact that to perform something is to accomplish something becomes deeply significant when you consider its broader implications. Imagine the things we do that trigger heightened alertness or vigilance: giving a speech or presentation in front of people, teaching or demonstrating a concept, even participating in a meeting or group discussion. Many people, when they raise their hands to speak or ask a question, silently rehearse what they will say when called upon because they want to make a good impression. Taking a driver's test in a new state? That's a performance. Sitting down for a job interview? That's a performance, too. First date? Definitely a performance. I'm sure you can think of other examples. Preparing for a dinner party, calling to cancel a credit card account, asking for a raise, ordering wine in a fancy restaurant, stepping up to your lane in a bowling alley . . . all are varieties of life performances.

This isn't to say that you should plan on being anything other than yourself. To "perform" doesn't necessarily involve any sort of acting or deception, but it does include a degree of role-playing and expanded awareness. Usually this awareness includes the ways in which others might view us or how we evaluate ourselves. Many people would feel more nervous performing music in front of an audience than taking a driver's test, but not everyone. Millions of people experience test anxiety, social apprehension, or general stress associated with the diversity of life's performances. Because we adapt to the various roles in our lives (musician, student, teacher, parent, employee, friend, partner), our performances vary depending on the roles we are playing at the time.

If you remember this, it may help to put some of your experiences and emotions into perspective. A professor friend of mine wanted to know why, after 20 years of college teaching, he still became unbearably nervous before the first class of each semester. He would fuss over his slides, tweak his lecture notes, and imagine answering every possible student question. Although he taught political science instead of music, I encouraged him to consider that these first lectures were actually public performances. My friend prepared for these classes in the same way that an actor learns his lines, acquires the perfect costume, and rehearses the blocking for each scene. When my friend goes home in the evening, I'm guessing he doesn't prepare dinner for his partner with the same degree of nervous hypervigilance. This is because he probably adopts a different role at home, sharing news about his day, listening attentively during conversation, offering supportive feedback, and planning activities for the next day.

The wisdom of Shakespeare is reflected in that earlier quote. If life itself is one grand performance, the world is indeed our stage. Stress can arise when we fail to distinguish between high-stakes performances and everyday events, believing instead that everything we do is some sort of performance worthy of scrutiny. Stress can also get the better of us when we become too wrapped up in how others might perceive us. Creative artists face special challenges when their art becomes intertwined with their very identities. While every human being experiences daily performances on the virtual stage of life, a musician has the added stress of performances on a real stage or its equivalent. This pressure can take its toll on the creative spirit. Musicians and other performers need to be particularly careful to monitor and care for their psychological health and well-being.

Musicians and Mental Health

> A man goes to the doctor. He tells the doctor that he's depressed, and that life seems harsh and cruel. He says he feels all alone in a threatening world where what lies ahead is vague and uncertain. The doctor says, "Ah, the treatment is simple. The great clown Pagliacci is in town tonight. You must go see him. It is impossible to feel depressed when you are entertained by the great Pagliacci." The man bursts into tears and says, "But Doctor, I am the great Pagliacci." —adapted from Alan Moore's *Watchmen*

Many musicians will identify with the great Pagliacci. Artistic performance sometimes requires that we adopt a stage persona, or figurative mask, that does not always accurately represent who we are or how we feel. Regardless of what we are experiencing on the inside, we are often expected to appear calm, joyful, or radiant on stage. The introvert might be expected to play the part of an extrovert. A tired frown must sometimes be replaced by a cheerful smile. Occasionally, we are obliged to evoke emotions that we don't really feel. As a result, the audience can potentially mistake the stage persona for a person's true identity. Often, the musician herself is the one who inadvertently blurs these boundaries. Is my stage persona genuine or imagined? If I am not what others think I am, then who am I?

Ah, the musician: a gifted, tortured soul! This romantic image exists in our culture, but does not feel very glamorous to the performer who is struggling on the inside. We can cite endless examples of creative geniuses who suffered from psychological distress. Some of these examples come from our popular culture, and many are of legendary personalities from decades past. Contrary to popular belief, it is not possible to diagnose accurately the mental health of composers and performers who lived well before our time. Psychologists can find evidence of diverse emotional challenges only based on the historical and anecdotal accounts of various individuals. Although creative people can suffer from any number of mental health issues, they most frequently seem to experience forms of anxiety, depression, bipolar disorder, and issues related to substance abuse and addiction. This was as true for those suffering from "melancholia," described by the ancient Greeks, as it is for contemporary performers such as the actor Robin Williams, a modern-day Pagliacci, whose suicide came as a terrible shock to many people.

Legendary cellist Pablo Casals wrote the following in his autobiography:

> I gave my first real concert in Barcelona when I was fourteen. My father, who had come to Barcelona for the occasion, took me on the tramway. I was terribly nervous. When we got to the concert hall, I said, "Father, I've forgotten the beginning of the piece! I can't remember a note of it! What shall I do?" He calmed me down. That was eighty years ago but I've never conquered that dreadful feeling of nervousness before a performance. It is always an ordeal. Before I go onstage, I have a pain in my chest. I'm tormented.

When the world's greatest cellist describes 80 years of performance experience as *torment*, the musical world should take notice. We can no longer brush away the topic of performance stress or allow others to convince us that it will only get better with experience. We need to be proactive in acknowledging and working through our fears and challenges.

Historians believe that Ludwig van Beethoven and Frédéric Chopin suffered from major depression throughout most of their lives. Sergei Rachmaninoff spoke openly about his depression and the help he received from a hypnotherapist. Mozart, Tchaikovsky, Schumann, and Mahler may have suffered from bipolar disorder, but so might have Nirvana's Kurt Cobain and Pink Floyd's Syd Barrett. Others from the classical, blues, rock, and jazz cultures have also wrestled with obsessive-compulsive behaviors, personality disorders, alcoholism, drug addiction, and have even committed suicide. These, of course, are serious examples. The bottom line is that musicians who struggle with anxiety or who frequently find themselves battling the dark cloud of depression are not alone.

In the past, mental health professionals considered music performance anxiety to be a type of social anxiety disorder or social phobia. In recent years, however, experts have asserted that the diagnosis guidelines of the widely used *Diagnostic and Statistical Manual of Mental Disorders* (DSM) need to be adjusted to take into consideration the special situations and needs of a creative performer, and to accommodate the growing body of research on this topic. Is performance anxiety really a mental disorder, or a natural by-product of having to perform in the public eye? Even performers who do not suffer any debilitating effects of performance anxiety are still vulnerable to the roller coaster of emotions that accompany the performing career of a creative artist. Performance anxiety is a very complex psychological phenomenon that often manifests in a cluster of challenges, including melancholy, introversion, perfectionism, shame, obsessive-compulsive tendencies, eating disorders, even panic disorder. The most common challenge to accompany anxiety in musicians is depression.

Sometimes it is difficult to detect the symptoms of depression in an anxious musician, because these symptoms are often masked or overshadowed by the more visibly distressing manifestations of performance anxiety. Some musicians experience situational depression; others struggle with dysthymia, a mild but persistent low-level melancholy that always seems to linger in the background. Clinical depression can be even more acute and serious. The symptoms of depression include frequent feelings of sadness, emptiness or isolation, hopelessness, pessimism, loss of enjoyment in hobbies and other activities, difficulty concentrating or making decisions, extreme and persistent fatigue, noticeable changes in appetite or body weight, trouble falling asleep (or staying asleep, or sleeping more than usual), and even persistent thoughts about death or suicide. If you feel that you are reading about yourself or someone you care about, please be sure to read the last section of this chapter.

Much of our contentment in life, as musicians and human beings, involves our cultivation of mental wellness. On the one hand, psychological challenges are impossible to avoid. On the other hand, failure to cope with these challenges can negatively affect every part of our lives. As you continue to read this chapter, I hope you will keep two things in mind.

First, there is a fine line between the universal challenges of performing music (including stage fright, low self-esteem, and occasional sadness) and more serious mental health issues. With mindfulness, musicians can learn to distinguish those challenges that they can address on their own through practice, and those issues that would benefit from the assistance of a health care professional. Second, since the rest of this chapter is devoted to the ubiquitous topic of performance anxiety, remember that the goal is to understand and manage the anxiety, rather than to eliminate it entirely. As you will soon see, a touch of adrenaline is advantageous and desirable during a performance! One of my students aptly described this preference as "some, but not none."

Regardless of the age, experience, or professional status of the musician, the most common psychological challenge is that of performance anxiety. Long ago, pianist John Browning said, "Nerves is a hard subject because nobody wants to talk about it." Luckily, times have changed, and many people today *do* want to talk about it. Music is supposed to be about creative expression and the communication of something artistic. Why on earth would that be such a frightful endeavor? To understand the answer, we have to consider some of the curious secrets of the mind.

Fears of Performers

We can't stop the waves, but we can learn to surf.—Jon Kabat-Zinn

Before we investigate what happens in the brain and body when we feel nervous, let's explore the concept of fear as it applies to music performance. Not too long ago, performance anxiety was known only as "stage fright." Many have abandoned this moniker, because the apprehension we feel frequently occurs offstage! Furthermore, we can make a nuanced distinction between fear (a response to an immediate threat) and anxiety (a general sense of apprehension). Today, *music performance anxiety* is the most current accepted terminology for the discomfort related to music performance. But what is it that we fear, exactly? The Greek philosopher Epictetus once said, "For it is not death and pain that is a fearful thing, but fear of death and pain."

The fears and anxieties experienced by musicians are complex and multidimensional. Often, as we begin to explore one possible fear, we uncover deeper layers of more complex fears. Here is one example: If I ask a musician what makes him so nervous about an upcoming performance, the initial answer is usually something like "I'm afraid I'll make a huge mistake." He may then choose to contemplate that response more deeply by exploring questions such as, "And then what?" or "So, what's the worst that can happen?" He might discover that the fear isn't really about making a single mistake, or even a series of mistakes, but that those mistakes will result in an overall bad performance. If he explores that idea further, he may find that the concept of a "bad performance" comes from his imagined viewpoint of one or more critical audience member. In other words, the situation has now expanded into the fear of criticism by others. If he searches more deeply, he can explore the perceived consequences of criticism, such as a negative response by the audience, or the publication of a bad review. He may fear he will be revealed as a fraud whose inadequacies become visible for the world to see. He may instead fear losing his own self-respect or losing the love and admiration of certain audience members. Whew! In this one example, the fear of making a mistake turned out to be, on closer examination, the profound fear of loss of love.

If you ever ask a large group of musicians to write down what frightens them about performing, you will get an unbelievably long and varied list. Common responses include fears of criticism, inadequacy, inauthenticity, embarrassment, failure, rejection, and on and on. Some psychologists believe that we can reduce those initial fears down to just a few fundamental or primary fears. These include the fear of the unexpected or the unknown, loss of control, and loss of approval. Anxieties related to music performance can certainly reflect and magnify these root fears. Fear of the unexpected may arise if one is performing in an unfamiliar venue, with a new band or accompanist, or to an unknown audience. Loss of control might involve potential missed notes, forgotten lyrics, technical problems, or lack of focus. Fear of the loss of approval or love is very common, and can refer to disappointing a teacher or mentor, a family member, critics or competition judges, even impressionable students or fans.

Ironically, sometimes the one thing a performer fears the most is . . . fear. It sounds silly, but if you think about it, it would make perfect sense for a typically anxious performer to begin to dread the anxiety she expects is waiting for her. In his first inaugural address, President Franklin D. Roosevelt said, ". . . the only thing we have to fear is fear itself—nameless, unreasoning, unjustified terror which paralyzes needed efforts to convert retreat into advance." Although he was talking about the state of the nation during the lowest point of the Great Depression in

1932, this statement directly pertains to musicians. Sometimes we spend so much effort trying to avoid the fear that we end up intensifying it and somehow giving it even greater power. Sometimes, fully experiencing the fear and going through it rather than around it can help tremendously. The line between fear and excitement, or anxiety and peak performance, can be a very thin one.

What Performance Anxiety Isn't

If you hear a voice within you say "you cannot paint,"
then by all means paint and that voice will be silenced.—Vincent van Gogh

Before we continue our discussion of stage fright, it will be good to clear a few myths out of the way. First, performance anxiety is not "all in your imagination," because it is a very real and universally experienced physical and psychological phenomenon. Second, performance stress is not the mark of a weak performer or a flawed musician. Some of the world's greatest and most successful musicians have spoken out publicly about their anxieties, especially in recent years as the old stigma surrounding performance anxiety has begun to diminish. Finally, discomfort on stage does not necessarily get easier the more you perform. Please remember this the next time a well-meaning person offers this advice. I work with many students and professional musicians, and it has been my experience that the mental aspect of performance anxiety (including self-criticism and negative self-talk) can sometimes increase as the performer becomes more and more accomplished and well known in her field. What can get easier with time is the ability to predict, recognize, and find ways to manage the anxiety. This does not happen without conscious effort and mindful, deliberate practice.

Importantly, I am talking about the sort of performance anxiety that occurs when a musician is prepared to do his best; the sort of anxiety that can sabotage the best efforts of a musician who has the potential to perform well. In other words, any discussion of anxiety management or mental skills training assumes that the performer has *practiced sufficiently* and *is well prepared* for the performance at hand. This is an extremely important point! Occasionally I will get requests for performance coaching from students who have an impending jury or recital and are struggling with their anxieties. When I meet with them, sometimes I discover that they simply aren't ready for the upcoming performance.

Perhaps they haven't fully memorized their music, translated their lyrics, or secured an accompanist. Sometimes they have not practiced enough and are panicking because they don't feel they have enough time left to "cram" for the performance. When this happens, I disclose (with a touch of gentle humor, I hope) that I have no magic wand with which to turn back the clock.

I don't mean to be harsh, but if you are nervous because you are unprepared for your performance, then it is probably appropriate for you to feel nervous about giving a substandard recital. This is what I would call a healthy and rational fear. In other words, if you have not fully memorized your Italian art song, then you are probably justified in your fear that you might forget the words. The exact opposite approach, perceived overpreparation, can actually help to mitigate performance anxiety. If you are so prepared for a performance that you know every beat of the music like the back of your hand, you will find it much easier to refine the mental aspects of peak performance. No performance coaching, no mental skills training, no nifty books or websites, no anxiety management techniques can compensate for a genuine lack of preparation. A comprehensive understanding of intelligent practice skills, combined with a sufficient amount of time and forethought, is nonnegotiable. We must be brutally honest with ourselves and understand that any fear stemming from a lack of preparation is simply valuable feedback for how to better prepare next time.

Another disclaimer to consider is that you need to be playing music that is appropriate for you. You should possess the adequate technical and musical skills required to perform the repertoire that you have chosen. This may sound like a no-brainer, but if your music is too difficult to perform well, anxiety management techniques will have little effect. Fear often arises when a musician or his teacher chooses a challenging piece that is beyond the realm of the musician's current abilities. I don't mean to imply that you must never stretch your potential with challenging repertoire, but you should choose your music wisely if it is intended for a public performance. I know a gifted organist who takes lessons and who plays for two churches in a large metropolitan area. He struggles with performance anxiety, so he developed the practice of performing only music that he has "lived with" for at least a year. So, the music he is preparing for his lesson this week may find its way into a church service this time next year. Even though he is an advanced musician, he knows himself well enough not to perform new pieces that push him to his technical limits. The most successful performers are well equipped, both technically and musically, to perform their repertoire with confidence and artistry.

Ideally, a musician will be physically and psychologically capable of performing her chosen repertoire. Any sort of physical limitation (including a recent injury, surgery, disability, or chronic condition such as arthritis) can understandably magnify performance stress. Depending on the condition, postponing a performance is sometimes the best course of action. Whether you are experiencing an ongoing physical challenge or a temporary setback, you may choose to modify your chosen repertoire to suit your present abilities. Psychological challenges, above and beyond the sort of performance anxiety discussed in this chapter, may also impair your ability to engage successfully in stress management techniques. These situations might include any number of learning challenges, behavioral differences, or diagnosed psychological disorders that would prevent a musician from performing with ease and confidence without professional guidance.

For dedicated musicians, I can offer one final opinion on what performance anxiety isn't: It isn't a good reason to discontinue your enjoyment of making music. If you are devoted to your music or to the idea of being a performer, then it is absolutely worth rolling up your sleeves, digging into the roots of discomfort, and discovering personal coping solutions. Too many fine musicians changed careers or gave up performing altogether because they lacked the information, resources, or support for dealing with the stress of performing. Others stopped playing because of the shame they felt at not being able to master their "problem" on their own. Luckily, much has changed over the last few decades, and resources for stress and anxiety management are now widely accessible.

What Performance Anxiety Is

Anxiety is the gap between now and then.—Fritz Perls

A young student once said to me, "Butterflies belong in a science project, not in my stomach." That image made me smile, but musicians will understand immediately what he meant. When a performer is under pressure and about to go out on stage, his unwanted symptoms may range from sweaty palms to a dry mouth to the aforementioned misplaced butterflies. Some musicians can feel these same symptoms while simply imagining a performance in vivid detail. Why do we experience these physical manifestations of fear, when performing music is seemingly such a benign activity? How is it that 25% of professional musicians report that their performances are needlessly *impaired* by performance anxiety?

A widely used definition of performance anxiety, developed by Paul Salmon in 1990, is "The experience of persisting, distressful apprehension about and/or actual impairment of performance skills in a public context, to a degree unwarranted given the individual's musical aptitude, training, and level of preparation." I like this definition because it contains some important key words: persisting, distressful, impairment, and unwarranted. Many musicians who struggle with performance stress are extraordinarily gifted individuals. Despite hours of practice and any number of outstanding preliminary performances, they are often not able to perform convincingly or confidently when in front of an audience. The symptoms of anxiety can override a good musician's excellent preparation, physical technique, and mature artistry, and can be downright devastating. For some performers, a few butterflies won't disrupt the overall performance experience. For others, this experience can become a major stumbling block.

Every performer, in order to be an outstanding and well-educated musician, must understand the basic facts about performance anxiety: what really causes it, how it affects the nervous system, and what techniques are most effective in managing it. It is no longer sufficient to rely on anecdotes from our teachers or peers, because what helps one performer may not work for another. We now know that silly solutions such as imagining the audience in their underwear will not magically alleviate a deeply rooted sense of dread. Performance anxiety is varied and personal, but also eminently manageable for most people. So, let's begin with what happens in your brain and body when a performance looms near.

When we experience a real or perceived threat, our bodies immediately respond in order to keep us safe from danger. If you have ever experienced a near accident on the highway, or have come face-to-face with a wild animal on a hiking trail, your brain probably initiated a stress response that allowed you to react quickly to keep out of harm's way. In fact, the physical symptoms you may have felt at those times (such as a racing heartbeat or shortness of breath) mirror the experiences of some musicians on stage. When a person experiences sudden fear for any reason, specific neurological and physical changes occur in the body. Perceived danger triggers a burst of adrenaline and other neurotransmitters in the bloodstream, and these manifest in the body in a number of curious ways.

To understand the body's autonomic stress response, I find it helpful to imagine that I am faced with a very real physical threat, rather than an upcoming performance. Of course, it is no fun to daydream about possible real-life catastrophes. Instead, I invite you to imagine that you are under attack by a seemingly benign fictional creature, such as a giant sugary marshmallow chick. Perhaps this hideous yellow monster is twice your size and about to engulf your body until you drown in its treacherously sticky goo. How would your brain and body fight to keep you safe from this ghastly demise? While many readers may be familiar with the fight-or-flight reaction, it helps to recognize the purpose behind the specific physical sensations we experience when under pressure.

At the earliest sign of attack, the sudden rush of adrenaline in your system will enable you to make a split-second decision—whether to run away from your sugar-coated attacker or to turn and fight for your life. No matter what you choose, you will need a great deal of energy in your body and the strength to fight or run. Chances are that your pulse will quicken, and blood will be redirected to the largest muscles in your limbs. Perhaps you will feel a pounding or racing heartbeat, or a sudden rise in blood pressure. Your hands may become cold, since the blood has moved away from your hands and feet and into the large muscles of your arms and legs. This happens so that you can use the maximum power of your arms and legs to fight and defend yourself, or to run away. (Of course, trying to play the guitar with those same cold fingers is a different story, but we will get to that later.)

In response to your high-fructose assailant, your respiratory rate may increase, since your body will need more oxygen to fight or flee. You may experience this as shallow or quickened breathing, even hyperventilation. The digestive system temporarily ceases its regular functions, and digestion comes to a screeching halt. Why? Because your body does not have the time or energy to digest your morning bowl of Hexachordal Crunch if you are fighting for your life. This causes that familiar "butterflies" feeling; you may also experience this as an upset stomach, nausea, or a vague cramping sensation. Since the salivary glands are a part of the digestive system, they can go on hiatus as well, producing a dry mouth for many people. Your muscles tighten, and you may feel tension in your shoulders, neck, or larger muscles. You may even experience a tension headache. Sometimes the muscles become tight enough to shake or quiver.

Let's imagine that you have opted to run away from this killer marshmallow. If you are rushing through a darkened forest, for example, you will need to have a keenly sharpened sense of vision. The pupils will dilate, and you may experience acute visual awareness, enhanced peripheral vision, or increased sensitivity to lights. If you decide instead to face your attacker and engage in battle, your body will still work hard to protect your life. Your perspiration rate might increase dramatically, regardless of the external temperature. Wet skin is slippery, and a slippery human is less likely to be caught in the clutches of a giant monster. Lubricated skin also reduces the chance of debilitating scratches and cuts. Tiny capillaries will pull away from the surface of your skin, and this will reduce bleeding if you are cut or scratched during the battle with your attacker. In a life-or-death situation, your body will also work hard to eliminate any excess waste as soon as possible in order to make you lighter on your feet to flee from danger.

If we fantasize that you vanquished your squishy enemy, we can reflect on how these physical symptoms manifest on stage during a musical performance. You may observe the irony that playing music is not a true physical threat, because you are not being ambushed by your cello or an audience member in the first row. It is important to realize that the part of your brain that initiates the fight-or-flight response doesn't always recognize the difference between a real threat and a perceived threat. In fact, since that part of your brain is separate from the part of your brain responsible for rationalizing events, you can rarely reason or talk yourself out of an episode of stage fright. Instead, you can learn to understand and appreciate why you are experiencing certain sensations. It might even alleviate some of the mystery surrounding those jitters.

When the brain interprets a musical performance as an imminent threat, those physical reactions can become distracting or even debilitating if left unchecked. Trying to play the piano with cold fingers or sweaty hands is as difficult as trying to play a clarinet solo with a dry mouth. Musicians who sing or play a wind instrument know how difficult breath control can become when under pressure. If your hands or legs start to tremble while you are performing, remember that you may not be shaking because you are terrified, but because your muscles are tense. When we try to control the shaking to make it stop, we end up tensing the muscles even more, exacerbating the problem. If a performer chooses instead to release those shaking muscles or surrounding body parts, the quivering is likely to diminish. If you experience heightened sensitivity to stage lights or increased visual awareness in your peripheral field, it may help to remember that the pupils are simply more dilated than usual.

While stress can definitely affect the quality of a performance, some symptoms are more aggravating the days and hours before the actual event. Many people experience a tension headache the day of a performance, which can be bothersome and distracting. Other performers feel an occasional rush of panic or dread in the days leading up to an event. Because the body attempts to eliminate waste when it senses a threat, many musicians find that they need to run to the bathroom constantly the day of, and even the days preceding, an important concert. Others experience full-blown gastrointestinal distress. This is a completely normal, if not altogether annoying, human response to perceived danger. The next time you are running to the bathroom in your fancy recital attire, you can marvel at how attentive and effective your body is at keeping you alive and safe from harm!

The body's stress response is not confined to physical changes in the body, because some of our most troublesome experiences are psychological in nature. When threatened, the neurons in the brain fire more quickly than normal, and the brainwaves accelerate as well. The resulting sharpened attention will help you make immediate life-or-death decisions when absolutely necessary. However, this increased neurological activity can also make musicians feel hyperaware or overly focused on their music or instrument. A boost in brain activity can escalate internal self-talk, particularly unwanted critical or negative thinking. That little voice inside your head that relishes commenting on anything and everything may suddenly become hyperactive, finding new things to worry about or contemplating every possible worst-case scenario. An overactive conscious mind can also initiate feelings of agitation, indecisiveness, self-doubt, detachment, even dissociation.

For some musicians, the psychological effects of the fight-or-flight response are far more debilitating than the physical symptoms. The physical annoyances are sometimes easier to manage, and it often takes more time and persistence to address the inner workings of that relentless critical mind. In addition, psychological challenges can affect our patterns of thought, which can influence our emotions and cause behavioral changes or mood disturbances. Since the body's automatic fear response bypasses the logical part of the brain, it is usually impossible to justify or rationalize the fear away. Good mental skills, particularly when grounded in mindfulness, can help bridge the divide between the anxiety we experience and the equilibrium we believe is possible.

The hidden symptoms of performance anxiety are subtler, and perhaps more difficult to detect. Often, these manifest in behaviors that might not seem to be associated with performing at all. Procrastination is a great example. We put off doing what we secretly fear or think we may not achieve, such as writing a paper, practicing our music, confronting an adversary, or paying the overdue bills. Instead, we distract ourselves with smaller tasks that we know we will do well, such as organizing our desk drawers, loading the dishwasher, and surfing the internet for cute hedgehog videos. If you find that you are avoiding a task by telling yourself that you're not ready, it's not time, or you don't feel like it, stop and ask yourself if you are really procrastinating out of stress or anxiety. Procrastination often stems from apprehension. The irony is that, assuming the task is something that you eventually must do, putting it off will only increase your stress level. If a project seems overwhelming, you may be more likely to tackle it small bits at a time. Mark Twain once said, "The secret of getting ahead is getting started. The secret of getting started is breaking your complex, overwhelming tasks into small manageable tasks, and then starting on the first one." Like getting to the gym or the practice room, getting started is often the most challenging step.

Other hidden manifestations of performance anxiety include general agitation, indecisiveness, or withdrawal. Some musicians may subconsciously sabotage their own efforts by forgetting their reeds, driving directions, or audition music. Think about it: If you are unable to perform because you show up to a competition without your mallets, you won't have the opportunity to get nervous or crash and burn on stage. It is impossible to fail if you deny yourself the opportunity to succeed. Anxiety can also surface as negativity, particularly through self-disparagement or negative judgment of others. People who judge other musicians harshly, especially as a recurring habit, may secretly be trying to boost their own self-confidence. After all, if you criticize someone else's ability to play a rapid scale passage, the unspoken assumption is that *your* ability to play a rapid scale passage is far superior. The truth is that, deep down, sometimes the harshest critics are the most insecure musicians.

Self-medication is further evidence that anxiety might be at the root of the situation. A musician can soothe herself using alcohol, prescription medications, over-the-counter drugs, or illegal substances. The dangers of substance abuse and addiction are very real concerns for many musicians. Realize that performers can also medicate themselves with food, tobacco, sex, indiscriminate spending, computer games, or internet use. Becoming a self-aware and prosperous musician means learning to identify positive and negative behaviors and consciously choosing healthy ways to adapt.

Negative Thoughts and Irrational Ideas

Not until we are lost do we begin to understand ourselves.
—Henry David Thoreau

Successful musicians need to be bravely self-critical. In fact, we are trained from a very early age to identify and correct our errors and to set high standards of excellence. Occasionally the boundary between constructive self-criticism and negative self-judgment becomes blurred. Sometimes we become preoccupied with mistakes and memory lapses, either making them or avoiding them. A musician who has played flawlessly for several minutes may suddenly begin to expect or dread an impending mistake. Some musicians are a bit superstitious about errors and feel relieved once they make the first one. We can easily focus on avoiding glitches rather than giving our attention to the expressive intent of our music. In other words, we can spend all of our energy worrying about what we don't want, rather than concentrating on what we do want. We can also react negatively to mistakes when they happen by becoming exasperated or embarrassed. We can even supplement our negative thoughts by engaging in reasonable-sounding notions that are, on closer examination, unhealthy and unhelpful.

In the next chapter, we will explore techniques of identifying and disputing many of the illogical thoughts that can trigger stress and unhappiness. As long as we're considering the concept of negative thinking, though, let's take a look at a few maladaptive ideas that we humans love to adopt. These might seem silly at first glance. Yet, they are widespread in our society, even when they dwell only in the subtle realm of our subconscious minds. You may be able to recall a situation when your thoughts or behaviors reflected some of these beliefs:

- I should succeed in everything I do.
- I need to feel loved and appreciated.
- I must secure the approval of others.
- It is terrible when things don't go my way.
- I have no control over my thoughts or actions.
- Other people and events determine my happiness.

Additionally, the following unhealthy beliefs can be embraced by musicians:

- I must never give a second-rate performance.
- If I mess up, I will look foolish.
- My value as a musician is reflected in the quality of my performance.
- If I play badly, I will disappoint my audience.
- I must never let people down.
- I'm not as talented as people think I am.

These thoughts can generate very specific emotions. An emotion is never senseless, because it reveals the truth of our internal experience at any moment in time. Thoughts, however, as products of the electrical activity in our brains, can be irrational if they are generated in the absence of conscious awareness.

How can we determine if an idea that we have is rational or irrational? Generally speaking, a thought or belief is not rational if it is illogical, inconsistent with reality, does not support our short-term or long-term goals for success, and/or does not promote an overall sense of happiness or well-being. Looking back over the preceding lists, can you see why each of these statements could be labeled as irrational beliefs?

Another unrealistic idea worth mentioning to perpetually stressed musicians is the belief that we can achieve happiness through inertia. When we are overworked or burned out, it can be tantalizing to dream about relaxing in a hammock while slurping a drink from a coconut shell or sprawling in our pajamas during a home movie marathon. And these are both great ideas for relaxation and rejuvenation. But once the body and mind are refreshed, sustaining that sort of inaction can make us feel restless, listless, even melancholy. We humans tend to be happiest when we are engaged in a meaningful activity, engrossed in a creative pursuit, or devoting ourselves to other worthwhile people or projects. We can experience a sublime state of consciousness when we are completely absorbed in an activity such as music making. Musicians don't always recognize, however, that sometimes they need to be engaged in order to stay happy. The creative mind can't turn itself off for very long.

Sometimes human beings will adopt ego defenses to cope with stress and other unpleasant situations. We all do this at some point. Psychologists consider these strategies to be maladaptive, since they often help us to avoid a negative situation rather than deal with an effective resolution. If we learn to identify these behaviors, we can be mindful of what we do, why we do it, and if we can find a better way to cope. If you're like me, you may recognize yourself in a few of these! With conscious awareness, we can learn to acknowledge these behaviors without judgment, before choosing healthier approaches.

Avoidance is a temporarily effective way of dodging an unwanted situation. We can refuse to face any number of unpleasant realities by escaping or by engaging in other activities. Since procrastination can be a hidden symptom of anxiety, remember that shopping for recital shoes instead of practicing could be an example of avoidance.

Fantasy is a favorite tactic of musicians, because we do it so well. In order to succeed, we need to engage our imaginations to envision future successes. If, however, we are too preoccupied with our inner fantasy world, or if we rely too frequently on imaginary or improbable achievements rather than actually doing the required work, it can negatively affect our progress.

Compensation is one way to cover up a weakness, or a perceived weakness, by emphasizing something else instead. This could involve counterbalancing the loss of a job or audition by overeating or indulging in alcohol. Or, a musician who struggles with a certain musical style might become a self-identified specialist in a more comfortable style instead, rather than working to overcome the weakness.

Identification with famous people, bands, orchestras, performance venues, or institutions can temporarily bolster our self-esteem. We musicians are masters of name-dropping, especially when our musical training is scrutinized by others, and when we really do associate with well-known performers. This doesn't mean that you are using an ego defense every time you mention to someone that you once had coffee with Prince's hairdresser's next-door neighbor. It becomes a problem only if you find that you are imitating someone at the expense of your own artistic development or if you are using the successes of others to boost your own reputation or esteem. Everyone knows a pathological name-dropper, and most of them are no fun to be around.

Projection can occur when we blame others for our struggles or failures or if we focus too closely on what we believe others may think. A music student will sometimes blame his teacher if he fails to meet a specific performance goal. Or, we can project our fears and insecurities onto someone else by criticizing that person for something that causes us apprehension. Prejudice and jealousy can also be related to projection.

Displacement is the act of taking out one's frustrations on others. This is very common in our culture, because we don't always have the opportunity to express our negative feelings. A person who finds herself in a stressful situation at work probably can't yell at her boss, so she may come home and shout at her spouse or children instead. Many events involving road rage are examples of displacement. Understanding displacement can be very helpful if you have a teacher, mentor, or coworker who sometimes takes his stresses out on you, or if you are unable to understand why you seem to lose your temper with the innocent people in your life. A favorite act of displacement is to take out one's frustrations on an inanimate object. Once, when I was leafing through a friend's copy of the Chopin *Études*, I came across a page that had obviously been ripped out, mangled, and then taped back into the book. My friend had gotten so angry at her inability to master a section of that piece, she told me, that she threw the book against the wall. That wasn't enough to satisfy her, though, so she proceeded tearfully to rip and crumple the page in question. In the end, this action made her feel worse instead of better. Not only did she ruin a good edition of music, but the tantrum left her feeling embarrassed and even more frustrated. How might she have better handled this situation?

Emotional isolation is a familiar technique for musicians. Performers occasionally like to withdraw into passivity, seclusion, even inactivity. Of course, sometimes solitude is good and necessary for the creative process. If you are composing an original piece of music, for example, you may need to focus quietly without the distraction of other people. When used as a defense mechanism, however, isolation can lead to loneliness or depression. *Intellectualization* is a more abstract form of isolation, particularly when someone distances himself from a painful emotion or situation by talking about it in only the most detached and analytical manner. When it comes to difficult personal situations, it sometimes feels safer to think than to feel.

Acting out is a way of avoiding stress through indirect, often subconscious actions. This can include the sort of self-sabotage mentioned earlier. If you have an intense fear of flying, for example, you might "accidentally" oversleep and miss your flight. If you are nervous about an important audition or competition, you might forget to bring your music or your mouthpiece. Some psychologists relate this ego defense to the concept of wish fulfillment. This idea implies that all behavior is purposeful. In the example of forgetting your music at the audition, perhaps your subconscious wish was fulfilled when you were forced to forfeit the audition.

Years ago, I was engaged in an email conversation with a friend about her most recent romantic crush. She was interested in a mutual colleague of ours, but was too nervous to tell him how she felt. After several email exchanges about this man, she accidentally forwarded her email response to *him* instead of to me. She was mortified, because he was then able to read our entire email exchange. To this day, I am convinced that a latent part of her did that on purpose, because it saved her the trouble of actually talking to him in person. (By the way, her mistake worked, and they went out to dinner the next weekend.)

When It All Becomes Too Much

And how high can you fly with broken wings?—Aerosmith

As you have read and probably experienced, music performance and mental health challenges often go hand in hand. Sometimes it is enough to adopt and diligently practice many of the mental skills described in this or other books. Other times, though, certain psychological issues are more deeply rooted than we may realize. Sometimes they have very little to do with music at all! While most sensitive musicians struggle with issues of self-worth, self-doubt, and perfectionism, sometimes the anxiety can be coupled with depression or can stem from deeper personal or family issues.

If left unchecked, anxiety can disrupt your sense of well-being in a number of different ways. Be aware if the stress related to music per-formance also manifests in other parts of your life as insomnia, eating disorders, acute social anxiety or shyness, obsessive or compulsive behaviors, extreme mood swings, or ongoing health issues. Physical symptoms can include stomach or digestive problems, headaches, short-ness of breath, or pounding or racing heartbeat. You or someone you care about might also experience recurring issues of self-esteem or self-worth, persistent irrational beliefs or unhealthy thought patterns, phobias or fears, or characteristics such as excessive or constant worry, tension, irri-tability, or restlessness.

Some musicians who struggle with stage fright have also experienced panic attacks on one or more occasion. A panic attack is a sudden episode of intense fear that can happen at any time and that may involve feelings of dizziness or lightheadedness, pounding heart, sweating, trembling or shaking, feelings of being detached from oneself, and/or overall feelings of terror or loss of control. Although panic attacks feel terrible and can be quite frightening, they are usually harmless and readily treated. Many of the performance preparation techniques addressed in this book can help prevent or mitigate a panic attack.

Musicians should learn to recognize the symptoms of depression, which are best treated in consultation with a licensed professional. As I mentioned earlier, these symptoms include regular feelings of hopelessness, emptiness, fatigue, a change in eating or sleeping habits, difficulty concentrating, and general loss of energy or motivation. If this has been your recent experience, please seek help by calling a trusted friend, teacher, spiritual advisor, or mental health professional. Don't assume that anyone is aware of what you are going through. I was devastated to lose a student to suicide many years ago. No one, not even his closest friend, had any idea that he was depressed, because he covered it up so well. It is ironic to think that although we are masters of musical communication, we aren't always able to communicate to others how we feel. Opening up, while scary at times, is sometimes the best first step we can take. In the words of Robert Frost, "The best way out is always through."

When should you (or someone you know) make an appointment with a doctor or therapist? This is a difficult question to answer, because no two people or experiences are exactly alike. Remember that, when it comes to performance anxiety management, the goal is not to eliminate the jitters altogether. Adrenaline is a little bit like fire. A small, controlled amount of fire can heat your home or cook your dinner, but too much fire will burn down your house! A small amount of adrenaline can give your performance an artistic edge, but too much can impair your ability to perform well or with confidence. While some people will be able to find their own stress management solutions, others will benefit from professional help, especially if they are experiencing deeper psychological issues.

Please consider a professional consultation if any of the following are true:

- You have been experiencing ongoing symptoms of depression or anxiety as described in this chapter.
- Your performance anxiety continues to be distressing and unmanageable, despite your regular practice of the mental skills techniques described in this or other books.
- Your emotions or behaviors are affecting other parts of your life, your relationships, or your ability to practice or perform.

- You have noticed an overreliance on alcohol, prescription medications, recreational drugs, or other harmful habits.
- Your current relationship, past relationships, or family environment have included alcoholism, drug abuse, violence, or physical or emotional abuse.
- You have been deeply affected by one or more significant upheaval in your life: the end of a relationship, the beginning or end of a job, a relocation, a stressful financial obligation or loss, or the death or serious illness of a loved one.
- You have recently experienced or witnessed a traumatic event, or you have been struggling with dreams or memories of a trauma from the past.
- You are interested in using medication to treat your depression or anxiety.
- You have received feedback from your respected friends or loved ones that you might benefit from professional help.

Every part of your life affects your mental health and your ability to perform well. We musicians (and all other humans) deserve to take as much care of our mental health as we do our physical health. If you are an instructor reading this book, please remember that teachers often represent the first line of defense for many students in crisis. When a student seeks the advice of a trusted mentor, it is our ethical responsibility to respond as best we can, while acknowledging our professional limits as experts in music, not experts in mental health.

The challenges discussed in this chapter are much to absorb! The Russian author Fyodor Dostoyevsky once said, "To think too much is a disease." This is true for many performing musicians who worry or overthink things unnecessarily or who allow just one or two maladaptive thoughts or tendencies to sabotage their successes. In the words of legendary boxer Muhammad Ali, "It isn't the mountains ahead to climb that wear you out; it's the pebble in your shoe." Sometimes it's just a matter of finding that metaphoric pebble. In the next chapter, we will discuss several solutions to these psychological challenges.

4 MINDFUL PERFORMANCE PSYCHOLOGY

The human mind is our fundamental resource.—John F. Kennedy

Now that we have taken a long, hard look at some of the many challenges facing musicians, let's begin to explore a variety of mental strategies for successful performance. Over the past hundred years, advances in Western psychology have completely transformed the way we look at the nature of human thought and behavior. Musicians who possess a basic understanding of how their minds work can begin to employ powerfully effective mindfulness techniques. This chapter considers a number of contemporary perspectives, many of them from the cognitive-behavioral models of psychology. Since these approaches address how we can handle stress and influence thoughts, emotions, and behavior, they are particularly well suited to artistic performers.

I Think, Therefore I Feel

Between stimulus and response, there is a space.
In that space is our power to choose our response.
In our response lies our growth and our freedom.—Viktor Frankl

During the middle of the 20th century, psychologists began to recognize that our thoughts, feelings, and behaviors are all interrelated. Patterns of thinking can influence our emotional responses to events, which can in turn affect our habits of behavior. This suggests that happiness does not arise as a result of external events or situations, but rather as a result of our reactions to those situations. If that is the case, then, the negative feelings we experience are often the results of our own thinking. Does this sound too simplistic? A deeper look at this reasoning can reveal some very profound implications.

Many people believe that stress is the result of outside forces beyond their control. Reflect for a moment on the life events that could potentially "make" you feel stressed. Imagine, for example, that you find yourself on the receiving end of someone else's outrage. Perhaps a friend, coworker, supervisor, or family member lashes out at you, maybe blaming or accusing you of something. Like many people in that situation, you might feel angry or insulted. Your thoughts about the situation ("How dare she speak to me like that?") would trigger beliefs about the situation ("What a rude and offensive individual!"), which would then lead to a variety of emotions ("I feel insulted and humiliated"). Those strong emotions may then fuel any number of behaviors. In this example, your actions might include those related to retaliation, such as quarreling, sabotage, or even physical violence. This may seem like an unfortunate but natural chain of events, given the situation.

Imagine, however, that you experienced a different reaction to this angry person. In this case, maybe your thoughts about the situation would be something like, "Why is she being so mean and abusive to me? This is completely unfair; what did I do to deserve this?" This perspective might trigger emotions such as shame, sadness, or guilt, leading to very different behaviors such as crying, apologizing, or escaping. In a third possible scenario, this situation might amuse you. If you believed that the enraged person was just being ridiculous, you might laugh or make light of the situation. In yet another scenario, you might react with empathy and compassion. In this case, a thought such as "I'm surprised by her anger" might lead to a belief such as "She must be under a lot of stress, or maybe there's more to this story than I know." Resulting feelings and behaviors might be related to sympathy, understanding, maybe even an act of kindness.

This was one example of a single event, a furious tirade, interpreted from four different points of view: anger, shame, amusement, compassion. In each example, the experience varied depending on the line of thinking. If stress isn't what happens to us, it must be the result of how we interpret what happens to us. And, while we can't always control what happens to us, we can often control our reactions. When possible, we do this by choosing our thoughts deliberately. With conscious awareness, we end up exercising some authority over our feelings. The idea that we essentially choose our own attitudes can be difficult to accept at first, but it also offers a perspective that can be immensely liberating. Viktor Frankl, psychiatrist and Holocaust survivor, wrote about this choice in his book,

Man's Search for Meaning. He said, "Man does not simply exist but always decides what his existence will be, what he will become the next moment. By the same token, every human being has the freedom to change at any instant." This mindset can be very effective toward encouraging happiness and mental wellness, because it gives us the space and the opportunity to determine the type of person we want to be. Windy Dryden's influential statement of emotional responsibility expresses this: "We are largely, but not exclusively, responsible for the way we feel and act by the views we take of the events in our lives."

A music performance is another good example of a situation that can be interpreted in multiple ways. Different musicians may view an upcoming concert as a source of achievement and prestige, or anxiety and dread, or procrastination and avoidance, or apathy. The list goes on and on, but if you think about the many musicians you know, you will probably be able to identify a wide variety of attitudes and emotions related to public performance. What emotions do you tend to feel? If you can identify these, you can probably trace them back to specific thoughts and beliefs you have about yourself and your musical abilities. And if a belief is more or less a pattern of thought, you can gradually learn to change negative beliefs by consciously changing those patterns of thought. In other words, you experience more of whatever garners your attention.

A few years ago, I experienced a striking example of this philosophy. I was returning from a conference in Albuquerque, but a bad winter storm interrupted my travel plans as well as the travel plans of several hundred other people. My flight to Denver was diverted 70 miles away to Colorado Springs, which caused everyone to miss their connecting flights. The series of events that unfolded was almost comical. Phone and internet connections were overloaded, so no one could get through to an agent to rebook a flight. The airport was so overcrowded with stranded travelers that lines were hours long, even to find a nearby hotel. It was so late that busses had stopped running, and the snow was falling so heavily that most taxis had given up as well. No travelers had planned for a snowpocalypse, so no one had packed a winter coat or boots. It would have been a great setup for a horror movie: *Airplane III: Snow Zombies.*

I was fortunate to have been stuck with several of my professional colleagues who were returning from the same conference. Because of the long lines and overall chaos, I had plenty of time to wait, which was an excellent opportunity to observe how different people handled this situation. On the plane I had been reading the psychological literature, so these ideas were fresh in my mind: Stress might be the result of our own thinking, and we get more of whatever we focus upon. While the general atmosphere in the airport was one of frustration and confusion, the diversity of human emotions seemed to range from humor to fatigue to irritation to utter rage. Some people shouted into their phones or at the airport ticket agents, as if the agents could do anything to stop the storms or create more flights. (I actually heard a man yell, "This is an outrage!" and I couldn't help but chuckle, because I suddenly imagined that he was scolding the frozen precipitation.) As I recall, a few people were trying to share or trade transportation opportunities with other travelers. Some people sat in silence, looking sleepy or bored. One woman was in tears, perhaps out of frustration, or maybe because she was going to miss an important event. As I walked around the terminal to kill time, I saw different groups of people playing cards, interacting with children, talking with other families around them, exchanging travel disaster stories, and telling jokes. One of my friends went on a mission to find a bottle of wine in order to make the best of the situation. I wholeheartedly approved.

For me, this escapade confirmed the wide variety of possible human responses to a single event: a disrupted airline flight. The fact that some people were laughing and some people were shouting validates that the canceled flight itself was not really the source of stress. The ways in which people were choosing to interpret an event beyond their control . . . now, *that* was the source of stress. I observed that those who were angry and shouting seemed absolutely miserable. Those who continued to read a book while standing in line seemed calm or indifferent. Those who were playing games and laughing with their friends seemed willing to entertain an unexpected adventure. I noticed that my own reaction seemed to cycle through feelings of boredom, irritation, and amusement. And those feelings were certainly triggered by my thoughts about the event. If I found myself thinking, "I bet there are no hotel rooms left," I felt more anxious. If I found myself thinking, "Maybe we can find a nice restaurant," I felt more optimistic.

In the end, my colleagues and I emerged from the experience unscathed. In fact, the unplanned overnight stay in snowy Colorado generated new friendships and a great story. Most important for me, it offered a priceless lesson on the nature of the human mind.

Healthy Minds

Slump? I ain't in no slump. I just ain't hittin.'—Yogi Berra

As we saw in the last chapter, the stereotype of the sensitive and tormented musician exists because there have been so many examples of brilliant, creative minds who have suffered publicly from some sort of psychological distress. While we can't simply think our way out of very real psychological disorders, we now understand that the thoughts and behaviors we choose can have a profound impact on our sense of well-being. This means that even the most vulnerable musicians can learn mindfulness skills that promote good mental health. Over the years, psychologists have identified several characteristics that happy, healthy people have in common. Some people seem predisposed to be happy without much conscious effort. Others, barring any limiting medical or psychiatric conditions, can develop and refine those same mental skills.

One indication of good mental health, according to some professionals, is the belief that we are able to take responsibility for our own happiness. This relates to the statement of emotional responsibility mentioned earlier: "We are largely, but not exclusively, responsible for the way we feel and act by the views we take of the events in our lives." Being responsible doesn't mean that everything we experience is our own fault, but it does imply that we can turn a negative situation around through conscious awareness. It may help, at first, to practice identifying your emotions, and then asking yourself whether you might be choosing these emotions.

Years ago, this idea fascinated me. I found great freedom in thinking to myself, "I feel happy right now, and I'm choosing to be happy. I could just as easily feel grouchy." Or, "I am angry right now, and I am choosing to be angry, because it feels pretty good at this particular moment." Whether I really believed I could have controlled my feelings at those times, mindfully identifying them and using the word "choose" encouraged me to become aware of the part I was playing in my own life experience. This feels much more empowering than a statement such as, "He makes me so angry!" It helps me to remember that no one can really make me feel anything, unless I allow that to happen. Sometimes, though, it is hard to convince yourself that you are actually choosing difficult emotions. This is because it is more accurate to say that we are choosing the *thoughts* that may be triggering those emotions. We will explore this idea later on in this chapter.

On those days when "choose" doesn't feel quite right, try "I am responsible" instead. Recently, when a restaurant server took 20 minutes to bring me a glass of water, I thought to myself, "I am feeling irritated and impatient, and I am responsible for those feelings." I was reminded that irritation and impatience were not my only options. An additional benefit of thinking "I choose this" or "I am responsible for this" is that I didn't judge my negative emotions so harshly. If I opted to feel outrage in a particular moment, I felt like that was okay, because it was my own conscious choice. I could always change my mind later. This process of emotional responsibility, while not always easy, is an excellent preparation for the more abstract practice of radical acceptance, described in Chapter 7. For now, the art of identifying emotions and considering the extent to which you may be choosing, agreeing to, or responsible for those feelings, is a valuable practice in conscious awareness.

Another indicator of good mental health, one of my personal favorites, is referred to as high frustration tolerance. A person who has developed this skill is able to bounce back quickly after a misfortune or disappointment. You probably know someone who never seems to get too ruffled or who is able to shrug off the stressors that would discourage the rest of us. A person with high frustration tolerance may still feel disappointment, anger, or fear, but may also have the resilience to put the situation into perspective more easily.

My grandpa was the very embodiment of high frustration tolerance. He seemed to take life in stride, always quietly and graciously, and always at an easy pace. I'll never forget the day that my grandma accidentally demolished their garage door. She had been parked in the garage; she threw her car into reverse, never bothering to look behind her, and drove *completely through the garage door*. The noise was deafening, and the damage was extensive. Metal shards were protruding from all sides, and the enormous hole in the middle resembled an escape scene from a cartoon. We all froze in silent horror, waiting for grandpa's reaction. He stood for a moment, thoughtfully chewing on a toothpick with his long arms folded, and quietly surveying the damage. He then went into the kitchen, poured himself a cup of coffee, and looked out again through the window. He said only, "Betty, that's the damnedest thing I ever saw." He quietly arranged for the repairs and never mentioned it again.

On the very opposite side of the spectrum, someone with low frustration tolerance would act according to a very different mindset. These people are very easily offended, and seem to become annoyed by the slightest thing. I once observed a patron in a restaurant send back a piece of cheesecake because it didn't "look nice enough." I even knew a cat who exhibited low frustration tolerance! She was fluffy and beautiful, but if you looked at her the wrong way, she would hiss at you. Of course, most people fall somewhere in between these two extremes. I find that I have an easier time with frustration tolerance depending on the context. For example, it is more difficult for me to tolerate frustrations related to aggressive drivers or noisy moviegoers than it is when dealing with unprepared students or grumpy cats. The fact that high frustration tolerance can be learned is good news for performing musicians who must deal with frustrations on a regular basis.

Our interpretation of what is perceived as "frustrating" is often cultural. I have witnessed this many times in my international travels. In the United States, for example, the pace of living is much faster than in many other parts of the world. We are accustomed to instant gratification through fast internet connections, immediate communication, and quick convenience. In many cases, running an errand is meant to be as efficient and effortless as possible. If any part of the errand is frustrated, for example, by long lines, downed computer systems, or slow service, many people react with impatience, frustration, or exasperation. In other parts of the world, though, time is perceived very differently.

A few years ago I was traveling through Jordan. I wanted to buy a gift before my trip ended, so I went into a small jewelry store. The shop owner immediately drew up two chairs and brought me a small glass of hot mint tea. At first, he seemed completely uninterested in selling me anything, which was a very new experience for me. We chatted at length for almost a half hour before he finally started showing me some of the jewelry he had for sale. By that time, his wife had brought out pastries to go with our tea. She was entertaining another group of shoppers, a few ladies who appeared to be family friends. The shop owner took great pains to explain each piece of jewelry that seemed to interest me, so that I would understand its history. Each piece seemed to have a story behind it. At one point, the other group of ladies came over to offer their opinions as well, and to joke with the shop owner's family. I began to feel like one of the family members myself.

I had expected to zoom in and out of that store in only a few minutes, but the adventure took almost 2 hours. At first, I had fought the temptation to glance at my watch. I didn't want to offend the shop owner, but I also hadn't planned to stay there for very long. When I noticed that no

one else in the shop seemed to be in any hurry and that the overall atmosphere was one of relaxed enjoyment, I settled down and suspended my
culturally indoctrinated perception of time and convenience. No one in
that shop seemed impatient or irritated. No one was frowning, looking
at their watches, or talking on their cell phones. To me, these people all
demonstrated the signs of happiness and relaxed well-being.

I didn't realize it at the time, but the shift from impatience to contentment had been my own conscious choice. I could easily have felt
inconvenienced, delayed, even trapped. Looking back, I can identify the
moment I decided to shift my focus. That moment is referred to in the
quote at the beginning of this chapter: "Between stimulus and response,
there is a space. In that space is our power to choose our response. In our
response lies our growth and our freedom." Of course, we can all identify
many more examples of times that we ignored that space and didn't consciously choose our response. By developing this awareness, anyone can
work to improve her level of frustration tolerance.

Optimistic people demonstrate a certain degree of mental flexibility, which includes accepting life's uncertainties. Music performance
can be unpredictable, since no one can anticipate how they will feel on
stage or how well they will be able to execute difficult passages when the
time comes. Other issues beyond a musician's control might include the
lighting or temperature of the performance space, quality of the facilities,
attention of the audience, and the actions of band members or other
collaborators. Mental flexibility allows us to adapt quickly, regardless of
the situation. It also allows us to relinquish control when necessary.

I once knew a pianist who was obliged to perform a classical concert on an old digital keyboard with no touch sensitivity; it was impossible for her to vary her dynamics while playing. She navigated this by
recruiting another musician to spin the volume knob up and down to
simulate crescendos and diminuendos! Another time, I attended a jazz
gig where the drummer failed to show. A brilliant friend of mine solved
this problem by playing the hi-hat cymbals with her foot while she used
her hands to play the saxophone! Although these are somewhat unconventional examples, they illustrate the benefits of mental flexibility and
optimism. Importantly, in both of these examples, my musician friends
did not dwell on their frustrations. They directed their energies toward
finding creative solutions instead. When people are able to recognize and
accept that not everything is within their control, they can begin to take
healthy risks without fear.

Purpose of Behavior

What you do speaks so loudly that I cannot hear what you say.
—Ralph Waldo Emerson

Our beliefs and emotions drive our behaviors. Consider for a moment that all behavior is purposeful. This means that everything we do (and everything we don't do, for that matter) accomplishes something for us. Our actions are often guided by a desire to create, avoid, or maintain a certain emotional state. Sometimes we hope to elicit a response or change our environment in some way. A person who gets up early every morning to practice his music is guided by any number of desires: to create music for his own enjoyment, to improve for self-satisfaction, to prepare for an upcoming concert, to avoid negative criticism or a bad rehearsal, to win an award or earn a positive review, and so on.

But the opposite is also true for someone who neglects to practice. Procrastination is a behavior in itself, and like other behaviors, it serves a purpose. Someone who puts off practicing may be guided by a hidden fear of success, for example. After all, success often leads to more pressure and even greater fears! Or, she may be acting out a secret fear of failure. Unbeknown to her, she might even be creating a convenient excuse for failure. Think about it; if you have practiced hard and have a bad performance, the disappointment can really hurt. But if you didn't practice much and have a bad performance, you can always blame the quality of your performance on the lack of time you had to prepare. It's not that you failed, because you didn't give yourself the chance to prosper.

When I work with musicians who struggle with stage fright, I occasionally ask them, "How has your anxiety benefitted you?" People are always surprised, and sometimes slightly offended, by this question. Frequently, the initial response will be, "It isn't benefitting me at all. It is affecting me negatively. Why else would I be seeking your advice?" But remember that behaviors associated with performance stress can also have meaning and purpose. If you have experienced nervousness related to performing, try to have an honest and open mind about it, and see if you can view it objectively. Consider for a moment how this fear may have served you in some unexpected way. For example, a musician who grapples with performance anxiety may acquire a good excuse when something goes wrong on stage. I have heard people say things like, "She would be such a great performer if it weren't for her nerves." The hidden benefit might be that any mistakes are beyond her control. Nervousness can also give us an excuse to back out of something that doesn't really interest or inspire us. I have seen young musicians develop symptoms of anxiety because they didn't really want to travel to a music camp or festival. For some people, fear can be a validation that, as they had suspected, they really aren't strong enough to triumph.

Another important benefit of nervousness is that it offers tangible evidence that we care about what we do. We want to do well, and we want others to enjoy the music we are offering them. One of my undergraduate piano majors, Caroline, said it best in an email to me:

> A little bit of nervousness shows that you care about the performance. It actually means something to you. This allows you to play with more emotion and really want to do well. Playing apathetically is, frankly, boring. And it's boring for the audience because they can tell that you're bored, too. I want to play with emotion. That is so important to me.

In this example, heightened adrenaline is a little like cayenne pepper. Just a pinch can give your performance that zesty edge.

Consider the feedback of a fine musician whom I met at the Van Cliburn International Piano Competition for Outstanding Amateurs several years ago. A cardiologist, he regularly prescribed himself beta-blockers to help cope with his performance anxiety. I asked him about that, because I was very interested to hear about his experience with the medication. His response was so memorable that I have quoted him many times over the years. He said, "Well, I mean, the good thing is that when I perform, I feel as if I am alone in my living room, and no one else is around, and I'm only playing for myself. The bad thing is that when I perform, I feel as if I am alone in my living room, and no one else is around, and I'm only playing for myself." For him, one benefit of excess adrenaline is that it connected him to the people in his audience.

I mentioned earlier that emotions are never irrational, because they are authentic indicators of our present-moment experience. Performance anxiety, in addition to having purpose and meaning, acts as an emotional barometer that can provide helpful feedback. Think about the fuel gauge in your car, and imagine a time when the fuel indicator light came on. That indicator light didn't signify that your car was broken or defective, it simply meant your car was in need of fuel. You probably didn't blame or criticize your car or plan to purchase a better, more resilient model. That would be silly. Instead, you probably stopped at a gas station, and then continued on your merry way. When we experience performance stress, we can interpret it as feedback that we could approach our practice differently, that we care about the quality of our work, or even that we are discovering some unseen benefit in the experience.

None of the hidden advantages of anxiety is bad or wrong. Each of them serves some sort of emotional purpose. Once we identify the purpose, it is easier to work on letting go of old thought patterns so that we can adopt new behaviors that serve healthier objectives. This can help us understand our own actions, including some of the maladaptive things we find ourselves doing without conscious awareness. It can also help us empathize with other people. When I was a freshman in college, my friend Emily would always come back to campus in tears after a visit home. She would have a nice weekend visit with her family, but just as she was getting ready to leave to go back to college, she would get into a huge fight with her mother. This would cause her to leave home in anger. After several months, Emily began to notice that it was her mother who would start the arguments. No matter how pleasant the visit home had been, Emily's mother would say something to anger my friend as she was loading up the car. Emily didn't understand why her mother was doing this, so we both decided that if it happened again, she should just ask. The next time she went home for a holiday, Emily became very aware of her mother initiating the argument. Instead of engaging, she said, "Mom, why do you always pick a fight with me just as I'm leaving?" Of course, this surprised everyone in her family, including her mother. It turns out that her mother was always filled with sorrow to see her daughter leaving home, and she struggled with controlling those emotions. She didn't want to cry in front of her family or make Emily feel guilty for leaving. Subconsciously, she had picked the fights because, as she finally admitted, "It's so much easier to be mad at you, when you leave, than to be sad." Even a hurtful action serves a purpose somehow, since each behavior is fueled by an underlying helpful intention.

Hold That Thought

A man has free choice to the extent that he is rational.—Thomas Aquinas

Musicians can establish their personal power when they are able to identify thoughts and beliefs as either rational or irrational. The previous chapter introduced this idea. The word *rational* has the same Latin root as the word *reasonable*, which presupposes thoughtfulness and good common sense. A rational thought would be one that is logical, consistent with reality, and that promotes an overall sense of well-being. Rational thoughts can help reinforce our progress when they support our short-term and long-term goals for success. The statement, "If I keep practicing, I will be able to play this passage up to tempo eventually," would be considered a rational statement in most situations. An irrational thought would be just the opposite: rigid, illogical, inconsistent with reality, and incompatible with psychological well-being. By these guidelines, the statement, "I miss this passage every single time; I'll never be able to play it well," is irrational. Can you identify what makes the sentence irrational? The observation about making mistakes is then followed by the unrelated and implausible conclusion that it will therefore never get any better. It is fairly easy to identify this statement as unreasonable when reading it with a sense of objectivity, but it is more difficult to observe irrational ideas at the moment we think them. Practicing mindful awareness of thoughts, as they unfold in the present moment, is the first step toward developing this skill.

Performers notoriously bestow harsh judgments on themselves in the practice room. Do any of these phrases sound familiar? "I always miss that note," "This shouldn't be so hard," "I can never control my tempo here," "I ought to be farther along by now." Phrases that contain the words *should, must, always, ought,* or *never,* or that sound fatalistic or extreme in some way, can offer evidence of self-defeating thinking. The word *should,* for example, is a favorite word of musicians. That auxiliary verb is most often used to express condition or to indicate duty. Consider the difference between the phrases "I should practice for one more hour" and "I will practice for one more hour." The second phrase is more empowering than the first and implies that the decision to practice is my own, without the added overtone of an impending chore. Because the second phrase implies personal freedom of choice, it contributes to a sense of well-being. Notice the difference in tone between "I missed that note" and "I always miss that note." The word *always* is a powerful word meaning every time and without exception. *Always* seems to indicate that if it has been true in the past, it will certainly be true in the future. Most of the time, a statement such as "I always miss that note" is untrue. Even if were true, that viewpoint does not necessarily cultivate healthy or supportive thinking. "Although I often miss that note, I know I can focus my practice and fix the mistake" reflects a much more positive spirit. Of course, identifying irrational thoughts is only the first step. Challenging or reframing those thoughts is equally important.

Negative thoughts can be disputed successfully using logic and reason. Arguing with yourself can also be sort of fun to do. You can challenge your own unhealthy thinking by asking yourself questions such as, "Is there a reason I am saying this?" "Is that always the case?" "Is that really true, or does it just feel true right now?" This can bring a sense of clarity and awareness to our own mental habits. How would you dispute and rephrase the following statement? "If my fingers slip during this performance, I will get totally lost and make a complete fool of myself." This sentence is not entirely unrealistic, because it is indeed possible that I might slip and make a mistake during the performance. The second half of the sentence is the part that needs some attention. "I will get totally lost," a statement of fear, is not a guaranteed truth. It is an example of an unlikely worst-case scenario and is not helpful in any way. The other part of the conclusion, "and make a complete fool of myself," is even more unlikely and self-defeating. Once you identify the irrational components of that statement, you can rethink the statement and restructure it so that it is truthful but also positively oriented. "Even if I make a mistake, I can still give a convincing and expressive performance." Or maybe, "I am prepared enough to handle any unexpected events."

You may have noticed that the most empowering statements are framed using positive language, without any negative qualifiers. The sentence, "Even if I make a mistake, I can still give a convincing and expressive performance," feels more confident and supportive than "Even if I make a mistake, I won't ruin everything or make a complete fool of myself." We will examine the power of language, in the context of creative imagery, more closely in Chapter 6. For now, realize that the mind does not easily distinguish between something that is wanted and something that is not wanted. The images that come to mind vary greatly when the two preceding sentences are read, all because of the language used. The first sentence features words such as *convincing* and *expressive*, while the second contains *ruin everything* and *make a complete fool of myself*. Even with the addition of the word "won't," the image that comes to mind is of that which is not wanted. This is why it is so essential to reframe negative thoughts and focus instead on the most positive possible outcome.

I call this phenomenon the Green Monkey Principle. (Of course, you could call it anything you want. You could call it the Plucky Petunia

Principle or the Monster Taco Principle, and the notion would be the same.) The idea is simple: Don't think about the green monkey. Just don't do it. Think about anything else, but not the green monkey. And whatever you do, don't imagine what sort of monkey it is, or what shade of green it might be. Don't even consider whether or not it is a giant monkey or a tiny little pocket-sized monkey. Hopefully, your mind is now completely and utterly free of the green monkey. Get the idea? It doesn't matter how many times you read the word *don't;* the image in your mind is strong because the suggestion is ever present. In fact, I bet even now a small part of you is still thinking about the you-know-what. I no longer have to name it, because the suggestion was so specific. Consider the images that pop into your subconscious mind when you remind yourself not to mess up a certain passage, not to forget something, not to sing out of tune, or not to drop your instrument. If you find yourself thinking about what you don't want, see if you can turn it around to express and imagine the positive outcome you hope to achieve. We can acknowledge and validate our fears with self-compassion, and at the same time, mindfully work to transform maladaptive patterns of thought.

Another version of an unhealthy belief is an all-or-nothing attitude. This might manifest in a thought such as, "If I bomb this next audition I might as well give up." It is not reasonable to expect that things will either be perfect or terrible, with no possibilities in between. Metaphorically speaking, music and life both express infinite shades of gray. Another example of irrational thinking, magical thinking, can be identified when the cause and effect aren't logically connected. An example might be, "If I don't get a full hour to warm up, I'll have a memory lapse for sure." Unrealistic expectations or demands, overgeneralizing, or judging someone or something as awful, as in, "It would be just awful if . . . " are other examples of imprudent thinking. It helps to remember that how we think and feel does not always represent the truth of a situation. Is it possible that the little voice in our head sometimes lies to us? Absolutely. That little voice can try to convince us that we aren't prepared, that we're disappointing someone, that we don't remember how a piece begins, or that we should just give up pursuing some of our goals. The vast majority of irrational thoughts are simply lies we tell ourselves. Awareness can be liberating!

For additional practice identifying and disputing irrational thoughts, check out the worksheets on the companion website (⊕ items 4.1–4.3).

Creating a Performance Mindset

yes is a world
& in this world of
yes live
(skillfully curled)
all worlds—e. e. cummings

Most people assume that beliefs, mental outlooks, and personalities are more or less naturally and permanently ingrained human qualities. We tend to identify people as glass-half-full or glass-half-empty types or as introverts or extroverts. As you have read, however, thoughts, beliefs, and behaviors are often choices that can be developed and refined over time. You might be skeptical at first, but research suggests that optimism is a learned behavior rather than a biological tendency in most humans. For athletes, musicians, and others who perform publicly, staying motivated and cultivating a positive mindset are essential mental skills for lifelong resilience and success.

A psychologist named Martin Seligman once discovered that, in a controlled laboratory environment, dogs could be taught to feel empowered or helpless. For example, dogs who received a punishment but figured out how to escape the situation would always try to improve their circumstance. They learned that they had the ability to control their environment. But dogs who did not have the option to escape soon gave up trying and just accepted their punishment. They had learned that nothing they could do would change their situation, and they became lethargic and indifferent. Seligman called this behavior *learned helplessness.*

Soon after, Donald Hiroto repeated a similar experiment with human beings. He put one group of people in a room, turned on a very loud noise, and gave them the opportunity to figure out how to turn off the noise by pushing a combination of buttons on a panel. A second group was put in a room with the same loud noise, but could not turn off the sound no matter how many times they tried to figure out the combination of buttons on the panel. He then put both groups of people in different situations involving other loud, annoying sounds that could easily be stopped. Amazingly, the people who had been in the second group, and who had learned that nothing they did would change their situation, didn't even try to stop the irritating sound in the second experiment. They just sat there. The people who had been in the first group immediately got to work to figure out how to stop the sound, and they were successful. Although both groups of people could turn off the sound if they tried, only the first group was persistent and eventually succeeded. They had learned that they could be in control of their situation. Psychologists would later call this behavior *learned optimism.*

Learned optimism is more than an extension of pop culture positive psychology. These revolutionary experiments showed how easily living beings can learn to think and behave like empowered individuals or like victims. We can easily find examples of similar situations in our own lives. Take, for example, a musician auditioning for an orchestra job. Even the greatest professionals are obliged to audition over and over again, often receiving rejection after rejection until they are finally hired. As in the experiments, some musicians might give up in defeat after the first few rejections, while others might look ahead to the next opportunity. One of my friends who worked in sales once mentioned that successful salespeople were highly optimistic. Otherwise, they would not be able to handle the rejection of uninterested customers day after day. Another friend of mine had the unenviable job of telemarketer. He maintained that, as long as he never hung up the phone after a rejection, he remained optimistic. In other words, he would immediately dial the next number without thinking, and refocus on his mission. If he did put the phone down after a rejection, it gave him the opportunity to ruminate about all of his failed attempts that day, and his average number of calls decreased significantly. Many other areas of life require persistence: getting a date, passing an exam, beating a computer game, or baking the perfect soufflé. My university colleague and I just happen to make the greatest chocolate martini on the face of this earth. Had we given up after our 14th or 15th try, we might never have achieved such decadent, frothy perfection.

Many psychologists now believe they can identify traits of optimism and pessimism based on how people explain their failures. How do you tend to view the concept of failure? We can, if we wish, shift our perspectives about unwanted events. For example, a perceived failure might simply be a form of feedback. If you make a mistake in the practice room, you can almost always find a reason for it. When you do find the reason (perhaps you were tense, or fatigued, or not paying attention, or out of physical alignment), the situation becomes more objective. Rather than viewing the mistake as a personal flaw, you can use it as feedback to diagnose and correct the error. Even if a mistake happens because of bad planning, such as not practicing enough or not getting enough sleep, it is still a form of feedback. Top athletes are trained to analyze their mistakes and use them as data to regroup and plan for future successes. Likewise, a musician can think to himself, "Okay, now I know what I need to do differently next time." Sometimes the shift needed is a small one ("Next time I will remove my watch, because it was really distracting me"), and sometimes it is more complex and involved ("I need to return to practicing etudes in order to refine my technique"). Either way, it can be viewed as a tool for improvement rather than a shortcoming.

We can observe three characteristics of optimistic humans, based on how they view unwanted events. According to Seligman and others, someone with a constructive outlook is likely to perceive a failure as an external event. In other words, she doesn't take an unwanted event too personally. She might, for example, attribute an unusually bad performance to her cold hands rather than to her lack of talent. Or, she might acknowledge that the piano was out of tune and beyond her control. A positively focused person may also see the event as a temporary situation. In an earlier example, we identified the phrase "I always miss that note" as irrational, because the word "always" implies a permanent situation. Consider that an observation such as "My technique is terrible" might more accurately reflect a temporary situation: "Today I have been playing unevenly" or "That last repetition was out of tune." Finally, a more optimistic person will recognize that unwanted events can be isolated, rather than pervasive. An optimistic performer might think, "I got off to a rough start," rather than "I blew the entire audition." When you experience negative feedback, either in your musical or personal life, experiment to see if it is possible to shift your perception of the event from personal, permanent, and pervasive to more external, temporary, and specific.

Imagine that a musician performs a lackluster audition for a music job. Perhaps he made a lot of mistakes or got delayed because of traffic and didn't have enough time to warm up. With a negative attitude, he might view the event as personal ("This was all my fault"), permanent ("I'll never be able to get a job"), and pervasive ("I just don't have what it takes"). Alternatively, he could see the situation more positively as external ("I wish I had had more warm-up time, but that couldn't be helped"), temporary ("I know this situation won't last"), and specific ("This is only one audition"). Just as with rational and irrational thinking, an optimistic focus tends to be psychologically healthier than a pessimistic one. A constructive outlook can better help someone achieve her personal goals, which can lead to a sense of improved well-being.

Earlier in this chapter, we focused on the idea that thoughts can become beliefs, which then affect our emotions and behaviors. An adversity can be a good opportunity to practice observing and reframing our own thoughts, before they become ingrained beliefs. Any time we encounter a problem, we react by thinking about the problem. At this point, we have an option (or, as Frankl said, we have the space between stimulus and response) regarding our reaction to the problem. With practice, we can learn to counteract negative, irrational, or pessimistic thought patterns by disputing those thoughts, offering evidence to the contrary. Plus, it can be entertaining to argue with the little voice in your head.

To deepen your practice of these concepts, see the sections in Chapter 8 on Thoughts and Emotions (pages 192–193), Emotion Regulation (pages 193–196), and Emotional Triggers (page 196–197).

Healthy Detachment

He who would be serene and pure needs but one thing, detachment.
—Meister Eckhart

When creative people express themselves through their music, they sometimes feel as if they are exploring aspects of their own identities through that music. This is a natural result of spending countless hours absorbed in something they feel very passionate about and in engaging their personality, emotions, and a deep sense of connectedness. Career musicians, especially, find themselves engrossed in their art throughout most of the day and night. One of my friends acknowledged to me that he envied his wife, a nonmusician, because she was able to put her work behind her at the end of the day and focus on other things at home. He said, "I am always playing or thinking about music, so it never feels like I'm *not* focused on my work!" Writers, artists, performers, and others who use their creativity during the day often find that they can't simply turn it off in the evening. Others have different jobs during the day, which requires them to focus on their music in the evenings and on the weekends. Many artistic personalities work odd hours, sometimes late into the night, because they need to honor and take advantage of their own spurts of creativity. These moments of inspiration don't always fit into a regular workday. Sometimes the boundaries between work time and personal time, or between creating music and just being a regular person, become blurred.

Challenges can arise when a musician struggles to distinguish herself, the human being, from herself the performing artist. When we become completely wrapped up in our musical lives, we often confuse the quality of our performances with our value as a person. This helps to explain why peak performances feel so exhilarating and bad performances feel so devastating to many musicians. If we lose a competition, for example, it is so easy to think that we are somehow deficient as musicians. Even the title of *musician* seems to label us. Sometimes it helps to remember that music is what we do, but is not who we are. We don't call ourselves sleepers, eaters, or bathers, but we do those things as well. The notion that our accomplishments define us can be illustrated in the unfortunate phrase, *I am what I do*. Author Wayne Dyer once asked, "If you are what you do, then who are you when you don't do it any longer?" In other words, the fundamental problem with *I am what I do* is that when I don't, I am not.

Do you ever drop your keys on the floor? Of course you do. And then you probably bend over and pick them up. Did you ever accidentally knock over your drink at home? Of course you did. And then you no doubt cleaned it up before going on about your day. My point is that you probably didn't think about those keys on the floor or that spilled beverage throughout your day or week. You probably didn't berate yourself or obsess over the mistake. "I can't believe I knocked that soda over. I am such a failure. I probably spilled an entire serving of root beer, not to mention the loss of so many innocent ice cubes. And I wasted so many paper towels, it's just embarrassing. Now the world knows what a klutz I am. I should stop talking with my hands, that's the problem. I'm not fit to drink anything. I should just give up drinking liquids altogether!" This example, while utterly silly, mirrors the way in which we often react to our own musical mistakes. If, for example, a musician botches a solo during a dress rehearsal, he might agonize over that mistake for the rest of the day. While we don't tend to associate our own worth with a glass of soda, we often relate it to the quality of our music. We might make reference to bombing an audition, but we don't talk about bombing a glass of root beer. We have established a sense of healthy detachment from the keys and the soda, and this detachment keeps us from taking things too personally.

When you gently detach from your music in a mindful, compassionate way, you can strengthen the perspective that you are not your performance. You are a completely separate entity from your performance. Most important, you are *more* than your performance, which means that you are more than any virtuosic feat or any mistake you might make. For many musicians, this idea makes sense, but is difficult to recall during moments of stress. It may help you to write down or think of a phrase that separates your identity from your musical accomplishments. This could be as simple as "I am not my music" or "I am more than my performance." It may be more specific, such as "I am not this recital" or "I am not this song" or "I am not my mistakes." Or you may prefer, "I play music, but I am not my performance." If you struggle with performance stress, you can think, "I feel nervous, but I am not my nervousness" or "I am greater than the part of myself that feels scared right now." If you can remember a similar phrase to repeat to yourself when it is most needed, it can provide a powerful sense of reorientation.

Detachment does not involve disconnecting or abandoning our passion, purpose, motivation, drive, or deep connection to our music. It is simply a mindfulness technique to help practice the compassionate separation of our sense of self from the quality of our work. For more examples, see the section on writing Disidentification Affirmations in Chapter 8 (pages 197–198).

What Can Musicians Learn From Athletes?

It's not whether you get knocked down; it's whether you get up.
—Vince Lombardi

Consider that musicians are the athletes of the small muscles. Performing arts medicine specialists like to remind us of this important principle. Like athletes, we undergo rigorous training for many years to become proficient in our field, and we practice intensely as we prepare for important events. Like athletes, we are often required to perform in public and under the pressure of public scrutiny or perceived criticism. Like the greatest athletes, the best performing musicians are able to maintain intense concentration and highly refined muscle movements while remaining alert and in control. For many decades, athletes have understood the importance of cultivating essential mental skills as part of their training. Sport psychologists who study peak performance have discovered that mental conditioning is as crucial as physical training.

Research suggests that elite athletes cultivate specific practice strategies and psychological skills to prepare for competitions. These approaches are equally relevant to performing musicians and other creative artists. In 2009, a group of researchers studied a number of highly skilled athletes in Italy. These athletes had competed in the World Cup, the Olympic Games, or other championships. The study concluded that the most successful athletes engage in a wide range of deliberate mental strategies to focus attention, detach or recover from mistakes, regulate anxiety, and exercise greater control over their emotions. They set short-term and long-term goals for success as they train. They practice observing and redirecting their emotions when under pressure. Many keep a written record of the feelings they associate with a good performance. They engage in competition simulation, practicing under the same sort of stress and environment they anticipate. They also use a variety of mental imagery techniques. They demonstrate, in their practice routines, personal characteristics such as perseverance, consistency, and commitment. They assess the quality of their performance both before and after a competition, observe their reactions to their mistakes, and practice handling criticism objectively. They sometimes demonstrate an unusually positive mental health profile, which includes high self-confidence and positive self-talk. Overall, they tend to be motivated, committed, focused, able to cope with adversity, able to excel under pressure, and able to pursue their goals in a deliberate and rational manner. While it may sound too good to be true, many of these qualities are skills that can be learned. You already realize this, or you would not be reading this book!

A common practice strategy for top athletes is *automatic execution*. This technique involves practicing specific physical movements until the performer is able to accomplish these at a high level without thinking about them. Have you ever had the experience, while making music, of not having to focus consciously on your technique or even your interpretation, because it just seems to happen automatically? Obviously, it takes a great deal of practice to be able to perform without thinking too much about it. Once a performer is able to reach that level, though, he is free to trust and let go.

We can remember and associate certain feelings with our best performances. Creative artists will sometimes talk about feeling "on," "connected," "in the zone," or in a state of "flow." Some musicians have felt this during a performance, while others experience great joy or flow only in the practice room. Still others have never personally experienced being in the zone, but know that it is possible. We occasionally recognize the thoughts (or sometimes, the perceived lack of thoughts) that accompany our finest performances. However, most musicians do not think to practice identifying their very individual emotional patterns. Once we learn to identify the specific feelings that are unique to us, we can deliberately contemplate those in practice. This is what many elite athletes do in their training. They purposefully seek and reinforce optimal feelings associated with outstanding performances, write these down, and then recall them before an event. Some will even watch a video of one of their best performances, so that they can relive the experience and reimagine the feelings associated with that experience. Think back to one of your best performance experiences, and see if you can capture your feelings in words. Write them down somewhere where you can easily add to the list when necessary. Even better, document your feelings immediately after a great experience. These are the words you can focus on before and during a performance, when practicing mental imagery, and perhaps even when setting goals for future success. For more practice, see the section on Best Performance Memory in Chapter 9 (pages 219–220).

Top athletes are always mindful of their physical bodies. They are conscious of their fatigue levels and are keenly aware of the need to rest, both physically and mentally, during practice. While good coaches schedule recovery time into practice and training sessions, my experience has been that far fewer musicians organize their rehearsals in this way. Very focused musicians may take a short break when they suddenly notice pain or if they become stiff or sore from being in the same position for a long period of time. By that time, it is too late, because fatigue has already begun to set in. When it comes to rest and recovery, most athletes tend to be proactive, while most musicians tend to be reactive. If we would schedule regular recovery time as needed, we might avoid tension, soreness, injury, and distraction more successfully.

All of these athletic strategies rely to some extent on the practice of mindfulness. You will recall that mindfulness is intimately connected to the concept of awareness, which includes awareness of the body, thoughts, and emotions during practice and performance. Mindfulness training emphasizes an objective, nonjudgmental approach, and a focus on the present moment. In recent years, a number of therapies combining traditional cognitive-behavioral psychology and mindfulness have emerged. Studies suggest that, when it comes to building resilience and developing a sense of well-being, the combination is more effective than either component practiced alone. While this book has emphasized both approaches to performance preparation, more advanced applications of mindfulness are discussed in later chapters.

Musicians and sport psychologists have begun to collaborate, sharing their strategies and studying similarities between the two disciplines. Popular topics in both areas include motivation, practice habits, goal-setting, time management, recovery techniques, mental rehearsal, focusing, and postperformance analysis. So far, studies involving the most effective behaviors of athletes have focused on their use of stress and anxiety management, guided relaxation, hypnotherapy, creative imagery, and breathing exercises. Researchers agree that more studies are needed for musicians, particularly on the most effective preperformance routines. Even with the current scarcity of research, the general consensus is that, at the very least, none of these practices can hurt or impair a musician's performance preparation. They can only help, and for many people, they help tremendously. This book addresses all of these topics from the viewpoint of a performing musician.

Mindful Communication

> *Darkness cannot drive out darkness: only light can do that.*
> —Martin Luther King, Jr.

Consciously or unconsciously, we are communicating with ourselves at all times. Much of this chapter has addressed the many ways in which we talk to ourselves. Language is a powerful tool, whether it is spoken, written, or silently thought. In addition to words and phrases, we communicate to ourselves and others through our body language, expressions, and actions. What we say, how we say it, and what we do reveal our underlying thoughts and beliefs. And, again, we can work to change those thoughts and beliefs if we wish.

Just as musical notation on a staff is not the same as the sound of music itself, our thoughts do not always represent our true situation. Musicians can consciously focus on positive, empowering thoughts and images while reducing or disregarding negative or enervating thoughts. Most people already possess the mental resources they need for success, but sometimes need to identify and develop these skills in a more constructive way. When failure is reinterpreted as feedback, a performer can identify what is working and what isn't working. And if something isn't working, it makes sense to do something else.

Albert Einstein's famous definition of insanity ("Doing the same thing over and over again and expecting different results") has been restated in the popular phrase, "If you always do what you've always done, you'll always get what you've always gotten." My hope is that you will discover some helpful mindfulness strategies that speak to you as an individual performing musician.

5 THE ART OF MINDFUL BREATHING AND RELAXATION

Breathing is a fascinating topic to consider, surprisingly enough. Since you are reading this, you must be alive, and since you are alive, you must be breathing. And yet, it would be silly of me to offer a chapter on "Digestion Techniques" or "Effortless Blood Circulation." This is because breathing is the only bodily function that we can do either consciously or unconsciously, voluntarily or involuntarily. With awareness, we can control our breath, but we rest assured that breathing will continue once we withdraw that awareness. For many musicians, breath control is an essential part of performing. For *all* musicians, conscious awareness of the breath is a simple and effective tool to develop concentration, focus, stress reduction, and comfort on stage.

Breathing as Awareness

Try this little experiment in mindfulness. As you continue to read, allow a portion of your attention to rest on your breath. Notice that you can observe the breath without actually trying to control the timing of the inhale and the exhale. This can be tricky, because the mind tends to want to control whatever it is giving its attention to. As much as you can, see if you can just observe your natural pattern of breathing. The idea is not to change the length of the inhale or the exhale or to alter the movement of the body as it breathes, but simply to sit in awareness.

There really isn't a wrong way to breathe, despite what your esteemed music, yoga, or meditation teachers might have taught you. If you are alive and well and reading this book, chances are that you are doing a pretty good job of breathing. With that in mind, see if you can release any urge to self-critique, and observe your natural breathing cycle with genuine curiosity. Notice the length of your natural inhale, as well as the duration of your natural exhale. Are they more or less equal in length, or does your exhale seem to be longer? What about the quiet gaps in between the inhale and the exhale? Do you immediately transition from one to the other, or is there a slight pause in between? If there is a slight pause, is the pause at the end of the inhale as long as the pause at the end of the exhale, or does one of them seem longer than the other? Where do you feel your breath most easily in your body? Do you feel the cool air enter your body at the tip of your nose, or at the back of your throat, or in the chest, or belly, or somewhere else? What part of your body moves the most when you inhale, the shoulders, chest, or abdomen? Do you perceive the sound of your own breath, or is it silent? What other aspects of your breathing are you able to notice?

Most humans do not pay attention to their breathing throughout a normal waking day, because they don't need to. The beauty of the autonomic nervous system is that the body functions naturally so that you can focus on other things. It would be a sad day if you had to turn down an invitation to a fancy dinner party because you had to stay at home and focus on your breathing. It can be extremely beneficial, however, to become aware of the breath periodically throughout the day. It is one way of bringing your awareness to the present moment, which can help assuage stress, worry, or rumination, even if just for a few seconds. It also encourages body awareness, which is essential for people who use their physical selves to perform music. It can serve as a way to focus the mind and build the skill of concentration. Finally, it can relax the body and mind, which helps alleviate anxiety and distraction.

Healthy Breathing

Listen, are you breathing just a little and calling it a life?—Mary Oliver

Although there is no right or wrong way to breathe, it is true that—at times—some methods of breathing can be more beneficial than others. Numerous studies suggest that breathing deeply from the diaphragm can not only improve our mental and physical health, it can actually bring about healing. *Breathwork* is the term used most frequently by health practitioners to describe the use of conscious breathing techniques for healing and stress reduction. Most of these involve diaphragmatic breathing, also called deep or belly breathing, a technique that is very familiar to singers and wind or brass instrument players. Even those who know how to breathe from the diaphragm do not always do this periodically throughout their day. Often, this sort of breathing is reserved only for making music. However, practicing this technique away from your music can help develop valuable mindful performance skills.

The diaphragm is a large domed muscle that extends the width of the body at the bottom of the rib cage. When you inhale, the diaphragm contracts, creating a vacuum that pulls air into the lungs. When the diaphragm relaxes, the elasticity of your lungs allows you to exhale. Diaphragmatic breathing is distinguished from chest breathing, which is experienced higher in the torso. The action of breathing deeply from the diaphragm actually stimulates the vagus nerve, which is an important part of the body's parasympathetic nervous system. This involuntary system slows the heart rate, counteracts the body's fight-or-flight response, and brings about a feeling of well-being in many people. In other words, diaphragmatic breathing can activate a natural relaxation response in the body.

Shallow breathing (also called clavicular, thoracic, or high breathing) can be associated with stress and anxiety. When we are nervous before a performance, the way in which we breathe can actually ease or exacerbate any negative experiences we may be having. If you would like to try another little experiment as you read, I invite you to move your awareness of the breath up into your throat, collarbone, and/or shoulders. As you breathe, allow these body parts to do most of the subtle moving with each inhale and exhale. For example, you may imagine that you feel your collarbone gently expand and contract as the upper parts of the lungs take in and let out air. You may notice that this manner of breathing does not allow for very full breaths. In fact, the breath will often become lighter, shallower, and slightly faster in order to take in sufficient oxygen. Because you are directing your attention to it, you may find this sort of breathing somewhat unsatisfying. Nevertheless, when we are worried or stressed, sometimes we begin to breathe in this way, even to the point of hyperventilation, which can result in lightheadedness or even a temporary loss of consciousness. I have seen musicians hyperventilate before a performance, and it can be a very scary experience for them, even though it is not life threatening.

Breathing shallowly can be helpful in order to experience the contrast of diaphragmatic breathing. If you tried the experiment in the last paragraph but then resumed your normal breathing, I would encourage you to return to the shallow thoracic breathing. Allow the very tops of your ribcage to expand and contract, as you notice the lightness of the breath cycle. Place your hand on your abdomen, around and slightly below your navel. Try to avoid moving the belly as much as possible in order to delegate most of the work to the upper body. After a moment, try the opposite approach, shifting your focus of the breath to the lower abdomen, filling the lungs up with air and allowing the abdomen to expand and contract with each breath. You should be able to feel your belly puff out with each inhale that you take, and return to neutral with each exhale. Hopefully, you can see your hand on your stomach moving out and in with each breath cycle. It can also be helpful and interesting to put your hands on the small of your back, or on the sides of your torso near your back, and feel those parts of your body moving in and out as well. Some people find it easier to imagine breathing into the small of their backs rather than into the front of their abdomens. Another great exercise to try is to lie on the floor, placing your hands on your stomach. The pull of gravity will require you to work a tiny bit harder to make the abdomen visibly expand and contract. It is even more fun to put a book on your stomach as you lie on the floor, breathing in a way that gently moves the book up and down. This is a great practice to try when you are feeling especially nervous or distracted.

Some people notice, as they practice this sort of deep breathing, that their breaths naturally become deeper, slower, and more relaxing. Since the process of breathing from the diaphragm can physiologically trigger the body's natural quieting response, it is not simply mind over matter. Dr. Herbert Benson coined the phrase "the relaxation response" in the 1970s when he taught at Harvard Medical School. We still use this phrase to describe the process of consciously activating the body's parasympathetic nervous system to bring about feelings of composure and well-being. You can activate the relaxation response by directing your thoughts mindfully, which is why it was an important early concept in mind-body medicine.

Diaphragmatic breathing has been used successfully, often in combination with mindfulness-based stress reduction techniques, by many holistic medical professionals. Some use breathing techniques to treat high blood pressure, irregular heartbeat, respiratory disorders, digestive disorders, nervous system imbalances, and other physical conditions. Breathing exercises are especially beneficial for psychological conditions such as anxiety, panic disorder, and depression. Most clinical uses of breathwork involve a more comprehensive program of relaxation exercises, yoga, nutritional changes, and/or cognitive therapy. The beauty of using the breath as a tool for stress management and good health is that it is accessible, easy to do, and doesn't require medical insurance! It is also a relatively invisible activity, since you can practice breathwork just about anywhere, at any time, and no one will even notice.

Although this chapter features a wide variety of breathing techniques for stress management, I would like to acknowledge the value of doing nothing other than noticing the breath. Paying attention is the very foundation of mindfulness practice. It is also a useful way to refine the skill of focusing, which is so important for musicians working to improve their performance skills. When you perform, your focus is primarily on the music you are playing or singing, but it is easy to become unfocused if distractions should occur. These distractions can be external events, such as a noise from the audience or a flickering lightbulb. However, the majority of distractions are internal, resulting from the roaming thoughts of an active and engaged mind. You may find yourself making a critical observation about something you just played or sang, or you may suddenly worry about an upcoming passage. Luckily, anyone can learn to regain focus after a distraction. I find it helpful to practice this mindfulness skill when I am not performing, using an object or a concept to refocus my mind. For many people, the breath is the most accessible point of focus. It is always with you, and it happens whether you contemplate it or not.

Creative Breathing Techniques

What we call "I" is just a swinging door, which moves when we inhale and when we exhale.—Shunryu Suzuki

The sheer wealth of information on breathwork techniques can be mind-boggling. You can find entire books about when and how to breathe! The following exercises are my favorite breathing techniques that encourage relaxation, focusing, or centering the mind, and that work well for performance preparation or performance anxiety management. If you have trouble falling asleep at night, particularly because of an active or apprehensive mind, these can be extremely effective. I suggest you try one or two per day until you find a breathwork technique that feels right for you. These require very little time commitment.

If you practice one of these breathing techniques for about 5 minutes a day, you may prefer to find a relatively quiet place where you will not be disturbed. Alternatively, since these are exercises that you can do at any time, you may choose to practice them when you are standing in line or waiting for your computer to power up. I find it helpful to associate a new experiment, such as a mindfulness activity, with an event that requires me to pause for a short period of time. This might include those times when I am waiting on hold, at a stoplight, or during a television commercial. You can choose to link a new habit (such as breathwork) with an established habit (such as warming up before practicing) to help to reinforce the consistency of the new habit. You can also use a mindful habit to substitute for, or suspend, your engagement in a less healthy habit. Examples might include stopping to practice breathwork when you feel the impulse to check your smartphone or eat an unhealthy snack. The choice is entirely yours.

You don't have to close your eyes, but you may feel more comfortable and relaxed if you do. If you first practice these when you are calm, they will be more effective when you are nervous, such as right before a concert. The more you practice, the more these exercises become conditioned responses, which means that your mind will soon learn to relax and focus quickly and automatically. If you try these only sporadically, or only when you are stressed or anxious, they will be less effective.

Remember that, no matter which of these you choose, each one should seem relatively easy. They should feel good. If the activity makes you feel stressed out, or if you feel like you are out of breath or working hard, you may be breathing too slowly or trying too hard to control the breath. If you feel lightheaded or dizzy, you may be breathing too quickly. Breathing is not a competitive sport, so you should only do what feels suitable for you. For each exercise, it works best to take deep, comfortable breaths from the diaphragm.

Check out the companion website for a mindful breathing worksheet, ⊕ item 5.1. Also see item 5.2, a guided introductory breathwork recording.

Finger Breathing

Finger breathing is a fun and easy way to observe your breaths while staying relaxed and focused. You have two options; both include using your hands to track your breath cycles. The first option is to use one hand, slowly sliding your thumb down to the tip of your index finger as you inhale, and sliding it back toward your palm as you exhale. With your next breath, move to your middle finger as you slide the thumb down and back. When you finish with the smallest finger, begin the journey back toward your index finger. If you find that your mind wanders more frequently than you would like, give a gentle squeeze when your thumb contacts each fingertip. The second option is to use two hands. Use the index finger of one hand to trace each finger of your other hand, starting with the thumb, down and back as you breathe. You may choose to slide up and down each side of each finger, tracing your hand as you go around and back. This is one of my favorite emotion regulation techniques for stressed adults, but children also respond well to this calming activity.

Bubble Breaths

This activity works well if you have only a short time to practice, if you feel frustrated or angry, or if you are working to ward off a panic attack. Inhale deeply through your nose, then exhale a slow and gently sustained breath through your mouth, pursing your lips slightly as if you were blowing soap bubbles through a bubble wand. You can also imagine that you are blowing out many candles on a birthday cake, blowing an enormous bubble gum bubble, or blowing the white seeds off a dandelion puff. Try to make the exhale a tiny bit longer with each breath. (You can also practice with actual soap bubbles, for added levity.)

Counting Breaths

For some people, the gentle repetition of counting breaths can induce a mild and healthy trance state, which can lead to deep relaxation. This technique involves counting breath cycles on the exhale. Begin by inhaling, then thinking "one" on the exhale. Inhale again, and think "two" on the exhale. I recommend that you count no higher than ten before repeating the pattern, because it is easy to lose count (and focus) as you become more relaxed. For some, counting from one to five is even more effective. After your last exhale, inhale and begin again with "one" on the exhale. This simple practice can feel deliciously hypnotic after a while. If you find that you tend to lose focus on the inhale, you may choose to insert a mental word on the inhale as well. For example, you may want to say "and" on the inhale in between the numbers of the breaths, or repeat the same number on both the inhale and the exhale. If you lose count, simply start over again with "one." At times, I have resorted to counting "one" on every single exhale, and that works just fine. No one is evaluating your ability to count your breaths. Remember that it is okay to lose track and start over, since keeping track of numbers is not the point. Gentle focused awareness is the point.

You may find that it feels significantly different to count inhales instead of exhales. Some people experience the inhale, in a very abstract way, as something leading or questioning. This may be because if you listen to the breath, it may sound internally as if the inhale ends with an upward inflection. By contrast, an exhale may feel more affirming, like a statement or an answer, because of its perceived downward inflection. You may learn that you prefer to draw your attention to the perceived rise of the breath more than its ebb, or vice versa. Again, if you lose count, just start over again with "one." If you find that you are especially distracted and keep losing count, you can assign a number to each inhale and exhale: one on the inhale, two on the exhale, three on the inhale, and so on. You may prefer instead to breathe the letters of the alphabet. Alternatively, you could simply repeat the phrases "breathe in" and "breathe out" for each inhale and exhale.

Measured Breaths

This technique involves regulating the length of your inhales and exhales by counting beats or pulses rather than breath cycles. For example, you might choose to inhale for five counts and exhale for five counts. Each breath should feel smooth, continuous, and comfortable; the measured pulses simply coordinate the speed of each inhale and exhale. The speed of your counting is not important, because you can choose any number you wish. If you start off with five counts for each inhale and exhale, the next week you could experiment with six counts for each. However, the goal is not to increase the number of counts each day, which would eventually become impossible. Instead, you might keep the same number of counts each day, but experiment with a slightly slower tempo. A former student of mine preferred to turn on a metronome with the volume adjusted very low, to help keep him focused on the pulses of his counting. Generally speaking, the slower the breath cycle, the more relaxing the practice. This is a good technique because it encourages regular patterns of breathing, and since it is so highly regulated, you are less likely to lose focus during the activity.

Triangle Breathing

Triangle breathing also involves counting and regulation of the breaths. It differs from the previous activity in that you inhale, exhale, and then pause gently for a certain number of counts. If you visualize an equilateral triangle pointing upward, you can imagine that you are breathing in a clockwise direction around that shape. The left-hand side of the triangle would represent the inhale rising, the right-hand side would be the exhale releasing, and the base would symbolize the pause in between. In this imaginary equilateral triangle, you would hold each "side" for the same number of counts. For example, you might inhale for three slow counts, exhale for three slow counts, and pause for three slow counts before beginning the cycle again. Be sure to choose a number that doesn't require you to hold your breath for very long. It should feel evenly spaced and very soothing. If you find you can hardly wait to begin your next inhale, you should probably reduce the number of counts for this activity. In this form of triangle breathing, the pattern is always inhale–exhale–pause, inhale–exhale–pause. If you were to imagine an isosceles triangle (remember those from geometry class?) with two long sides of equal length and a shorter base, you would practice longer breaths with a shorter pause time. For example, you might inhale for six, exhale for six, and pause for three. Or you might inhale for seven, exhale for seven, and pause for only two. The ratio of counts is not as important as that you find something that feels relaxing and somewhat natural.

You might prefer to try what I call *inverted triangle breathing*, which is basically the upside-down version of triangle breathing. If you imagine the triangle turned on its head, you would inhale for a number of counts, pause at the top of the inhale for a number of counts, and then exhale for a number of counts. The only difference, then, is the timing of the pause in each breath cycle. You could practice by inhaling for four, pausing for four, and exhaling for four. Or you might inhale for six, pause for three, and exhale for six. Sometimes people will experience this activity, with the pause at the top of the breath, as a more energizing form of triangle breathing. That just depends on your personal preference.

The 4:7:8 Breath

The 4:7:8 technique comes from integrative physician Dr. Andrew Weil, who sometimes refers to it as the Relaxing Breath. In this variation of inverted triangle breathing, you inhale for four counts, gently hold the breath for seven counts, and exhale for eight counts. Dr. Weil does offer a few additional suggestions for this practice. Throughout the exercise, experiment with placing the tip of your tongue against your hard palate, just behind your front teeth. When you inhale, inhale through your nose. When you exhale, exhale through your mouth with an audible "whoosh" sound, as if you are inflating a balloon. As you practice, you may choose to imagine that your breaths become slower and deeper. Dr. Weil suggests that you repeat this for four breath cycles only, aiming to practice twice a day or more. This is an easy and convenient breathing technique that has been effective in clinical settings. The speed of your counting is not important, but maintaining the 4:7:8 ratio is the essential component of the exercise.

Breathing With Imagery

Depending on your preference, you may wish to include a creative visualization of an image in motion during breathwork. You could imagine, for example, a figure 8 symbol, where the inhale rises to the top of the 8, looping back down toward the exhale. This slow imagined movement of a pattern can help keep the mind focused and tranquil at the same time. If you are practicing triangle breathing, you may wish to visualize the breaths moving slowly around the sides of the imagined shape. Or, perhaps you prefer to imagine a structure such as a ball, an accordion, or a large coiled spring, expanding and contracting slowly as you breathe. I sometimes like to imagine that I am standing on a beach looking out at the ocean, and my breaths are like the waves lapping onto the shore. When I inhale, the water pulls back into the ocean and builds up, and when I exhale, the waves roll forward and break upon the sand.

Some people favor sensations more than mental pictures. You might choose to perceive that each breath washes over your body, rising up the front and over your head with each inhale, and sliding down your back with each exhale, or you could reverse the direction. You could imagine that you are inhaling through the bottoms of your feet, all the way to the top of your head and back down again. Or, you might imagine that with each inhale your body's energy expands outward in all directions, and with each exhale it draws itself back in toward the body. A friend of mine imagines that she is sitting on a large playground swing, swinging back and forth in slow motion with each breath cycle. You are limited only by your creative imagination.

Alternate Nostril Breathing

An ancient practice, alternate nostril breathing is one of the most powerful breathwork techniques for restoring a sense of physical balance and emotional well-being. As you breathe comfortably through your nose, rest your left hand in your lap and raise your right palm to your face. Allow your index finger and your middle finger to rest comfortably on the bridge of your nose and between your eyebrows. These two fingers serve simply as an anchor; your thumb and your ring finger will be the only fingers you need to move. (I resisted the urge to call this the Facepalm Breath.)

With your right thumb, gently close your right nostril so that you inhale through your left nostril. The inhale should be slow and easy, without forcing the breath. At the top of the breath, allow your ring finger to close off your left nostril, and release the thumb so that you exhale through your right nostril. Without shifting the hand, inhale through your right nostril; at the top of the breath, close your right nostril with your thumb as you release your ring finger. The pattern of one breath cycle is this: Inhale right, exhale left, inhale left, exhale right, as you use your thumb and ring finger to help close off the opposite nostril. Repeat this cycle for as long as you wish. This technique can induce a profoundly peaceful state of consciousness.

I will be the first to admit that alternate nostril breathing can be a little bit of a challenge at first, especially if you suffer from allergies or nasal congestion. If you find that you absolutely cannot breathe through one of your nostrils, approach the exhale very slowly and try not to force the breath. You can cheat a little if you need to by allowing the other nostril to open just a tiny bit. Be patient with the practice, even if only one side of your nose seems to be cooperating at first. I have found that if I am slow and gently persistent with the breath, both nasal passages will eventually open up. On a few occasions, I have been surprised to find this holistic practice more effective than a decongestant.

Release Half

I have adapted this breathing technique, one of my very favorites, from a practice taught by aikido expert Paul Hirata. It works especially well for relieving stress, nervousness, even anger. Because it centers the mind very quickly, it is also a good rescue technique for people who feel suddenly overwhelmed. Suppose you are waiting to be called in for an audition, and you feel exceptionally apprehensive about it. You know that it is unrealistic to hope that all of your anxiety will go away, but you can imagine that you are able to release about half of it. So, you inhale slowly, and as you exhale, you think to yourself, "release half" as you surrender half of your anxiety and allow it to fade away. You may pause for a moment to see how you feel. If you wish, you may inhale deeply once more, and on the exhale think "release half" as you relinquish half of whatever anxiety was left behind. You can do this as many times as you wish, always releasing half, appreciating that the negative feeling will diminish, but it may not vanish entirely. This technique also works with impatience, hyperactivity, even some cravings. Imagine that you are practicing your music, and you become irritated with yourself. This would be the perfect time to take a short break and practice this technique, releasing half of your annoyance or frustration. When you do resume your practice, you will be in a more objective place to evaluate and improve your progress.

Breathing Affirmations

Many people enjoy repeating a meaningful word or phrase during each breath cycle. You could take a deep inhale, and on the exhale, think of an adjective that suggests how you want to feel or be, such as "calm," "relaxed," or "prepared." Or, you could think of a verb or phrase that suggests gentle action, such as "release" or "let go" or "just breathe." An esteemed colleague of mine uses a similar technique, which I really enjoy, when he guides a group meditation. He will offer the phrase "just this moment . . . " on one breath, followed by "and this moment . . . " on the next breath, followed by "and this moment . . . " on several subsequent breaths. It is a wonderful means of drawing the attention to each moment as it unfolds in time. Other people prefer to repeat a short affirmation, prayer, or inspirational quote that gives them a feeling of peace or security. As long as the phrase is short enough to be repeated with each breath cycle, anything can work. What inspires us can be deeply individual.

The Centering Breath

This powerful technique is an adaptation of *Ten-Second Centering,* an activity developed by creativity coach Dr. Eric Maisel. The title of his exercise refers to the idea that each deep breath cycle takes about 10 seconds, 5 on the inhale and 5 on the exhale. This is an excellent performance anxiety management technique.

On the inhale, think of the word "I" plus a verb. An easy one to start with is "I am." On the exhale, think of a word or phrase that represents what you need to hear in the present moment. If you feel worried, for example, you could think "I am . . . " on the inhale, and ". . . at peace" on the exhale. Repeat this pattern a few times, once per breath cycle. If you are anxious, you might think "I am . . . " on the inhale, and ". . . completely safe" on the exhale, or perhaps even ". . . okay." If you are suddenly agitated or enraged, you can think "I am . . . stopping now." If you are having trouble falling asleep, you can try "I am . . . letting go." If you are getting ready to perform, your affirmation might be "I am . . . " followed by ". . . courageous," or anything that helps you feel reassured. Other variations of this technique might include phrases such as "I am . . . prepared to do my best," "I am . . . free," "I am . . . empowered," or anything else that feels right. One of my meditation students came up with a wonderful idea of thinking "right here . . . " on the inhale, and ". . . right now" on the exhale. With each breath, she reminded herself that there was nothing else to do and nowhere else to be, because all she had to do was breathe right here, right now.

One Conscious Breath

Several years ago I was watching a televised interview with meditation teacher Eckhart Tolle. Toward the end of the show, a woman called in with a question. She detailed her experiences with various meditation teachers and expressed her confusion about the conflicting advice she had received. This woman was interested to know how many minutes she should spend in meditation every day. She described several of the suggestions offered to her, ranging from 20 minutes to an hour and a half or more each day, and she asked Tolle if he had an opinion. He sat quietly as she spoke, and I remember reaching for a pencil, because I wanted to know the answer, too! I will never forget his response. He smiled and said simply, "All it takes is one conscious breath."

He went on to explain that one moment of pure awareness can be more valuable than an hour of meditation. As a musician, I understood immediately what he meant, because I knew that a few minutes of intensely focused practice is more effective than an hour of mindless repetition in the practice room. The only challenge related to one conscious breath is remembering to practice it. I have a good friend who sets an electronic reminder so that, at random moments throughout the day, the word "breathe" will pop up on her laptop or mobile phone. As I mentioned earlier, I find it works well to link a new habit with another activity that I do every day. For example, I have experimented with taking one conscious breath before checking my email, after brushing my teeth, and when switching to another piece of music to practice.

I often think about the idea of taking one conscious breath, because it is a complete paradigm shift from everything I was originally taught about mindfulness. The power of this technique comes not from the single deep, rejuvenating breath, however. It comes from the single moment of true awareness, as you look up from what you are doing, and are completely aware of the present moment, including your surroundings and your physical self, with minimal thought. That short pause creates a space for introspection, self-realization, even transformation. I sometimes wonder, how might humans think or act differently when coming from a place of pure consciousness?

***

These represent only a small sampling of the vast possibilities of breathwork. You may come across or invent another breathing technique not mentioned here, and it might be an excellent fit for you. Once again, it is a good idea to practice these breathing activities when you are calm, so that they may work effectively when you feel stressed. No one learns to swim in a stormy ocean. As you discover which breathing techniques work best for you in different situations, you may begin to reap more benefits than simply calming and centering the mind. One of the most perceptible advantages is that the physical body tends to relax in response to the breathwork. This offers an important benefit to musicians who tend to be tense or anxious before a practice or performance.

Conscious Relaxation

Tension is who you think you should be. Relaxation is who you are.
—Chinese proverb

The concept of relaxation is a paradox for all musicians. While excessive muscle tension can interfere with healthy technique, keeping certain muscles engaged is necessary for optimal performance. When a teacher or colleague suggests that you *relax* when you play or sing, be silently aware that this would be impossible, unless you want to spill onto the floor like a blob of gelatin dessert. In fact, for many musicians, the directive to relax is problematic in itself. The idea of relaxing may evoke images of lounging by a pool with an eye mask of cucumber slices. To sit or stand upright with good alignment, however, requires a degree of complex muscle activity. Singing or playing an instrument may oblige a performer to engage large and small muscles in the abdomen, arms, jaw, and many other areas. The problem arises, of course, when habits of excessive tension develop in certain areas of the body. Instead of thinking about tension and relaxation, it helps many musicians to think instead of releasing certain muscle groups while engaging others.

Because we are integrated beings, imbalance in one area of our lives deeply affects other areas as well. Tension and stress are very tangible examples of this, particularly for performing musicians. For example, psychological stress and worry often bring about needless physical tension in the body. The reverse is also true: An excess of muscle tension can trigger feelings of anxiety. Often, performers get caught in an unfortunate loop of feeling tense, which sparks a sense of apprehension, which in turn tightens the muscles even more, which subsequently magnifies our nervousness, and so on. The result can be unwanted performance anxiety and even physical impairment. Since superfluous tension in the upper body, especially, can cause problems in the hands and arms, managing that tension is a crucial skill for any musician.

When performers injure themselves in the practice room, needless tension is often one of the culprits. The best way to develop body awareness, of course, is to address it before you even begin your practice. Professional athletes warm up before practicing, but musicians often neglect this component of self-care. This is illogical, considering that musicians may spend hours a day practicing or rehearsing in one position, engaging the same groups of muscles in repetitive motions. Since the muscles should be warm before you begin to play or sing, plan to take a minute or two to move the body and increase circulation before each rehearsal or performance. Swinging or circling the arms, rolling the shoulders, even wiggling the fingers can be beneficial, because these movements lubricate the joints and prepare the muscles. For this reason, musicians are advised to warm up at their instruments as well. No professional singer would launch headfirst into the "Queen of the Night" aria (or, for that matter, "Bohemian Rhapsody") without first preparing the voice with vocalises and other exercises. Cooling down is essential as well and should include gentle stretches appropriate for musicians.

Stretching after each rehearsal or performance is a vital part of physical and mental well-being. During long rehearsals, it is also important to stretch during breaks. The body should be warm before stretching, which is why it is best to stretch during or after a practice session. If you always keep in mind that musicians are the athletes of the small muscles, it is will be easier to remember the importance of caring for even those smallest muscles that are capable of performing virtuosic feats.

The best stretches for a musician, depending on the instrument, often involve the muscles of the shoulders, neck, forearms, wrists, hands, and back. Of course, full-body stretching is also wonderful for any human being. But in this chapter, I have focused on stretches that you can do during a practice break or after a performance. Each stretch should last about 15–20 seconds and should never feel painful. Stop or ease up on the stretch if you feel discomfort. Stretches should also be performed while stationary, or should involve only very slow, deliberate movements, but should never include any sort of bouncing or jerking. Ideally, these stretches can also be combined with some of the breathwork activities just described. Focusing our attention on various body parts, as we stretch them in the present moment, is excellent mindfulness practice.

Stretches for the Neck, Shoulders, and Upper Back

· Keeping your shoulders still, gently turn your head to the right as far as is comfortable and hold for a few seconds at a point of gentle tension. Repeat by turning your head to the left.
· Gently lower your chin toward your chest until you feel the stretch in the back of your neck and upper back and hold for several seconds.
· Keeping your face forward, gently bend your right ear down toward your right shoulder and hold. Repeat on the left-hand side.
· Draw one straight arm across the chest and gently hold it in place with the other hand. Repeat on the other side.
· Shrug your shoulders up toward your ears as far as comfortably possible, and hold. Allow the shoulders to drop back to a neutral position. Repeat as often as necessary.
· Clasp your hands behind you, and gently pull your arms away from your back.

- Hold your arms out in front of you as you clasp your hands together. Allow the upper back to round over slightly, creating a gentle stretch. Move your clasped hands overhead, or slightly behind your head, holding the stretch.

Stretches for the Hands, Wrists, and Forearms

- Extend your right arm out in front of you, with your palm facing forward. With the opposite hand, *gently* pull the fingers up and toward the ceiling and your body until you feel a mild stretch in the wrist. Repeat on the other side.
- Extend your right arm out in front of you, palm down, with your fingers pointing forward. With the opposite hand, *gently* pull the fingers down and toward the floor until you feel a mild stretch. Repeat on the other side.
- Using both hands, spread your fingers out as far as you comfortably can, and hold for just 1 or 2 seconds. Contract the hands into an easy fist. Repeat this 5 to 10 times.

Good health and wellness practices contribute to a holistic model of musical development, one that addresses the performer as a whole being with complex and interrelated parts. The next sections focus on disciplines that intentionally unite the mind and body for improved well-being.

Beginning Yoga for Musicians

Blessed are the flexible, for they shall not be bent out of shape.
—Unknown

The practice of gentle, restorative yoga can be tremendously benefi-cial for musicians. Not only is the entire body stretched in a slow and deliberate way, but the practice often ends with a short meditation that encourages feelings of peace and tranquility. An ancient discipline, yoga develops strength, balance, and flexibility through postures and breathing techniques. Today, yoga is widely practiced in the United States to promote health and wellness. Some yoga emphasizes static poses that are held for several seconds or even minutes, while other forms of yoga involve slow, deliberate movements. This chapter highlights only a few static poses that are easily described in a book and implemented in a small space such as a practice room. If you are more interested in a practice involving gentle movement, check out a flow or vinyasa yoga class.

Musicians should be careful with yoga poses that strain the wrists and arms or that require the wrists to support the weight of the body. Most musicians should be fine with an introductory yoga class taught by a reputable and certified instructor, but everyone should feel confident asking for modifications for more strenuous poses. You should not try any pose if you have recently had surgery or experienced an injury, unless you consult with a medical professional. Yoga, like breathing, is not a competitive sport. A professional musician's physical body is his or her livelihood and should be protected as the valuable resource that it is.

The following yoga poses are those that I believe are the gentlest and of greatest benefit to the majority of performing musicians. I have used the common English terms for these poses, rather than the original Sanskrit names. Feel free to try any of these, or to explore the many available yoga apps, websites, and video tutorials. Just keep in mind that you will receive more personalized attention, assistance with proper alignment, and suggested modifications for your body if you take a class with a certified instructor. Hold each of these poses for several breath cycles, and stretch only to the point of gentle tension. Eventually you may discover that you can practice your breathing exercises while holding a yoga pose.

Mountain Pose

The easiest *looking* yoga pose, an exercise in good alignment, can actually be tricky to master. If you practice or perform standing up, this would be a wonderful way to align the body before picking up your instrument. If you practice while seated, you can try a modification of this pose while sitting on a chair or bench. Stand with your feet hip-distance apart and your toes pointing forward, and see if you can balance your weight equally between the feet. Keep the knees soft or slightly bent, and tuck your tailbone slightly forward. Roll your shoulders down and back so that they do not slope forward, and let your arms hang softly at your sides. Stand tall but comfortably, imagining your spine gently lengthening toward the ceiling. See how much unnecessary muscle tension you can release as you allow the bones of your body to support your weight.

Standing Forward Bend

Stand balanced with your feet hip-distance apart and your toes pointed forward. Bend the knees slightly, and slowly bend forward from the hips as if they were hinged. Only bend as far as your hamstrings will comfortably allow you, keeping your knees soft. Place your hands on the floor in front of you, or on the front of your shins, or clasp your elbows with opposite hands and allow your arms and head to hang gently. After holding for several seconds, slowly move yourself up from the hips, keeping the back relatively straight. You can also do a version of this pose seated in a chair, lowering your head between your knees and wrapping your hands around your ankles. This seated stretch is particularly excellent after a long rehearsal or marathon performance.

Cat and Cow

This fluid pose, which requires you to get down on the floor, is an excellent way to warm up the spine and promote flexibility in the back muscles. On a patch of soft carpet, a towel, or a mat, get down on your hands and knees. Align your arms so that they are straight and directly under your shoulders, and position your legs hips-distance apart. As you inhale, lift your hips and your head toward the ceiling, arching your back slightly. This is the cow. As you exhale, round your back, lower your head, and tuck your chin under. This is the cat. Repeat gently for several breath cycles. If you need a practice break and you are starting to get fatigued or frustrated, this pose is a fun and meditative activity. Animal noises are completely optional.

Legs Up the Wall

This is a good one to try if you are exhausted or if your back is sore from practicing or sitting all day. It is exactly what it sounds like, so you will need to find a nice, smooth wall. The idea is to lie on your back on the floor, and rest your legs vertically up the wall so that your body forms a 90° angle. The easiest way to get into this pose is to curl up on your side in a fetal position, facing away from the wall, scooting your backside as close to the wall as you can, then rolling onto your back while sliding and straightening your legs up the wall. You can try to press the length of your legs against the wall, or just your ankles or calves. You can also put a blanket or two under your lower back or hips if it is more comfortable. This can be a very therapeutic pose.

Astronaut Pose

This isn't exactly a yoga pose, but it is used in meditation as a restorative posture and is wonderful for your back. You will need a bench or a standard-sized chair with an open back. Lie on the floor facing the front of your chair, as if you were going to do *Legs Up the Wall*, but this time bend your knees and rest your legs on the seat of the chair. Your back will be flat on the floor, and your calves will rest flat against the seat of your chair, with your feet poking through the back of the chair. This is actually an inverted form of a seated position. Again, you can use blankets or pillows to support your head or back.

***

You can easily practice breathwork exercises while you are hanging out in these poses. When you combine mindful breathing with yoga stretches, you may find that the stress reduction benefits are greatly increased.

Other Practices for Musicians

Not all those who wander are lost.—J. R. R. Tolkien

Although yoga is probably the most universally accessible mind-body practice available to musicians, other approaches are equally beneficial, or perhaps beneficial in slightly different ways. I encourage you to explore any of the following practices that pique your interest. Practitioners of these techniques should be well trained and certified, and, in the best of all possible worlds, should have some experience working with musicians. The following list is far from exhaustive, but represents some important and widely practiced disciplines.

Alexander Technique

The Alexander Technique was developed to increase body awareness, relieve excess tension, understand correct alignment, and learn to move freely and with mindful awareness. This technique involves the practice of body mapping, or developing an understanding of human anatomy in order to move with greater ease and efficiency. Alexander teachers often emphasize freeing the neck and spine from tension and bad habits of alignment and engaging only the most necessary muscles when in motion. Musicians have found this technique to be extremely beneficial, and, in fact, many colleges and universities now offer Alexander Technique classes to music majors. In a class or lesson setting, a certified instructor may watch you sing or play your instrument and may help you incorporate the techniques into your practice.

The Feldenkrais Method

Feldenkrais is a form of somatic education, which means that its primary focus is the internal perception of motion. Key components of this method are body awareness, improved physical function, and ease of movement, all of which are essential to good musical technique. Feldenkrais practitioners often emphasize slow, repetitive movements to develop better habits of using the body efficiently.

T'ai chi ch'uan

This gentle Chinese martial art, as it is most commonly practiced in the United States, involves very slow and meditative movements that can help a musician calm and focus the mind. Most t'ai chi instructors teach a series of traditional movements that the entire class performs together in silence. Musicians who are interested in Eastern philosophy combined with meditative movement may enjoy the quiet and disciplined nature of t'ai chi.

Qigong

This practice, pronounced "chi-gung" and spelled a number of different ways in English, is another Chinese practice of moving meditation. It differs from t'ai chi in that it is specifically a spiritual practice, originally intended to cultivate and balance the life energy known as *qi* (chi). Qigong practice may include choreographed fluid movements, holding static postures as in yoga, rhythmic breathing, and/or seated meditation. In contemporary practice, qigong is perceived as the ultimate balance of body, breath, and mind.

Laban Movement Analysis

Also referred to as LMA or Laban/Bartenieff, Laban is a multidisciplinary approach to studying and practicing human movement. Practitioners explore the physical characteristics of the body in motion, attention to the quality and timing of movements, the ways in which the body changes shape when it is in motion, and a person's perception of the space around her. Dancers frequently use Laban principles, although actors and musicians can benefit from this practice as well.

Progressive Relaxation Techniques

Some of us think holding on makes us strong, but sometimes it is letting go.
—Hermann Hesse

Musicians can learn how their bodies function best during an optimal performance. Unlike professional athletic coaches, most music teachers do not take courses in anatomy and biomechanics and do not learn how and when to teach stretching, relaxation, or the proper care of important muscle groups. Fortunately, a few mindful relaxation techniques can make a huge difference in physical and mental comfort and ease.

The first technique works especially well with very tight muscles and is very easy to do. Simply tense each muscle group as tightly as possible, hold for a few seconds, and then let go. For example, try clenching one of your fists as tightly as possible as you read this paragraph. (I especially encourage you to try this if you are reading this book in a public place, because it may appear to others as if this book is making you very, very angry. No one will mess with you after that.) If you clench your fist tightly enough, and hold it just long enough, the muscles in your arm will probably begin to quiver. When you suddenly release those muscles and allow the arm to drop, you may notice that the muscles feel warmer and more relaxed than before. You can try this with any body part, but it works best with the large muscles that carry tension. The shoulders respond well to this technique, particularly if you shrug them both up as far as possible toward your ears and hold them in that state of tension for several seconds before letting them drop.

Another technique, quieter and more meditative in nature, is particularly effective for performers who struggle with stress or anxiety. This activity involves bringing about relaxation through mental suggestion. Notice how your body reacts when you read the following passage very slowly and deliberately: "My shoulders feel warm and heavy. I feel the muscles gradually releasing, as gravity pulls my shoulders down into their natural, relaxed position. As a result, the back of my neck begins to soften, the muscles on the sides of my neck gently release, and my shoulders become even heavier and more comfortable." Your body will often respond to mindful suggestions made to it, particularly in a comfortable and unhurried environment.

The beauty of this technique is that no one can see you doing it. You can be standing backstage, silently coaxing your jaw and your neck to relax and let go, before you go out on stage to sing. This practice is very effective if you are able to recline or lie down, giving yourself enough time to relax the entire body one muscle group at a time. This only takes 5 or 10 minutes and is a great activity to try in bed before you fall asleep. You would breathe deeply from the diaphragm, and softly visualize each part of your body becoming more and more relaxed. You might start at the top of your head and work your way down to your feet, or experiment instead with the opposite direction.

Here is an example of what your internal voice might sound like, if you were practicing this relaxation exercise while lying down on your sofa or in another comfortable place. You might think each sentence very slowly to yourself, perhaps even repeating it once or twice. Pausing for a few seconds in between each phrase gives your body the opportunity to respond slowly and naturally to your suggestions.

> My body is quiet. This pillow feels lovely. I am beginning to feel quite relaxed.
> My feet feel heavy, warm, and relaxed. Even my toes feel relaxed.
> My ankles feel warm, relaxed, and comfortable.
> My calf muscles feel warm and relaxed.
> My knees feel loose and relaxed.
> My thighs are releasing any excess tension.
> My hips are releasing, letting go.
> My abdomen feels soft, warm, and relaxed.
> My chest feels heavy and comfortable.
> My back is beginning to relax and unwind.
> I allow each muscle in my back to release and let go.
> My arms feel heavy, warm, and quiet.
> My hands feel warm and relaxed. Even my fingers are releasing and letting go.
> My shoulders feel warm, relaxed, and comfortable.
> My neck feels loose, relaxed, and free.
> The muscles in my face are beginning to relax and let go.
> My jaw feels loose, heavy, and relaxed.

> My eyes feel heavy and comfortable.
> My forehead and scalp feel smooth, soft, and relaxed.
> My whole body feels warm, heavy, and comfortable.
> Gravity is gently pulling my body down, and I am able to surrender to it.
> I am comfortably relaxed.

You may notice that in this example, the same words and combinations of words are varied and repeated in an almost hypnotic fashion. With a small amount of practice, you can learn to coax your body and mind into a very tranquil state. Sometimes I like to intersperse the same phrase, almost like the refrain of a song, in between each statement just listed. For example, you could repeat something like, "I am becoming more deeply relaxed" after each phrase. That way, as each body part begins to release, you are reminding yourself that the entire body is letting go and becoming more comfortable with each breath.

Several progressive relaxation recordings are available on the market, often in the form of meditation or self-hypnosis exercises. Some of these are excellent, and you can allow yourself to listen and follow the suggestions offered by the voice on the recording. A few smartphone apps offer free programs as well. You can even read the sentences just listed into your own recording device, and play it back to yourself! The secret is to speak very slowly, with frequent short pauses, as if you were sleepy. The body responds easily when there is no hurry.

Many of the audio recordings for this book begin with a short breathing exercise, followed by a progressive relaxation exercise, followed by a visualization for peak performance. This formula represents what is, in my opinion, the "triple whammy" of mindfulness practice for performance success. You have already learned two of the components, breathing and relaxation, in this chapter. We will explore the third element of creative imagery in the next chapter.

The following is an abbreviated transcript of one of the progressive relaxations I recorded for this book. This differs from the previous example in its narrative approach and its use of imagery. You may choose to read it to inspire additional ideas of how you might practice these suggestions yourself.

Allow yourself to feel deeply relaxed as your body is completely supported by the earth. Imagine that, in this lovely place, a feeling of warmth begins to surround you. This is a peaceful and healing warmth that relaxes every muscle and cell that it touches. Imagine that this warm sensation moves slowly from the top of your head to the tips of your toes, relaxing every part of your body. As the warmth gently surrounds the head, feel the scalp softly relax. The small muscles in the forehead and around the eyes gently soften as the face relaxes and tiny stress lines disappear. The eyes feel heavy and comfortably relaxed. The jaw becomes loose and heavy, and as it relaxes you are able to feel the resulting space between the teeth. The muscles in the front and back of the neck begin to release, as all tension dissolves. As the warmth moves slowly down your body, your shoulders become loose and heavy, and you allow gravity to pull them down toward the earth into their natural position. As the back begins to relax deeply, feel each vertebra in the spine slowly unwind, as all tension and tightness are released. The front of the torso feels quiet and heavy, and the abdomen becomes relaxed and comfortable. Allow the mind to relax and unwind, simply letting go, releasing all fears, problems, or pressures. The feeling of warmth makes its way down your arms, relaxing the elbows, the wrists, and the hands. The hips feel relaxed and comfortable. Feel the large muscles in the thighs and calves begin to loosen and become heavy. The knees are relaxed. The ankles, even the feet and the toes feel warm, quiet, and very deeply relaxed. Imagine that this comfortable warmth envelops your entire body, helping you to feel safe, secure, and at peace. It gently releases all stress, concerns, and worries that may have been held in the body, and allows the body to go deeper into this feeling of relaxation. Feel the pleasant sensation of becoming deeply, peacefully relaxed.

Check out the companion website (⊕ item 5.3) for a progressive relaxation audio recording.

In addition to presenting a number of healthful breathing and relaxation techniques, this chapter also serves as an introduction to the powerful practice of creative visualization, which is discussed next. As we continue to explore various applications of mindful awareness, we will also begin to discover the boundless potential of the musician's mind. The secret lies in how and when we use our imagination.

6 IMAGERY FOR PEAK PERFORMANCE

Everything you can imagine is real.—Pablo Picasso

Consider that, for every moment that you are not aware of the present, you are visualizing another reality. If you are ruminating on a past event, you are replaying that reality. If you are nervous about an upcoming situation, or even imagining a worst-case scenario, you are visualizing that reality. Psychologist Rick Carson said it best: "In every moment you devote your life to something. You do so via your awareness." How have you devoted your life today? Are you consciously directing many of your thoughts, or are they directing you? The mind is an extraordinarily powerful tool, and we often forget that we can retain tremendous control over how we use it. We can create powerful, positive experiences with the mind, but we can also use it as a harbinger of negativity and worry. As Mark Twain once quipped, "I've experienced many terrible things in my life, a few of which actually happened."

The brain and nervous system cannot distinguish an event that occurred in real life from one that was only imagined. When you visualize the physical movements of an outstanding musical performance, then, the nerve cells involved in moving all those necessary muscles are stimulated. Your mind and body believe the fantastic performance was a real event! In that moment, you will have consciously directed the mind to expect a specific positive outcome. But it is also true that if you habitually focus on all possible disastrous performance scenarios, your mind may believe those catastrophes happened in real life. The constructive and deliberate use of imagery, then, is one of the most powerful applications of mindfulness that any musician can use to train for peak performances. It is fun to do, and you are limited only by your creative imagination.

What is Imagery?

Imagination is more important than knowledge.—Albert Einstein

Imagery refers simply to the formation of mental images and is virtually synonymous with visualization. Some professionals like to distinguish between imagery and visualization, since visualization can sometimes imply an emphasis on mental pictures, while imagery can refer to a whole host of internal experiences. Many people are not particularly visual by nature, preferring to engage emotions and other experiences in their mental practice. Because of this, contemporary sport psychologists tend to view the word imagery as more inclusive. In practice, though, the two terms are used interchangeably to describe the creation of an imagined reality.

Although authors have explored creative visualization since the 19th century, the concept erupted in popularity a hundred years later with the publication of books such as Maxwell Maltz's *Psycho-Cybernetics* (1960) and Shakti Gawain's *Creative Visualization* (1978). Maltz was a plastic surgeon who noticed that many of his patients continued to experience low self-images even after cosmetic reconstruction. He discovered that if people first visualized a positive outcome, they were much more successful at changing old negative thoughts patterns and beliefs. In other words, he believed that we must set constructive inner goals before we can successfully achieve positive outer goals. Today, many writers, coaches, and performers use these same concepts to achieve success in a variety of fields, including business, sports, health care, and artistic creation and performance.

Anyone who can focus on an idea can learn to use imagery successfully. Some people find it difficult to imagine an upcoming performance in vivid detail at first. In this case, I find it very helpful to practice this skill by focusing on a memory. If you can remember an event from the past, you can learn to imagine a future event. Some people have very visual memories, while others focus on the facts, feelings, or aural recollections of a past event. It doesn't really matter, as long as the experience feels engaging and realistic. The short exercises in this chapter can help you strengthen the skill of using imagery for performance preparation, or for any other goals you choose for yourself. If any of the activities feel particularly challenging for you at first, it is a good idea to practice them daily until they become easier. It only takes a minute or two.

We must distinguish imagery from daydreaming. When someone is daydreaming, fantasizing, or simply absorbed in thought, the mind can wander aimlessly without specific intention. Often, a daydream or fantasy can take on a life of its own, with little or no conscious control, which is why people sometimes refer to being "lost in thought." When using visualization as a tool for successful performance, the idea is to focus the imagination consciously and deliberately on an objective with the intent of achieving that objective. It is also important to distinguish the use of *imagery* for peak performance with the act of *mental practice* to learn and refine specific passages of music. These two skills engage different parts of the brain and are intended for two different outcomes. (You may prefer to review our discussion of mental practice in Chapter 2.)

Top athletes rely on imagery to enhance their performances. In fact, research suggests that highly confident athletes use imagery more often and more effectively than athletes with lower levels of self-assurance. The fact that imagery has been found to be more effective in tasks that are highly cognitive (such as playing a game of chess), rather than purely motor (such as doing abdominal crunches), makes it an ideal tool for performing musicians. Other studies suggest that mental imagery combined with physical practice is far more effective than either mental imagery or physical practice alone. This means that imagery is not a substitute for practice, but can greatly enhance what we accomplish in the practice room.

When practicing imagery, we can develop personal control by focusing on positive or self-enhancing experiences as often as possible, rather than on those that are negative or detrimental. Imagery that you practice while relaxed tends to be particularly effective, so it will be helpful to set aside a time and place where you can take a few minutes to breathe and relax before beginning the activity. Professional athletes document their goals, emotional states, and experiences using imagery, and this can provide essential feedback over months of training. I encourage you to keep track of your imagery experiences by tracking them in some sort of a journal or log. Far from being a waste of time, this sort of record keeping will help you refine your mental practice by adjusting it as needed.

Successful performers are able to engage both internal and external mental perspectives when they practice imagery. They can visualize themselves performing from a first-person perspective, as the performer, as well as from the viewpoint of the spectators who are watching the event. In other words, a musician can imagine himself on stage with his instrument, looking out into the audience; but he can also imagine himself from the perspective of a seated audience member. With practice, he can even imagine that he is observing himself from behind, from the side of the stage, or even from above. Some people become so adept at this skill that they can easily switch perspectives back and forth in their minds. The idea of shifting imagined viewpoints is beneficial in practice because it satisfies a performer's desire to feel confident on stage in her own body, as well as to project a deliberate appearance and body language to others.

Musicians can easily improve the skill of mental imagery with regularly applied mindfulness practice. Studies suggest that in some cases, athletes who could barely use imagery techniques at first were able to learn these skills and eventually develop them to a very high level. Furthermore, when it comes to mental training, we have learned that one size does not fit all. Since performance experiences are as unique as the individuals themselves, standardized training programs do not work as well as strategies that are highly individual and personalized. Keep this in mind if a technique that helps another musician does not seem to work well for you. With experimentation, you can find what clicks with your particular situation and personality.

The practice of mental imagery can generate remarkably vivid experiences. In fact, the more imagined senses we use during imagery, the deeper and more effective the experience will be. As an experiment, take a moment to focus your mind on an upcoming performance event. Imagine that you are standing on stage, moments before you begin to play or sing. Your first response might be to visualize what you look like on the stage, the objects or people near you, and the appearance of your physical surroundings. This healthy mental picture is only a small part of the experience, however. If you consciously engage the other senses in your imagination, you may experience the feel of your clothes or shoes, the temperature of the room or stage, the warmth of the stage lights on your skin, even the feeling of holding your instrument, music, or microphone. You may also experience internal sensations such as nervousness, excitement, or restlessness. You might imagine that you can hear the rustling and whispering of the audience members, the sound of other instrumentalists tuning or warming up, or the voice of someone introducing you. If you go even deeper into the experience, you might pick up some familiar aromas, such as the distinct smell of musty stage curtains, your instrument case, resin, cork grease, or your own soap or cologne. In this sort of mental activity, it is almost impossible to run out of things to imagine.

It is worth mentioning that this sort of mental training necessitates realistic and healthy expectations, as well as a generally positive mindset. It also assumes that you are practicing well, and frequently enough to ensure a successful experience on stage. Mental imagery can greatly enhance performance and can even help bring about a peak experience, but it can't substitute for adequate time in the practice room. Be patient with yourself. Remember what it was like to be a beginner in your music lessons, and allow yourself the opportunity to make mistakes, and to learn and grow. At the same time, be a good self-coach, and push yourself to stay focused and motivated.

Practicing Imagery

> *Change your mental imagery, and the feelings will take care of themselves.*
> —Maxwell Maltz

Even if you already have some experience with creative visualization, the following activities will help you develop and refine this skill. Although the tendency of most readers is to want to read from paragraph to paragraph without stopping, I invite you to pause after each exercise and try it, even if only for a minute. Since the mind loves to remember and daydream, this should be entertaining. If you treat these activities with a playful sense of adventure, rather than trying to "get it right," you will be more successful at developing mental flexibility and imagination. You may be surprised at how quickly your abilities improve with practice. Treat it like a game.

Theme and Variations on a Memory

When you finish reading this paragraph, close your eyes and choose a short happy or pleasant memory to recall from your childhood. This will be only a brief snapshot in time. Don't spend too much time choosing a memory, because the memory itself isn't that important, as long as it evokes a neutral or positive emotional response. See if you can imagine what it was like to be that young again. Do you remember what you were wearing and what you were doing? Or can you imagine your surroundings, including the people around you? Take just a moment to relive this short memory.

***

You may have been able to recall much of this childhood memory. Like many people, though, you probably struggled to remember some of the smaller details. This is perfectly fine and normal. When using a memory to practice creative imagery, your mind may need to fill in some of the gaps by making up a few of the details. If, for example, you couldn't remember the color of the carpet or what you were wearing at the time, allow your mind the freedom to complete that mental image for you. What is most important is that you focus on the first-person experiences of that event. If the memory was too distant or vague to be vivid, try this exercise again with a more recent happy memory before continuing.

While it is still fresh in your mind, imagine that you are no longer the child in your memory, but that you are watching the same scene unfold in colorful detail on a movie screen in front of you. This may take a few moments as you adjust your mental perspective, but you can imagine that "older you" is sitting in a movie theater watching "younger you" on the big screen. By doing this, you can observe other details about the child (you) that you might not have noticed earlier. For example, you might have a different or more objective view of how the child interacts with others nearby.

***

If that last activity was challenging, practice it daily by choosing a different memory to recall. If you find you have difficulty imagining the pictures in your mind, it may help to look at an actual photograph from that scene in your life. If you close your eyes and focus mentally on the photograph, you might be able to imagine that it slowly comes to life. With practice, the visual detail will gradually become sharper and more specific. If you find that you are having trouble managing what happens in this mental scene, remember that you are in control as the director of this mental movie. You can freeze the frame and refocus on a still image, or you can experience the scene in slow motion until you regain control of the images.

On the other hand, if the activity seemed particularly easy to you, return to the memory and try this variation. As you watch the child version of you on the mental movie screen, begin to imagine that the child is not you, but a child actor playing the part of you. Perhaps the child actor resembles you somewhat, but doesn't look exactly like you. This may take a few moments as you imagine subtle changes in your child's physical appearance. Or, imagine that this movie is no longer in color, but in black and white. The people and events are the same, but the scene somehow feels even older, perhaps more distant. Finally, imagine that the movie is paused on one scene, which is frozen before you like a large black-and-white photograph. Maybe the photograph begins to fade just slightly, or even becomes slightly wrinkled or discolored with age. Does this feel any different from the original memory?

***

The simple activity of recalling a memory in detail, and then applying any number of creative variations, will help develop mental flexibility and will strengthen your ability to control your mental experiences in any way you choose. Notice which variations feel more vivid and alive to you and which ones seem more distant or detached. This can be very helpful when you are remembering a past performance or anticipating a future one. During visualization, you can take the idea of a positive performance experience and make it even more vivid in your imagination. You can imagine that the colors are slightly brighter and more saturated than they are in real life or that any positive emotions feel amplified.

Images in Sound

Choose a familiar sound which is not a melody, a rhythmic pattern, or any type of music. This should not be something you can actually hear as you read this. It could be a sound from nature (birds, crickets, a stream, a thunderstorm), a manufactured sound (traffic, a siren, a printer), or the sound of an activity (pouring soda into a glass, shuffling cards, bowling). Try to re-create the sound as vividly as possible in a gently repeating mental loop. Most performers do not think to practice aural recall with nonmusical sounds. If you do practice this way, you can develop the skill of audiation without relying on the added psychological and emotional elements of music. Remember that a performer's ability to imagine multiple sensory modalities can greatly intensify a creative visualization experience.

Images in Sensation

Mentally choose an object with a unique and interesting physical texture. This could be a pinecone, hairbrush, baseball glove, or anything else that appeals to you. Close your eyes and imagine that you are holding the object or that you are able to run your hands and fingers around it. How many details can you imagine? Don't be alarmed if you find you can't remember certain details or if you can't entirely re-create the object in your imagination. Consider the size, shape, material, temperature, and texture of the object. Once you are able to re-create what it feels like in your hands, can you imagine how it might feel against the inside of your arm or against your cheek?

A good activity for an instrumentalist is to repeat this exercise using your musical instrument as the object in question. This is a fun and familiar exercise for many musicians, and it can be a challenge to imagine the feel of touching the keys, strings, or drumsticks without mentally creating the resulting sound. You might also focus on one area or component of an instrument part, such as the headstock of a guitar, the frog of a violin bow, or a mouthpiece.

Images in Thought and Emotion

In the very first exercise, the recollection of a childhood memory, the goal was to emphasize the visual details of that past event. For this activity, you will choose another memory, this time focusing on the thoughts and emotions surrounding the event. Since the first activity focused on a happy memory, you may wish to try this one with an event that was not particularly pleasant for you. Emotional experiences can be especially vivid if the memory was one that caused any number of unwanted thoughts and feelings.

Usually we try to avoid or forget negative emotions. With mindfulness, however, we can learn to experience these feelings with objective awareness. For musicians, it can be a very powerful skill to learn to observe and release negative performance experiences, including the unhelpful criticisms of other people. The memory you choose to work with can be a memory from the past, or something very recent, just as long as you can still vividly recall your emotions surrounding the event. It is important that you refrain from choosing an event that caused you significant grief, trauma, or despair. Instead, choose a memory that was only moderately uncomfortable or negative, such as an argument, disappointment, or mildly embarrassing mistake.

Recall the details of the event while casually exploring each of your imagined senses. See if you can remember the visual details of your surroundings, including the objects and people in your vicinity, your clothing, the feel of your physical body, the lighting, colors, and anything else you can think of. Try to re-create the sounds of the event, including voices and ambient noise, and any possible scents in the air. Once you have created the overall image in your mind, pay particular attention to the array of emotions associated with this event. You don't need to identify or name these emotions, but do try to put yourself back in time as if the event were happening right now. Since feelings can be quite visceral, see if you can feel these emotions once again in your body. Try to remember the thoughts that were associated with these emotions, whether the thoughts were about you or about someone or something else.

Occasionally someone will report that they remember the thoughts and emotions, but can't re-create that feeling. ("I know I was angry at the time, but I can't seem to remember how that felt.") If this is the case, perhaps choose a more recent or vivid memory, one in which you can mentally experience at least some of the emotions. Here, the idea is not to shy away from past experiences, but rather to relive them as mindfully as possible. Human beings tend to cling to negative experiences, which can sometimes make those unpleasant memories easier to work with. Consider the advantage of being able to re-create vividly your own past feelings of performance stress. If you can imagine your fluttering stomach or increased heart rate, you are in a position to create a very realistic performance experience in your mind. You can practice managing those feelings, or experiment with positive thoughts that might change your perspective the next time you perform.

If you were able to recall the feelings of an unpleasant memory in striking detail, you may find that you can gently dismiss that memory and go on about your day. If, however, a particular memory continues to trouble you, you can use any number of visualization techniques to help detach from the negative emotion and reframe the memory more objectively. We explored a number of these in a previous exercise. You might choose to imagine that you are watching the memory as an outside observer, as if the memory were playing on a movie screen and you are in the audience. You may even choose to visualize the movie in black and white, or with other actors playing the parts, both of which can offer a greater sense of detachment. Sometimes I like to imagine that an upsetting memory is just a photograph, or even a pencil drawing in my hand, rather than a scene unfolding in front of me. Mindfulness makes it easier to remember that memories are not real, except as imagined events in our minds. This offers us complete control over how we choose to replay those experiences, if at all.

***

The next step is to anticipate an emotion you are likely to feel in the future. This naturally presents more of a challenge, since the event has yet to occur. However, you are able to draw from the emotions of past experiences. For example, are you excited about an activity you have planned this weekend? Or do you feel apprehensive about something you need to do? Can you identify the emotions surrounding an upcoming music event? Is there something coming up in your life that fills you with a sense of gratitude or appreciation? If you have trouble grasping any of these imagined feelings, focus on the thoughts surrounding the feelings. Remember that thoughts trigger emotions. The ability to anticipate a future event in vivid detail is an incredibly valuable tool for any performing musician.

Imagery for Peak Performance

And the walls became the world all around.—Maurice Sendak

In my experience, the most successful imagery involves a combination of thoughtful preparation, relaxation, concentration, suggestion, and positive expectation. Good preparation involves finding a relatively quiet place where you are not likely to be bothered. You can sit comfortably or recline, and the activity often works best if you close your eyes. If you have a tendency to fall asleep, you will not want to lie down. Mindful breathing and physical relaxation, as discussed in the previous chapter, will greatly enhance the experience and will help train the body and mind to relax before an actual performance. Concentration involves deliberately focusing on your objective rather than allowing the mind to wander and daydream. If you do notice your mind wandering, gently guide your awareness back to the visualization. If your mind continues to stray despite your best efforts, you may choose instead to listen to one of the recordings provided on the companion website (⊕ items 6.1–6.4). A good creative visualization takes only about 10 minutes to practice. However, if you find this exercise as relaxing and engaging as many musicians do, you can take as much time as you like. As you imagine your successful performance experience, the suggestions you make to yourself should be both optimistic and realistic.

Before the Performance

As you guide yourself through the activity, I suggest you begin the visualization by imagining yourself in an offstage location where you would be waiting to perform. Depending on the performance venue, your options might include your practice space, a dressing room or green room, or an area just off the stage. Using ideas from earlier in this chapter, you can imagine what your backstage surroundings may look like, including the lighting and decor of the area, your fellow musicians, or your own in-strument, music, and clothing. When practical, it is advantageous to visit the performance venue several days before the actual performance. I have even found it helpful to revisit familiar performance locations, because I always notice additional details to incorporate into my visualization. Fine details add a realistic edge to your mental practice, which will intensify your preparation. If you are able to choose your performance attire well in advance, use this to aid your visualization. You can imagine looking down at your shoes, for example, or perceiving other features of your clothing. Don't worry if you're not exactly sure what to expect. Remember that, since this is your own visualization, you can dream up anything you wish.

Once you have established a mental picture in your mind, begin to en-gage your other senses. You might imagine various sounds that you will hear from the audience (talking, rustling) or from the stage (musicians tuning, an announcer speaking). See if you can envision some of the pos-sible physical sensations, such as the temperature or humidity, the feel of your clothes, or anything you may be holding in your hands before you perform. Pay particular attention to the *internal* sensations you expect to encounter. These will most certainly include your emotions, both posi-tive and negative, and the many thoughts associated with those emotions. Consider that your internal dialogue varies depending on where you are in the performance process: before, during, or after a concert. Think care-fully about how you can turn each of these moments to your advantage.

If you normally feel apprehensive before a performance, engaging a few of these emotions can create a very vivid and realistic virtual expe-rience. The difference is that in your relaxed state, you have the luxury of handcrafting your preferred experience. The relaxed and engaged mind is very flexible, and can entertain the paradox of acknowledging and accepting all of your feelings, while simultaneously directing your mind to focus more frequently on positive, healthy habits of thoughts. For example, if you normally feel jittery or restless before you perform, you can experiment with recognizing those feelings and reframing them as indicators of excitement or enthusiasm. In other words, you can prepare your mind to interpret excess adrenaline in your body as eagerness and confidence rather than fear or worry. You can even suggest to yourself that you begin to feel more relaxed and comfortable as time goes on. If your mind tends to race before a performance, you can imagine that you feel alert, energized, and focused. You can plan to discover a peaceful core of confidence and stability beneath all the excitement. Since you are in control of this mental experience, you can imagine any thoughts or feelings you desire! We will practice constructing healthy affirmations a little later.

During the Performance

Your framing of the preperformance experience is important, and will only take a minute or two. The very core of an imagery exercise is the performance itself. Allow yourself to imagine any logistics related to the start of this virtual performance. These may include walking out onstage, perhaps speaking to your audience, playing or singing your program, bowing, and leaving the performance area. You can imagine the brightness of the lights, the sound of your shoes as you walk to your performance spot, your view of the audience, and of course, your performance. As you visualize yourself performing, you might experiment with the technique of shifting your viewpoint. For many musicians, a first-person perspective (imagining themselves on stage, looking out into the audience, feeling the sensations of singing or playing an instrument) is the easiest and most realistic perspective to start with. However, you can also imagine yourself from the position of an audience member sitting in the front row, an interested observer standing in the very back of the room, or someone watching from backstage. Experiment to see what feels helpful to you. The amount of time you spend on your imagined performance isn't as important as the quality of details you are able to imagine.

I recommend that you do not imagine yourself performing any piece note-for-note from beginning to end. As I mentioned earlier, that sort of mental practice is an excellent way to learn new repertoire, check memorization, clarify interpretation, and refine physical technique. It involves a very alert and active conscious mind and a specific set of attainable practice goals. However, that type of practice does not allow the mind to become deeply relaxed, focusing exclusively on the thoughts and feelings surrounding the art of performance in general. While mental practice might be impractical to do every day, the type of creative imagery described here is intended to be part of your daily preparation. It is designed to prepare your mind for multiple successful performance experiences, regardless of the venue or the specific repertoire performed.

When visualizing yourself performing music, you might first direct your imagination to the beginning of a piece. Perhaps you can imagine feeling focused and energized as you begin to play or sing; you might even hear the opening notes of the music in your mind. This is your opportunity to practice feeling engaged and optimistic as you start to perform. You can then allow your imagination to drift to a less specific performing experience for a few moments. Although your mind will not hear every note of your music unfold in real time, you can still feel the style, tempo, and overall character of your music. If a specific passage such as a virtuosic solo worries you, you can imagine playing that passage with complete confidence and ease. In this sort of mental performance, your focus is less on the actual music and more on your positive thoughts and emotions about the performance itself. You might prefer to visualize the very end of each piece as well, right before you acknowledge your audience. In regular imagery practice, only the beginnings and endings of actual pieces will change, depending on your repertoire. The middle portion of the imagery, where you are performing with confidence and security, may be similar for many of these exercises.

What would a best-possible performance experience look and feel like to you? If you could describe how you want to feel, and how you want your music to sound, how would you articulate that? Take a moment to consider this, if you haven't already, because you will want to be able to direct your mind in a very specific and positive way. Think about the words and phrases you might use in a future imagery exercise. For you, this may mean feeling secure and confident, performing with ease and accuracy, having the freedom to express yourself creatively, feeling connected to your music or your audience, or anything else. Once you identify your ultimate performance goals, you can craft these into affirmations for before, during, and after your virtual performance.

After the Performance

Before you conclude your imagery activity, be sure to visualize yourself moments after the performance, whether you will be alone with your thoughts or greeting friends at a reception. The time immediately following a performance is when many musicians feel the most self-critical and vulnerable. You might imagine hearing the sounds of enthusiastic applause from your audience, as well as the positive comments people offer you afterward. You can imagine that you feel satisfied with your performance and are genuinely appreciative of the supportive feedback from others. You can reflect on how pleased you were with your quality of focus and confidence on stage or how grateful you were for the opportunity to share your music with others.

On rare occasions, a musician will have the experience of unintentionally visualizing a mistake or some sort of performance mishap. Don't worry too much if this happens to you. Realize that your subconscious mind is just trying to work out its fears in the same way it does when you dream at night. Remember that your conscious mind is always in control, and you have the ability to pause the visualization, rewind that segment in your mind, and try it again. You can even imagine yourself in slow motion, if that's easier, performing the passage flawlessly. Try to "override" an imagined mistake with a positive visualization, to be sure you are consistently training the mind to expect success.

For more practice with different types of performance imagery, see the sections in Chapter 9 on Multiple-Perspective Imagery (pages 223–224) and Spotlight Imagery and Practice (pages 224–227).

Imagery and Self-Talk

Keep your face to the sunshine and you cannot see a shadow.—Helen Keller

I once had a high school student named Kate who was very tall and beautiful, but also very clumsy. You would never guess by looking at her that this refined and elegant-looking young woman was the sort of person who could, and often would, trip over a wrinkle in the carpet. She was a talented musician who performed in several recitals and competitive events each year. I began to realize that every single time she walked to the piano, she would stumble. She never actually fell down, thank goodness, but there would always be an awkward moment when she seemed to trip over one of her own feet. One day I asked her what she was thinking to herself as she walked out on stage, and her answer was, "I hope I don't fall on my face this time." In other words, Kate had established a mental expectation and somehow programmed her feet to falter! So, together we came up with the new affirmation, "I walk slowly and mindfully with confidence and grace." I never saw her stumble again.

Musicians understand that the quality of self-talk before a performance can make a powerful impact, but we often forget that we can consciously direct that internal dialogue. In fact, how we speak to ourselves moments before going on stage often mirrors how we have been talking to ourselves in the days leading up to the performance. Think about how you normally feel a few minutes before performing. Are you looking forward to the experience, or do you just want to get it over with? Are you excited or terrified? Distracted or focused? Confident or miserable? Or somewhere in between? Then reflect on how you want to feel before you go out on stage. Consider the difference in these two statements: "I feel more anxious and jittery with each passing minute," or "I can feel the excitement build as I prepare to do my best." Both of these could be describing the exact same physical sensations, but the second statement frames them in a way that is constructive. Most musicians experience excess adrenaline before a performance, but while some describe those sensations as fear or apprehension, others interpret them as positive indications of energy, excitement, even ex-hilaration. Plácido Domingo is known to have said, "My strength is my enthusiasm." I have seen professional musicians transform their own experiences, in the course of only a few short weeks, by regularly reframing their thoughts in this way.

You can also use this technique to substitute unwanted thoughts and feelings with more beneficial ones. The observation, "My hands won't stop shaking" might become "I am pleased to notice that my hands are be-ginning to feel warm and relaxed." In this example, you directed the mind away from an anxious observation to an expected positive outcome. Or instead of, "My mind is racing a mile a minute," you could think, "I begin to settle down as I focus on the music I am about to play." Remember that, during a creative visualization, a deeply relaxed mind is very open and re-ceptive to positive suggestions like these. You alone determine the objects of your focus. Recall that unless you direct your thoughts mindfully, they will entertain whatever randomly comes to mind. I sometimes imagine that my mind is a toddler. If I don't keep a watchful eye on her, she will certainly wobble toward the hot stove.

Language is a powerful tool, and healthy self-talk requires some degree of advance preparation. Sport psychologists know this well, which is why they place such importance on daily goal-setting and positive affirmations. When I am thinking about or writing affirmations, I give myself enough time to find the perfect words for my mind to hear. I often use a thesaurus to spark my own creativity. For example, if my goal is to feel excitement rather than nervousness, I can work to find much more specific and col-orful expressions. Some of my favorite words for excitement are adventure, dynamism, ebullience, passion, spirit, vivacity, and zest. If I hope to feel a sense of positive energy on stage, my mind responds more readily to the freshness of words such as intensity, exuberance, or sparkle. Years ago, I used to "collect" fantastic words and write them down on index cards in order to remember them. The simple act of deliberately cultivating language is an effective mindfulness practice.

You may decide to follow the advice of some sport psychologists, and write down all of the emotions you tend to feel before and during a performance. You could potentially list all of these thoughts in two columns, separating the optimistic thoughts from the more fearful or negative thoughts. The idea is not to judge yourself, but simply to practice mindful observation of your thoughts. When you have finished, you can begin to add to the first column, writing down any additional positive emotions and thoughts that you hope to experience. As you learn to identify your more apprehensive or negative thoughts, you can begin to reframe these into positive outcomes. For example, if you tend to view your audience as critical or judgmental, you can focus instead on your eagerness to express your music in a personal way or to share your artistic ideas with the people who came out to support you. If there is a passage in your music that makes you feel anxious ("I hope I don't start the third movement too fast"), you could focus instead on the best possible outcome ("I will take a moment to set the perfect tempo").

The subconscious mind, that part of us that is most receptive during meditation and visualization, will accept and incorporate only suggestions that it believes to be true. Mental programming can fail when people make the mistake of establishing lofty or unrealistic expectations. So, if you create an affirmation such as, "I will give the most flawless and awe-inspiring performance of my life," your mind may write it off as a distant fantasy. If you say instead, "I am well prepared and ready to do my very best" or even "I can do this!" you will create a more truthful and adaptable expectation. You may find it beneficial to avoid thoughts and affirmations about impressing others, and to focus instead on those that foster personal satisfaction and growth. Therefore, instead of, "I will play better than anyone else on the program," think, "I have something exceptional to communicate, and I am excited to perform this music for others."

The best affirmations are expressed using motivating and realistic language. Take some time on a regular basis to reflect on the sorts of phrases that will resonate with you. If a great idea pops into your head unexpectedly, write it down for later. These statements are as diverse and personal as each individual. Remember Salam from the very beginning of this book? He created one of my all-time favorite affirmations: "Whether it's a good experience or a bad experience, it's an experience worth having." I love the idea that any performance experience is worth having, no matter what happens.

For more examples, see the section on Affirmations in Chapter 9 (pages 234–235).

You can use imagery to improve or enhance any part of your life. Its use is not restricted to musical performance or professional achievement. In fact, some of the finest athletes hone their mental skills by practicing them spontaneously outside of training or competitions. You might try visualizing an upcoming interview, conversation, or social event. Or you can imagine simple activities in great detail, such as cooking a special meal, changing a tire, or running on a park trail. Even if you choose to visualize yourself eating a piece of five-layer chocolate cake, you are developing and refining an essential mental skill! Of course, the most powerful use of creative visualization will be to create a detailed scenario of your own best-possible future performance.

Performance Visualization Script

This example, a variation of one of the recordings included on the companion website ⊕, can help give you a place to start. This exercise uses terminology specific to solo pianists, although it is simple enough to substitute words and phrases that are relevant to your own experience. Reading a script is not a substitute for doing the exercise, but it can be very helpful to study as you begin to engage in your own imagery activities. You can echo my organization and choice of language, or you can start from scratch. With practice, you will refine your future experiences and add new techniques to your creative toolbox.

*** *

I am standing backstage, getting ready to perform. As I look around, I can see the colors and patterns of the wooden floor, the heavy folds of the stage curtain, and many tracks for lighting overhead. Although it is somewhat dark where I'm standing, I can see the stage light streaming in between cracks in the curtain, creating stripes of light on the floor. There are some scratches and scuff marks on the floor, from furniture and instruments being moved around over the years. I look down at my feet and notice the shoes I'm wearing; I can also see the clothes I picked out to wear. I have to say, I look terrific! I can feel the soft ridges in the water bottle that I'm holding. The temperature backstage is comfortable, a little on the cool side, and I know it will feel even warmer under the stage lights. I can smell the familiar musty scent of the stage, and even the faint scent of a banana I snacked on a few minutes ago.

I can feel the familiar flutters of excitement in my stomach and chest. My hands feel a little cool, so I put down my water bottle and warm my hands in my pockets. I notice that my body wants to move around, so I quietly pace backstage, slowly walking back and forth, mindfully observing the floor and focusing on my music. I breathe slowly and deeply, allowing my mind and body to become centered. In the past, I would have interpreted my body's fluttery sensations as nervousness or doubt, but now I realize this is just my way of feeling the energy and enthusiasm of a performance. I feel almost impatient to go out on stage and perform. I have practiced for many, many weeks, and I know I'm as ready as I can be. I will be happy to finally have the opportunity to present this music. Even with the excited flutters and quiet pacing, I feel self-assured, confident, and fairly relaxed. I am a successful musician, and I know that every-thing is going to be just fine.

The time has come to walk out onstage and perform! I feel great. I walk easily toward the center of the stage, toward the piano, feeling the bright stage lights shining down on me. My awareness feels heightened, and I am happy to hear the sound of enthusiastic applause from the audience. As I near the piano, it seems like a familiar friend, waiting eagerly for me. I turn to face my audience, and I am able to see a few familiar faces smiling at me. I smile back at them and bow graciously. I feel welcomed and appreciated. As I sit down at the piano and hear the applause die down, I take a few moments to breathe and center my mind. The black and white keys seem to be greeting me cheerfully. When I look at the keyboard, I almost feel as if I have come home again. I am aware of a pleasant feeling of gratitude. I think about how my music begins. I can hear it in my head, at the perfect tempo, and with my own choice of style and character.

I begin to perform. My body is poised, my fingers feel strong and secure, and my shoulders and arms are free. Even the larger muscles of my legs feel comfortably relaxed. As I play, my body seems to move easily, and my mind is steady and gently focused. The sound that comes out of the piano is rich and beautiful. My technique feels solid and confident, and I find that it is easy to express the meaning of each phrase of music. I really do feel at home on this stage, at this instrument, and with this music. I am enjoying this moment, and I seem to play effortlessly. I feel like a natural performer. My hands seem to know exactly where to go, and I am able to trust them, surrendering, focusing on my interpretation as I listen. This is an enjoyable and exciting experience, because I am able to concentrate on what I am choosing to communicate to the audience. I am able to express the full and profound range of this music and of myself. In a way, I am thanking the audience for this opportunity to share my music with them.

I find that my program is nearing the end. Time seemed to fly by! As I finish this performance and stand up from the piano, I hear the appreciative applause that seems to grow slightly louder at times. I smile, bow, and walk comfortably offstage. I did it! I am standing backstage once again, and I feel completely exhilarated. My hard work really did pay off. I had something to communicate, and I did so effectively and artistically. I feel elated from performing with courage and confidence. I also notice feelings of accomplishment and freedom. I am aware that I am now greeting members of my audience. Smiling people are coming up to me, congratulating me, and telling me how much they enjoyed my performance. As they shake my hand, I believe them, because I truly did play well. I am thankful to have had this experience. I feel a sense of deep satisfaction and peace.

Other Creative Uses of Imagery

An artist is an explorer.—Henri Matisse

Best Performance Scenario

I encourage you to take the time to write out a great performance imagery script based on the guidelines presented in this chapter. You would ideally write this in first person, just as in the previous example, walking yourself step-by-step through your imagined experiences before, during, and after a performance. You can develop your own narrative and affirmations, or you can model your script after mine. The most important thing is that your performance scenario should be specific to *you*—your instrument or voice, your upcoming performance situation, your music, and your personality. The greatest benefit of writing out a narrative is that it will be fresh in your mind when you practice your creative imagery. You don't have to read it to yourself, unless you want to, and you don't have to feel as if you need to start from scratch each time you visualize. You have already put some excellent thought into the experience.

If you would like to use a template to write your own script, you will find one in the section on Mental Performance Script in Chapter 9 (pages 221–222). You may wish to turn your script into a personal recording; check out the Guided Imagery Recording activity in Chapter 9 (pages 222–223). You will also find a variety of guided imagery recordings on the companion website (⊕ items 6.1–6.5).

Visual Anchor

Your affirmations may embrace characteristics such as courage, security, strength, or self-compassion. Many performers find it beneficial to create a single mental image that represents that quality of confidence, serenity, or anything else. This could be an abstract mental picture, a symbol of something meaningful to you, or it could be an actual object. I knew one athlete who would draw his symbol on the inside of his wrist to keep himself focused and positive. You can incorporate this image in your mental practice, maybe before you walk out onstage, or you can focus on this anchor any time you feel stressed or anxious. Here are some ideas I have gathered from other musicians:

- An animal emblem, symbolizing a specific individual quality.
- A steady flame or ball of gold light, brightly glowing from the center of the body.
- A pink lotus blossom floating quietly on a still pond.
- A magical box filled with good surprises and possibilities.
- A young willow tree that bends with the wind but never breaks.
- A personally meaningful symbol of power, faith, or strength.

Safe Boundaries

Some musicians look forward to connecting with the public during a performance, but others would prefer to cultivate a feeling of safety and protection while on stage. If the idea appeals to you, you can have fun imagining something that surrounds or protects you while you're performing. This could be an invisible force field, an imaginary ring of fire, or even a protective moat filled with alligators. I know one opera singer who imagines two giant sentry guards, such as dragons or lions, one on each side of the stage. I have been surprised at the success I have had with some younger musicians, creating a ring around the piano bench using masking tape on the carpet. Of course they realize the ring offers no actual physical protection. But sometimes the mental image of being in a safe, enclosed area can encourage feelings of having their own personal, sacred performance space.

Stress Management

Mental imagery is a fantastic way to handle stressful situations in daily life. The earlier example of the willow tree works especially well, because you can imagine that a difficult situation allows you to bend flexibly, but will not break you. Or, if you find yourself in the path of an angry person or confrontation, you can imagine that your body is transparent, and the negativity passes right through you but doesn't affect you. Many years ago I worked with a colleague who was always complaining bitterly, so I frequently imagined an invisible energy field that deflected her angry words away from my personal space and back on to her!

You will recall another good stress management technique described earlier in this chapter, involving the process of detaching from a negative memory. This method can be a very therapeutic way of dealing with a negative or traumatic experience. Remember that you can imagine a difficult situation unfolding on a movie screen, or in black and white, or frozen as in a photograph. This can also work well with thoughts and events in the present moment. Years ago, while observing two strangers arguing, I suddenly wondered how they might look if they were animated cartoon characters. That technique worked so well, creating a feeling of healthy detachment, that I still use it from time to time. After all, if someone is scolding you, it is hard to take it personally if you are secretly imagining them as a giant cartoon hippopotamus. When remembering a recent stressful event, you might prefer to envision it as few illustrated pages from a comic book. I once knew a guy who talked incessantly, mostly about nothing. It never bothered me to be around him, though, because I would imagine the words coming out of his mouth and falling to the floor in huge piles of jumbled letters. I would then imagine an old-fashioned circus sweeper coming along with a giant push broom, shoving huge mounds of random words out the door. As long as you can keep from giggling inappropriately, creative visualization can be a tremendous mechanism for managing stress.

Thought Management

Anyone can use imagery to acknowledge, validate, and temporarily set aside stressful thoughts or situations. For example, if you notice that you are berating yourself, you can stop and be aware of your thoughts at that moment. You can imagine that you take those critical thoughts, put them inside a box or bottle, and paste a label such as "mind chatter" or "random judgments" on the front. Then you can mentally place the box or bottle on a shelf out of sight. This practice encourages mindful awareness, detachment from unhealthy thoughts, and a lighthearted attitude. Personally, I enjoy sealing my unhealthy thoughts inside canning jars and putting them away in an imaginary pantry. I label them with imagined words written on little adhesive stickers. I have a friend who imagines putting his destructive thoughts in a cardboard box, setting the box on fire, and releasing it into a river to float away in smoke and flames. One of my students imagines kicking her little boxes of negative thoughts, one by one, over the side of a cliff. You can use these creative ideas when someone offers you a hurtful comment or unwanted negative criticism. If you mentally externalize the words, label the container as "worthless opinions" or even "assorted crap" and mentally set it aside, it can help you feel less vulnerable. This technique also works with musical mistakes and bad performance experiences. If you have a hard time letting go of those thoughts, you can always give yourself permission to open the box and think about them later.

Safe Place

You may have heard people joking about going to their "happy place" in times of stress. In truth, creating a safe and comfortable mental sanctuary can be extremely effective for stress management and mental well-being. If you create an imaginary place that is very pleasing to you, and if you "visit" it regularly in a relaxed state, you may condition your mind to relax whenever you think about this space. As you read this, you might begin to envision a place, either real or imagined, that will make you feel happy and relaxed when you pretend you are there. It can be outdoors, indoors, or completely fictitious. Here are some ideas from musicians I know:

- On a sandy beach looking out at the ocean.
- In the mountains near a waterfall.
- On a lake dock, watching a beautiful sunset.
- Inside a cozy log cabin in front of a roaring fireplace.
- Inside a sacred temple or sanctuary.
- Inside a genie bottle, surrounded by colorful pillows and cushions.
- In a meadow or flower garden on a warm, sunny day.

I'm sure you can think of many other lovely places. My personal safe place is one that I have created over the course of many, many years. I have had a lot of fun "decorating" my place with specific trees, minerals, and flowering plants, and I feel that each time I return, I can see it more vividly in my mind. When I sit down to visualize an upcoming performance, I first hang out in my safe place for a minute or two, which automatically puts me in a relaxed and focused state.

Fine-Tuning the Process

As you continue to practice the skill of mental imagery, you will probably discover that you want to change up the activity as your mindset and situations change. For this reason, I believe it is beneficial to keep track of your experiences and to adjust your practice as needed. You don't need to take lengthy notes about your visualizations, since this can become time consuming. All you need to do is jot down the date, your primary target of focus or your affirmations, and how you felt during and after the experience. It is also tremendously helpful to keep track of your real-life practice and performances, and see how those experiences change and evolve under the positive influence of mental imagery. You may find that you no longer need to focus on certain elements, or you may need to add something new to your visualizations. Because the mind is flexible and dynamic, it is natural to adapt your mental practice to your current state of being.

I once had a friend who was finishing a doctoral degree in music performance. A vocalist, Jessica struggled with stress-induced physical tension in her neck, shoulders, and abdomen, making it difficult for her to sing well. Sometimes the tension was so great that she had to stop in the middle of her practice. She was anxious about an upcoming degree recital, which was going to be judged critically by the music faculty. At first, the visualizations I created for her emphasized how relaxed, warm, and loose her neck and shoulder muscles might feel during a performance, and how easy it would be for her to take deep and comfortable breaths. After a couple of weeks, Jessica was happy to report that she was becoming more relaxed when singing for her teacher, and her vocal technique was improving as a result of the imagery work. However, as the unwanted physical sensations subsided, she began to be more aware of her own thoughts, which turned out to be exceptionally negative and critical. Even when she felt physically relaxed, she was mentally uptight. We then turned her focus to observing and releasing negative mind chatter, and replacing those thoughts with specific positive expectations. Often, negative thinking will create or exacerbate uncomfortable physical symptoms. Or, the physical symptoms may serve as an indicator of the underlying fears. Getting to the root of a problem is sometimes like peeling off layers of an onion, and a musician can address each of those layers as they come into focus. Incidentally, Jessica passed her degree recital with flying colors and was thrilled to acknowledge that she actually enjoyed the experience.

Our minds continue to develop, evolve, and learn throughout our lives. Since we easily adapt to patterns of habitual focus, it is inspiring to remember that we can train our minds just as assuredly as we can train our hands, fingers, or voices. For this reason alone, mental imagery is one of the most powerful skills any musician can cultivate. If you would like to explore additional applications of creative thinking that do not involve the structured practice of mental imagery, you will find many of those activities in Chapter 9.

***

Musicians are well acquainted with the concept of paradox, two true but seemingly contradictory circumstances. For example, performers spend years learning to straddle the fine line between being in control and letting go on stage. In the practice room, we value relaxation, knowing full well that performance requires strong, engaged muscles. We seek a balance between the parameters of stylistic performance practice and personal expressive freedom. I believe that musicians who acknowledge and embrace the contradictions inherent in our art possess a creative advantage over those who seek only black-and-white answers. Sometimes the best course of action involves an unfamiliar way of thinking, even a significant paradigm shift.

Why do I mention this? Because in the next chapter, we will begin to explore mental skills development from a completely different perspective, a perspective that is contradictory in many ways. Now that you are armed with a comprehensive (and possibly overwhelming) summary of ideas and information on using imagery to create the reality you want, I am now going to suggest that you simultaneously learn to let all of that go. We can often find a larger truth between two seemingly opposite practices. My hope is that, as you continue to read, you will appreciate and embrace this paradox of the mind.

7 MINDFULNESS PRACTICE AND MEDITATION FOR MUSICIANS

Wherever you are, be all there.—Jim Elliot

The goal of this book, as I have mentioned, is to approach the topic of mindfulness from a truly integrated perspective. Some forms of mindfulness involve *directing* our awareness with a significant degree of personal control. In the previous chapter, we practiced this manner of directing the thoughts through creative imagery activities in order to train the mind and body to expect and achieve successful performances. This represents a very robust and enterprising way of conditioning the mind for performance success. The musician who is able to set conscious goals, make deliberate choices, and visualize optimal performances has an incredibly powerful set of mental skills at her disposal.

Other forms of mindfulness involve *observing* what is, with a greater sense of objectivity and acceptance. We explore this purest type of mindfulness in this chapter. You may remember from the first chapter that traditional mindfulness is simply the deliberate and gentle focus of awareness, without judgment, of thoughts and events of the present moment. We are continuing to direct our awareness, as in the previous chapter, but with a much softer touch. The concept of mindful awareness is fascinating in that it is the simplest of all the skills presented in this book, but it can also be the most abstract and challenging. For the stressed or self-critical musician, mindfulness is an especially valuable component of success, both on stage and off.

The Art of Awareness

If the doors of perception were cleansed, everything would appear to man as it is, infinite.—William Blake

Earlier, we considered that in every moment we devote ourselves to something through our awareness. As you read this paragraph, you are (I hope) mostly aware of the meaning of the words on the page. Assuming that something or someone is not distracting you at this very moment, this gentle stream of awareness is in the forefront of your mind, commanding the bulk of your attention. As your eyes skim the lines of text, your mind pays close attention in order to understand each sentence. While the eyes do not focus on the details of each word, letter, or punctuation mark, the mind groups the most important words and phrases together in order to grasp their larger meaning. This is the same type of attention we engage when we are learning something new, such as a piece of music or a topic in a workshop. If at any point your attention drifts, or if you suddenly realize that you don't remember what you just read, you will probably refocus your attention and reread that passage of text.

If you pay even closer attention to the activity of your mind, you may discover three or four other layers or streams of consciousness in the background as you continue to read. For example, a second path of awareness might involve the observations of the imaginary mental commentator who dwells in the back of just about every human mind. This would be the part of your awareness that offers personal opinions about how these ideas may or may not pertain to you, or how you may or may not choose to apply them for yourself. In other words, there may be a continuous stream of assessment in the background, offering thoughts such as, "Yes, I understand" or "Where the heck is she going with this?" This subtle voice may take on the role of mental critic, a role that is strongly developed in most creative artists. My mental critic usually works overtime when I read nonfiction, offering welcome or unwelcome analysis of the author's content, writing style, or potential contributions to my own very subjective point of view. This ongoing commentary can be helpful in developing critical thinking skills or in filtering out the least relevant subject matter. However, if you have ever watched a movie at home with the audio commentary turned on, you may agree that at times the narration can drown out or detract from the primary storyline.

As if that weren't enough, it's quite possible that you may observe other layers of awareness. A third stream of consciousness might include periodic awareness of your physical surroundings, particularly if there are any distinct sounds, visual stimuli, or scents in the area. When you are absorbed in a good book or movie, you are probably unaware of your surroundings until you perceive a distraction. Then, of course, there may be the inevitable "path of randomness" in your consciousness. I sometimes think of this stream of arbitrary thoughts as the mental equivalent of on-line pop-up ads. Perhaps a part of you suddenly wonders what you should have for dinner, how you will respond to a recent text message, or whether or not you should be practicing instead of reading this book. Right now, as I write this, I'm also wondering if there is any Dr. Pepper left in the vending machine. (Oh, I do hope so.)

The more closely you pay attention to each moment, the more aware you may become of these distinct streams of consciousness. It is as if you have three or four radios turned on in the room. Although each radio might be tuned to a different station, you have the ability to direct most of your focus to the channel you choose at any time. When you deliberately direct your attention to one channel, the others will seem to drop in volume. This is similar to having a conversation with one person at a noisy dinner table. Performers who learn to filter out the distracting paths of thought and focus more clearly on the task at hand tend to feel more secure on stage.

In fact, you may have noticed similar streams of consciousness during a performance. On stage, you will be most keenly aware of the music you are performing. However, you may also be aware of your physical sur-roundings, the audience, or other musicians. Your awareness may be drawn at times to the critical commentary in your mind, or even to those wandering pop-up thoughts. If you have ever had the experience of being in a flow state, you may have noticed that everything extraneous seems to fade away, leaving only the music. Mindfulness practice can help guide you to the most desired path of consciousness, which ultimately leads to a more gratifying performance experience.

The Present Moment

The point of power is always in the present moment.—Louise L. Hay

Consider, for a moment, the concept of time. (That is, consider the phe-nomenon of how we humans perceive linear time, whether or not it actu-ally exists in reality. The latter is a conversation for another day, preferably over a bottle of Château Margaux.) Do you think we spend most of our lives contemplating the past, the present, or the future? I'm not sure there's a definitive answer to that question, but I am certain that most people tend to focus their consciousness *away from* the present moment.

I once heard a psychologist remark that depression is rooted in the past while anxiety is rooted in the future. For a long time afterward, I was fascinated by the idea. When focused on past events, sometimes we recall a happy or pleasant memory, but we also replay our negative experiences, missed opportunities, and regrets. This sort of rumination can encourage negative emotional states, including isolation and sadness. We can focus on a future event, such as an upcoming vacation or long-awaited occasion, with eager expectation. But we can also worry about the future with apprehension or anxiety. Musicians, especially, spend much of their time in anticipation of an upcoming performance event such as a recital or recording session. While planning is a necessary part of successful goal-setting, the problem arises when we allow our minds to wander away from the present moment without our conscious awareness. It becomes even more problematic for a musician struggling to stay in the zone while performing onstage.

Music exists only in the present. Although we may own recordings and printed scores of music, music as an aural art is perceived only from moment to moment as we listen. When we are in a flow state of consciousness on stage, we too are focused in the present, aware of each musical gesture in the moment we create it. If, however, something goes wrong and we start to lament or obsess over a missed note or a memory lapse, we are no longer paying attention to what we are creating in the present moment. The same is true if we are apprehensive about an upcoming difficult passage, such as an approaching cadenza or solo. This is not to say that we shouldn't think ahead in our music, to anticipate an important change of tempo or key, but allowing the mind to drift frequently into the unknown future can sometimes trigger stress or anxiety. If we worry about an upcoming passage or fret over a recent mistake, we are not allowing ourselves to fully experience the music that exists only now.

We can take this idea one step further to acknowledge that, like music, life exists only in the present moment. The past is gone forever, and the future will never be now, because we will always be in the present moment. As long as we are preoccupied with real or imagined past or future events, we are not fully experiencing life. Consider the simple but profound notion that, as you read this paragraph, your life is right now. This means that your purpose in this life, right at this moment, is to sit here and read this paragraph. It isn't to ruminate about something you should have said or done, or worry about something that needs to be accomplished. All you need to do is read these words, because this present moment is all you will ever have. I relish the fact that the skills we will practice in this chapter apply to all areas of life, not just music.

Principles of Mindfulness

What a liberation to realize that the "voice in my head" is not who I am. Who am I, then? The one who sees that.—Eckhart Tolle

Musicians engage an impressive variety and combination of mental skills in the practice room and on the stage. So far, this book has stressed the importance of mental focus and control, goal-setting, and intentional striving for optimal performance. But we will now consider how to let all of that go, because it is also possible to investigate the side of human experience that involves awareness without regulation. Let's explore a few of the philosophies of mindfulness in the context of music making.

Nonjudging

There is nothing either good or bad, but thinking makes it so.—Hamlet

Releasing judgment is one of the hardest things anyone can strive to do. Musicians and other creative artists, especially, have been conditioned to expect and embrace criticism on a regular basis. After all, analysis is essential for developing the highest possible level of artistry. Not only do we seek out constructive criticism from mentors and other trusted musicians, but we are obliged to exercise continual self-criticism during practice and rehearsals. Critical listening and keen self-evaluation are nonnegotiable for performing artists. The problem comes when our inner critic offers unhelpful or destructive thoughts or when it doesn't know when to be quiet. Learning to become aware of those inner judges and to release thoughts without assessment can bring a tremendous amount of clarity and freedom.

Indiscriminate self-judgment can hinder creativity when it counts the most. While there is a time and a place to be diagnostic, there is also a time and a place to feel the freedom to experiment and try new things without worrying about being wrong. Jazz musicians often reveal that their best solos featured "errors" that were transformed into ingenious melodic twists. Saxophonist Ornette Coleman famously remarked, "It was when I found out I could make mistakes that I knew I was on to something." Pianist William Westney often talks about "juicy" mistakes, sometimes referring to them as *unexpected events*. When practicing mindfulness, unexpected events are neither good nor bad, because they simply are what they are. It may be helpful to think of these events as feedback for another time. As Shakespeare's Hamlet observed, judgment is simply a mental perspective. The most direct way to offset an overactive inner critic is to become a detached observer of your own mental activity.

If you are able to stand back and witness your own natural process of thinking, you may experience the relief that comes with the realization that *you are not your thoughts*. As meditation teacher Bhante Gunaratana observed, "There is a difference between being aware of a thought and thinking a thought." Detached awareness gives you the ability to acknowledge a thought and then set it aside. Imagine how helpful this would be during a musical performance, particularly if you make a mistake. With practice, you may cultivate the ability to acknowledge the mistake, but then immediately set your thoughts aside and return your focus to the music you are performing. Great athletes are able to do this during a competition; they recognize their errors, and then choose to analyze them *later* as a learning experience. If an Olympic skater falls on the ice when landing a triple axel, he has no time to ruminate about what just happened. To stay in the competition, he must instead concentrate on the present course of action.

This technique works well even when there has been no mistake at all. With mindfulness, when a negative thought pops into your mind, you can observe its presence and say to yourself, "that's just a thought." You are then free to return your focus to the present moment, or to perception and emotion instead. You may prefer to plunge into your own special space, ungoverned by thoughts, to experience the pure joy and pleasure of making music. I'm not suggesting that it is desirable to repress all criticisms and unwanted thoughts, but I do propose that you can exercise some authority over whether to think about them. This is an important distinction. It means the difference between denying the natural activity of the mind, which is not true mindfulness, and choosing instead to direct your awareness elsewhere. Again, the idea is not to control or restrict thoughts, but to guide the mind with conscious intent.

As you travel even farther down the metaphorical rabbit hole of nonjudgment, you may find the need to practice nonjudgment of your ability to practice nonjudgment! If you catch yourself wondering whether you are doing a "good job" at it, this is just another example of the inner critic trying to evaluate your progress. If you're like me, you may also need to practice not criticizing yourself for . . . well, criticizing yourself. After literally hundreds of hours of meditation practice, I still feel disappointed when I recognize my inner critic at work. But whether or not we are engaged in self-criticism is not the point, because success happens at the moment we *observe* those thoughts unfolding. Rick Carson offers my favorite paraphrase of the Zen Theory of Change. It goes like this: "I free myself not by trying to be free, but by simply noticing how I am imprisoning myself in the very moment I am imprisoning myself."

Acceptance

> *The boundary to what we can accept is the boundary to our freedom.*
> —Tara Brach

The ability to notice and release thoughts without judgment includes, at its very core, the practice of unconditional acceptance. It is easy enough to accept positive thoughts, praise, and validation, because those things make us feel good about who we are and what we do. It is much more difficult to accept mistakes, negative thoughts, and criticisms from ourselves or from others. Any musician reading this may feel resistance toward the idea of accepting mistakes. After all, accepting mistakes in the practice room will eventually lead to careless and amateur-sounding performances, right? The distinction here is that accepting a mistake and fixing a mistake are two separate processes.

Earlier, we considered that all life exists in the present moment and that the present moment is all we will ever experience. If something unwanted happens in the present moment, it immediately becomes part of our past. In other words, by the time we notice it, it has already happened. And nothing we think or do will change what has happened in the immediate past. We can either accept what is and move on, or we can beat ourselves up over it. On stage, this means releasing it and returning our attention to the music we are performing. In the practice room, this may mean pausing to diagnose and fix the mistake and using it as a learning experience to improve our craft. Musicians, athletes, and other performers who are able to accept mistakes and refocus on the present are less likely to experience the snowball effect of multiple errors that can occur when frustration or disappointment starts to creep in. Acceptance involves acknowledging faults, confronting fears, and appreciating that not everyone will like or approve of us. Author Tara Brach refers to this as a "radical acceptance" of all that happens.

The other day I was late to a meeting because of roadwork on the highway. Construction workers had closed all lanes but one leading into the city, and traffic had come to a complete standstill. Immediately irritated, I experienced a whole cocktail of exasperated thoughts. (Why would they choose to close *all these lanes* during rush hour? Why hadn't they arranged a detour to reroute traffic? Why hadn't I read about this construction in the local news? If I had known about the scheduled roadwork, I would have taken another route...) Then, in a moment of mindfulness, I became aware of these thoughts. I tried not to criticize myself for being impatient and irritated, acknowledging that these are natural and valid feelings. I decided to see if I could practice acceptance, knowing that I had no control over the traffic or over my arrival time at the meeting. I considered that if I were on my way to get a root canal instead, I might be thrilled by the delay! Whether I was irritated, elated, or neutral, my thoughts and feelings would not change my situation, so I decided to accept it and turn on the radio. In that moment of uncharacteristic awareness, I was able to release unwanted emotions by consciously redirecting my thoughts. Even when we are at our most anxious or distraught, the truth is that we are often okay in the present moment. Unless I am in excruciating physical pain or my life is in imminent danger, the answer to the question, "Are you *okay*, right now, in this moment?" will usually be "Yes."

Once, while on a meditation retreat, I found myself in an interesting situation involving the practice of acceptance. A group of us were asked to offer constructive criticism (a euphemism for negative feedback) to each other. We were to choose something we perceived as a fault or shortcoming in each person, and to share our thoughts with kindness. Interestingly, our only acceptable response to this feedback was the phrase, "thank you." It didn't matter if we agreed or disagreed with the comment, or whether or not we felt defensive or insulted, because the only thing to say was "thank you." This was difficult for me to do, but it was also a strangely liberating experience. Think back to a time when someone said something negative about you, and then imagine thanking them for that feedback.

As my teacher pointed out, when someone cares enough to offer their opinion about you, whether positive or negative, the most revolutionary response is one of gratitude. Even if you believe the comment to be false or misguided, there comes an unusual sense of detachment and compassion with thanking the person who offered it. Sometimes, that appreciation is best expressed only internally. In that moment, someone has given you a precious glimpse of how you appear through their eyes, for better or worse. Any chance at a new perspective of yourself is a gift. "Vanessa, your performance sounded weary and uninspired." "Thank you." Radical acceptance!

Patience

> Rivers know this: there is no hurry. We shall get there some day.
> —Winnie-the-Pooh

Just as nonjudgment requires a certain degree of acceptance, learning acceptance requires a measure of gentle perseverance. Patience does not come naturally to most of us, and practicing patience with ourselves is an even greater challenge. Musicians spend hours each day practicing, repeating, and refining musical passages. Those who are patient with their own process tend to make the best progress. Perhaps you've experienced a time when you became angry with yourself during practice. When negative emotions get the best of us, our progress decreases significantly. Luckily, when it comes to practicing patience, life is our best classroom.

I mentioned earlier that one psychological concept related to good mental health is high frustration tolerance. People who are able to accept or tolerate obstacles, misfortunes, or their own shortcomings tend to be happier people overall. Although personalities and behavioral tendencies vary, the concept of patience can be practiced and learned. When I was stuck in that traffic jam, I consciously shifted my thoughts away from frustration and toward patience and tolerance. However, that would not have happened without an essential moment of mindful awareness. Let's face it, very few of us are patient by default.

Often, patience develops when we focus on the process of our experiences, rather than on the product of our desired goal. While it is crucial to have those goals and to keep our highest ideal in mind, patience inevitably dwells in the present moment. If you are learning your first bebop scales in quarter notes but can only think about playing like Charlie Parker, you can't wholly experience the journey of getting there. If you are truly in the moment with each of those quarter note pulses, though, you create room for nonresistant awareness. We will explore a few mindful practice techniques later on in this chapter.

Beginner's Mind

In the beginner's mind there are many possibilities, but in the expert's there are few.—Shunryu Suzuki

If you have ever watched a baby discover his own hands, you know that he will stare at them with endless fascination before stuffing them in his mouth. If he had the same cognitive abilities as an adult, he might think, "What is that curious pudgy object with those five little stubby things? I wonder what will happen if I wiggle them around. Let's see what they taste like." Beginner's mind is the philosophy of exploring something as if for the very first time. It is a way to practice awareness from a fresh, impartial perspective. This is easy to do when you really are discovering something for the first time, such as a new form of music or art, a new movie, or a new culture. Even if something is not new to you, though, you can endeavor to experience it more deeply and objectively.

I often write in a coffee shop that exhibits the artwork of local artists. There is a photograph directly in front of me featuring two cows in a field, and I have glanced at it on and off for an entire week. The first time I saw the image, I thought, "neat, cows," and then I proceeded to look around at the other prints on the wall. Because I recognized the animals, my mind immediately labeled them as cows and moved on, seeking another experience. I had engaged my own preconceived notion of what cows are and what they look like, and after only a couple of seconds, I directed my gaze elsewhere. After that, any time I glanced up from my laptop and saw the photograph, my mind registered it as "that cow photo" and didn't pay much attention. Because, you know, cows.

But just today, I walked over to the picture and looked at it more closely, practicing beginner's mind. I went as far as to think to myself, "What are these strange and curious beasts?" The more deeply I looked, the more I realized that I was seeing the image for the very first time. The two cows were very different from each other, with contrasting colors and patterns on their bodies, reflecting different angles of the sun. They even sported two different expressions, revealing two very distinct personalities. They weren't just facing the camera; they were lumbering toward it, challenging the viewer with their slow and fearless advance. I hadn't really seen that photo until today. It was more than just two cows in a field.

You can practice beginner's mind with something you experience every day, such as your toothbrush or your morning toast. If you pick up a common object lying near you right now, such as a pencil, coffee cup, or your own watch, you can practice observing it with fresh awareness, as if you are sensing it for the first time. Right now I am staring at my left thumbnail with great curiosity, having already acknowledged that the owners of this coffee shop think I'm nuts. I just noticed that the subtle pattern of ridges across the surface of the nail looks almost like a transparent barcode. You may find it helpful, when you notice yourself identifying something by its name, to eliminate its label altogether. So instead of "these keys on this keychain," I can think "what's up with these groovy dangly things?" It may seem silly, but if you think about it, removing the label from something can help diminish our preconceived notions of it. Eckhart Tolle goes as far as to suggest that we practice removing labels from all the things we observe. Instead of thinking, "this is a dandelion," we can think, "this is called dandelion."

Beginner's mind is easily applied to musical experiences. When you hear a band start to perform a cover of one of your favorite songs, for example, you already have a conception (and probably some very strong opinions) of how the song should sound. If it just so happens that you hear something you don't like, you might assign the mental label "bad version," and essentially stop listening. When this happens, you don't fully experience the moment, just as I didn't fully experience the two cows. When I judge a piano competition, beginner's mind is my secret weapon for writing a good critique. If I happen to see that one of the musicians is playing a piece that I have taught or performed many times, I try to think to myself, "What an interesting-looking piece. I wonder what it sounds like?" Then, as the performance unfolds, I am able to listen with full presence. I can judge the performance on its own merit, rather than in comparison with another interpretation or my own preferences.

When listening to yourself play or sing, you can try to listen as if for the first time without comparing your performance with anyone else's. When repeating a passage in the practice room, you can listen closely to each repetition with interest and curiosity, rather than spacing out and accidentally drifting toward autopilot. Releasing assumptions and expectations can offer clarity and depth of awareness. Experiences become fresh and genuine because they are rooted in the present moment.

Nonstriving

How wild it was, to let it be.—Cheryl Strayed

Musicians struggle with the concept of nonstriving, because working for success is what we do every day of our lives. At first, it may be beneficial to think of nonstriving in contexts that don't involve learning new skills or setting goals. Striving connotes effort and exertion, which is not always the best mindset for a musician. Perhaps you have been in a performance situation where you wanted the music to sound effortless, as if you weren't forcing anything or trying so hard. These are examples of nonstriving on stage. It doesn't mean not trying your best, but it means not pushing so hard. The same is true if you find yourself in a job interview or on a first date. Although you want to make a good impression, nonstriving means that you prefer to be comfortable with who you are.

Nonstriving is especially valuable when practicing mindfulness. We are so conditioned to improve and achieve, and this sort of evaluative mindset can hinder the acceptance that comes with moment-to-moment awareness. For example, when I criticize myself for not being present enough, or meditating long enough, or focusing clearly enough, I am caught in the trap of striving to be something other than what I am right now. If I am striving for something other than what *is,* I am not accepting the present moment. Nonstriving means there is no goal in mindfulness practice except for the practice itself. Striving implies trying, and mindfulness implies only being. As the enlightened Yoda said, "Do. Or do not. There is no try."

The irony, of course, is that we will never truly be successful at practicing nonstriving. In one way or another, everything we do is a means to an end. Many goals will necessarily involve some sort of effort and drive. If all you do is flop on the sofa and watch TV, you are striving for something, even if just entertainment or relaxation. You may sit down to meditate and to practice having no goal, but that in itself is a goal! It amuses me to think that we strive to be nonstriving. Rather than a continued state of being, nonstriving is more of a philosophy of mind. If you are fully aware of the present moment, you are probably not striving to achieve anything else.

Nonstriving can help facilitate the attitudes of trusting and letting go. A well-prepared musician may experience a sense of liberation during a performance, fully trusting in her abilities. While trusting and letting go require a great deal of practice, you can explore these at any time in your life. My traffic jam experience gave me the opportunity to practice letting go of negative emotions. Very often, in fact, the thing we are letting go of is the need to feel in control. On stage, we want to feel a certain degree of technical control, but we also want to be able to let go of the self-criticism and fear that prevent us from becoming wholly engaged in the music. The next time you find yourself in a mildly stressful situation, notice when and if you feel temporarily out of control of that situation. Like acceptance, letting go can provide a great deal of emotional relief. Trust is a reminder that everything will eventually work out.

Self-Compassion

> It ain't what they call you, it's what you answer to.—W. C. Fields

Musicians can be the most sensitive and kind-hearted people around. On the other hand, we also tend to be remarkably hard on ourselves, and unsympathetic toward our own shortcomings. How is it that we can regard others with empathy and tenderness, but we don't always offer ourselves the same degree of compassion?

Some of our self-disparaging thoughts are rooted in our earliest experiences as children or as young musicians; others develop as we become highly skilled artists in a competitive environment. In a society that celebrates busyness, high achievement, and harsh evaluation of weaknesses, it is easy to confuse self-compassion with coddling. This is an illusion, though, since self-compassion is not related to self-esteem, self-worth, or even self-indulgence. It exists, as all other mindfulness practices, outside the realm of judgment. In fact, it can serve to break the trance of perpetual achieving. As Kristin Neff says, "Continually feeding our need for positive self-evaluation is a bit like stuffing ourselves with candy. We get a brief sugar high, then a crash."

Compassion begins with the recognition that human experience involves suffering and that, on some level, we are all suffering. If we can acknowledge the heartache in the people around us, we can learn to nurture tenderness toward our own emotional struggles. It is easy to appreciate ourselves when we succeed or when we impress others. With mindful awareness, we can recognize that we are also worthy and lovable when we fail, when we are uninspiring, and when we are mediocre at best. Self-compassion can be one of the most foreign feeling and difficult skills to learn. It can take a lifetime! On the other hand, in the words of Jack Kornfield, "If your compassion does not include yourself, it is incomplete."

All of the mindfulness practices described in this book can help develop self-awareness and sensitivity. When exploring the idea of self-compassion, a good place to begin is to observe how we speak to ourselves in moments of stress. We can be surprisingly harsh with ourselves when we are imperfect, and language, even when unspoken, is powerful. While we can often hear and assess how we speak to other people, it is more of a challenge to listen to our words and feelings when speaking to ourselves. It can be beneficial to imagine that you are talking to a dear friend of yours, instead of to yourself. How do you speak to someone you care deeply about when they are troubled?

I like to pretend that I am interacting with a much younger version of myself. It may sound silly, but I am particularly drawn to 4-year-old me, who (in an old photo, at least) wears a pink rosebud dress and little lacy white socks. If, for example, I am baking cookies and I happen to drop an egg on the kitchen floor, my automatic reaction differs greatly from my mindful and compassionate response. Left unchecked, I will experience a sudden flash of frustration or irritation; my mind will unleash a barrage of creative and colorful insults. As I reach for a paper towel, I might call myself any number of names, or I may just scold myself for not paying closer attention. If I had been baking cookies with a young child, though, my response would be very different. If 4-year-old me had dropped the egg, grown-up me would respond very carefully and with great kindness. I would cheerfully explain to 4-year-old me that everyone makes mistakes and that we can make a game of cleaning it up together. If other people had witnessed my original hateful response, directed toward a 4-year-old child, wouldn't they consider it hostile and abusive?

Years ago, I noticed this in my own music practice. If I repeatedly missed a note or confused one passage with another, I would write a snarky message to myself in the music. (My default scribble was "duh—oink!" with or without a little pig sketch.) Occasionally, the word "stupid" would appear above a circled note or chord. But I would never, ever call one of my piano students stupid. I wouldn't even think it. I resolved to be as compassionate with myself as if I were my own student, friend, or child. If you walk offstage after a lackluster performance, how might your reaction to yourself change if you were speaking to 4-year-old you? You can always practice reframing your self-talk as if you were speaking to someone you love and cherish.

All of the principles of mindfulness—nonjudging, acceptance, patience, trust—culminate in the deeply healing practice of self-compassion. Interestingly, from a practical standpoint, objective self-care can heighten an artist's ability to be creative and productive. Lucille Ball once quipped, "You really have to love yourself to get anything done in this world."

Practicing Mindfulness

Knowledge speaks, but wisdom listens.—Jimi Hendrix

Since the essence of mindfulness is awareness, we can be aware of our actions, our thoughts, or our surroundings at any time. As you read this, for example, you might choose to become aware of your left foot. My guess is that you don't normally focus on your left foot while you read a book, so this would be a good way to practice noticing something that would normally go unnoticed. Without trying to adjust your posture or move your feet around, simply observe how your left foot is positioned and how it feels. You could draw your attention to the bottom of your foot, noticing which areas are in contact with your shoe, sock, or the ground. You could mentally follow the periphery of your foot, to see if you experience physical sensations in some areas more than others. Can you feel the back of your heel? What about each of your toes; are some more sensitive than others? Do you find yourself wiggling your toes around, or trying harder than usual to be still? In the short minute it took for you to observe these and other characteristics of your foot, chances are that your mind was focused primarily in the present moment.

As mentioned earlier, mindfulness often involves more than one channel of awareness. While part of your mind was reading these words, another part was focusing on the physical sensations of your foot. Were you aware of anything else? Your surroundings? Your thoughts about this topic or activity? Other areas of your life? If you don't remember or aren't sure, gently bring your attention back to your left foot. Are you able to feel the arch of your foot or any sensations on the top of your foot? If you are able to notice your thoughts about this activity, acknowledge those as well.

This is a good time to point out the truth that when it comes to practicing mindfulness, *no one does it right.* Nobody does a "good job," because there is no goal except to do it. Because of this, there is no such thing as a bad mindfulness practice. Even if you are distracted and your mind keeps wandering, simply noticing that truth is the point. You cannot fail.

Consider something we do every day: breathing. If you want to, you can control the length of your inhale and exhale, the depth or shallowness of each breath, or whether you breathe through your nose or mouth. But how often do you criticize your breathing or praise someone else's breathing? Chances are that you never find yourself saying to a friend, "I wish I could breathe like Steve. He is the most talented breather I ever met!" The absurdity of this example arises from the fact that there is no correct way to breathe; breathing is the point. Mindfulness practice is the same, because there is no correct way to observe. To notice that you haven't been noticing is in fact a form of noticing, right?

Observing a body part, such as your foot, is only one of many possible ways to practice mindfulness. You can also choose to focus on a routine activity such as walking, driving, or eating. Normally, when we walk, our mind is focused elsewhere. To practice mindful walking, you would focus on every movement in your feet, legs, hips, and arms. You would feel each foot come into contact with the ground, and you would feel your weight shift to, and then from, each foot. This is much more difficult than it sounds! I find it easier to start by walking very, very slowly, as if in slow motion. This gives me more time to notice and appreciate each of the many complex events involved in walking. Walking very slowly up or down a flight of stairs is also an interesting and intense way to practice. I suggest that you try this for no more than ten minutes at first, because of the degree of concentration required. If you are walking or running for exercise, paying attention to the sound and rhythm of your steps can be very meditative, almost hypnotic at times. In fact, researchers discovered long ago that repetitive activities can bring about a relaxation response in the brain.

Mindful eating can also be an unpredictable experience. In my mindfulness classes I like to facilitate an activity borrowed from Jon Kabat-Zinn, who developed the influential Mindfulness-Based Stress Reduction program. This activity involves the practice of eating one raisin. After reading this description of the activity, you may wish to try it yourself. Consider, if you will, the humble raisin. I think it makes an ideal focal point for mindfulness because we usually don't pay much attention to a raisin. We may find one as an inconsequential ingredient in a cookie, but we rarely notice it as a singular bit of dried fruit. A raisin's appearance is interesting, and no two raisins look alike. In my classes, we take a full 10 to 15 minutes to eat one raisin in silence. We spend several minutes just looking at our raisins, turning them over in the palms of our hands. The wrinkled texture of a raisin is fascinating, as is the change in color depending on how the light hits its surface. If you take the time to sniff it, you may discover that a raisin has a delicate scent. To feel a raisin in your mouth without biting it, turning it over on your tongue to experience its texture and subtle flavor, is a fun way to explore the concept of beginner's mind. You can bite it in half to experience a sudden explosion of raisin flavor. You can observe the sensations involved in slowly chewing it; the possibilities are endless. Participants frequently remark that they had truly never experienced a raisin before. (Of course, in my adult classes, we then try the exercise with a piece of dark chocolate or an ounce of Sonoma Coast sparkling wine.)

Mindful cooking can be an excellent practice for some people, particularly if they are not rushed for time. You may have sliced a carrot many times before, but it is quite a different experience to observe fully the sound of the knife and the colors and textures of each carrot slice. Or you may choose another activity that you normally do without paying much attention, such as tying your shoe, checking the mail, or flipping channels with a remote control. The beautiful fact is that you can practice mindfulness anytime, anywhere, while doing just about anything. Why not focus the mind for 10 minutes a day, and strengthen this essential mental skill?

Mindful Music Making

Sell your cleverness and purchase bewilderment.—Jalal ad-Din Rumi

Mindfulness and music practice were made for each other. Music making is an incredibly complex task, when you consider the various large and small muscle movements, breath control, and highly advanced cognitive skills required. For the ideas that follow, I suggest setting a timer for anywhere between 10 and 30 minutes at first. This would be the duration of your mindfulness practice, of course, not your entire practice session. I would also suggest starting with short phrases, studies, or excerpts rather than entire songs, movements, or pieces. It is often better to repeat a shorter passage mindfully than to try to maintain concentration throughout an entire piece, at least at first.

Body Awareness

The most fundamental application of mindfulness is often overlooked by even the finest musicians. Awareness of the physical body is indispensable to proper form, balance, and healthy technique while making music. Yet, most of us become so wrapped up in the music that we lose our sense of our own physical selves. This can be a good thing when in a flow state during a concert, although it is also true that body awareness during a practice session can help keep us grounded and focused.

You might begin by standing or sitting as you would when you play or sing music, but without holding or touching your instrument. To do a short body scan before you practice, you may direct your awareness to the top of your head and then slowly move that awareness down your body until you end at your feet. At first, you would simply notice how your face, jaw, neck, and shoulders feel as you sit or stand in a preperformance posture. You would continue to observe your back, abdomen, arms, hands, hips, legs, and even your feet. See if you can become fully aware of the sensations in various parts of your body. You may be surprised to discover that you are thirsty, need to use the bathroom, or are still holding tension from earlier in the day. Most of us are just preoccupied with the musical ideas running through our minds.

The next step might be to adjust your posture so that it is balanced and free from excess tightness. Remember that the idea is not to judge or criticize, but to observe and shift if necessary. There is a tremendous difference between thinking "I am still hunching my shoulders . . . will I ever learn to stop doing that?" and "I notice my shoulders are high, so I will allow them to settle down and back." You might shift your weight from one foot to the other, or, if you are seated, back and forth between the sitting bones. By doing this, you can find a good central point of balance, but even more important, you can sense what that feels like. A great many musicians do not take 30 seconds to find an aligned and stable performance posture. Imagine the benefits to both the mind and body when we become aware of the self that performs.

For some musicians, a good next step is to engage the body with the instrument. This would mean picking up your instrument and holding it as if about to play, or placing your hands on the keyboard, holding mallets or drumsticks, and so on. This will most likely change the alignment and tension level in parts of the body, and you may again need to adjust. You might try a variation of slowly shifting back and forth between an "incorrect" posture and one that is healthy and balanced. (Often, it is difficult to notice what *good* feels like unless you compare it with what *not so good* feels like.) Not only does this activity focus awareness, but it also reduces the risk of performance-related injuries. Another variation involves "air playing" a short musical passage on your instrument, or mouthing lyrics, without actually making a sound. This can be helpful because you are not distracted by the sounds or sensations involved with performing, and you can continue to notice how your body is moving and feeling. Again, if you gently shift from correct to incorrect postures, you can train your mind and body to recognize and be mindful of healthy alignment.

Mindful Repetition

The mindless repetition of a musical passage can be the biggest waste of time in the practice room. Yet, all of us have accidentally engaged in this sort of practice, often when we are fatigued or distracted. Just as it is possible to reach your exit on the highway without remembering how you got there, it is equally possible to reach the end of a musical passage without remembering having played it. If you choose to practice mindfulness at the beginning of your rehearsal, you will be cultivating important mental skills even before you become distracted.

When I was an undergraduate student, I arrived to the music school very early one morning to drop off an assignment. As I passed by the practice rooms, I observed that a graduate student whom I greatly admired was slowly practicing the opening of Beethoven's piano sonata Op. 81a. Actually, he was practicing the first three chords of the piece over and over and over again. He seemed completely lost in thought as he played those chords in slow motion, almost as if underwater, with a few seconds of silence in between each repetition. I regarded that as very interesting, and went along my merry way. When I returned about 30 minutes later, that same student was still practicing those *same three chords*. I couldn't believe it! How could someone practice three quarter-note pulses over and over again, for a full half hour? I asked him about it later, and he replied that it was a form of early morning meditation for him. At the time, I only partly understood. When I practiced, my mind was so engrossed in all that needed to be done, that that sort of repetition seemed like a colossal waste of time. Years later, I realized that he was focusing his awareness as much as he was refining those opening chords.

The truth is that this sort of meditative practice, when adapted to your particular instrument or situation, can be incredibly mesmerizing and gratifying. My one recommendation is that you don't try it for 30 minutes, with all respect to my friend. In fact, 1 or 2 minutes is challenging enough at first. The goal is not to work up to longer and longer stretches of time, either, because the *quality* of focus is more valuable than the duration. On the one hand, if you notice that you are becoming frustrated or irritated, it is time to stop and switch to another activity. On the other hand, you may notice that on some occasions you become so wrapped up in awareness that you continue the activity in a flow state of consciousness.

Play around with a note, interval, or chord that is not easy to master right away, but that is not extraordinarily frustrating or difficult. Before you play or sing, hear it clearly in your mind, with the ideal tone and volume. Then play or sing once, listening closely, and pausing afterward. As a pianist, I like to completely drop my arms in between repetitions, so that each note is approached as if for the very first time. By the third or fourth repetition, you may find yourself in a slow sort of rhythmic groove. Observing the activity of your mind is as helpful as the external listening. Are you able to release self-criticism? If not, are you able to acknowledge that, and set it aside? Are you able to focus on the note each time, or is your mind wandering? If your mind is wandering, can you simply notice and accept that?

Another technique involves the mindful repetition of a short musical unit. This would be a passage no longer than a scale, a single measure of a piece, or a phrase requiring no more than one breath. As you repeat your chosen passage, see if you can perceive it as a single gesture rather than a string of individual notes or rhythms. Observe the activity of your own mind with patience and compassion. After all, it is easier to find fault with a longer sequence because so much more is happening. See if you can acknowledge all repetitions equally. Contemplate mistakes ("unexpected events") as feedback that you need to adjust something in your body or mind to play differently the next time. And if you're unable to do that, accept that as well.

Consider assigning a specific focal point for each repetition. This is helpful for avoiding mindless reiteration, which can happen when we don't have a purpose for the passage, other than "play it better." You can vary the shape of the phrase, dynamics, color, articulation, style, or tempo, to name just a few. You may find it helpful to express your intent out loud before each repetition. Since research suggests that speaking our goals out loud helps the brain consolidate and remember them, experiment to see what is most helpful. Incidentally, setting short-term goals for each repetition will almost always discourage mindless practice and will make your practice time much more productive and enjoyable.

Depending on your instrument, the slow practice of longer passages can be tremendously meditative. When you practice slowly, you give your mind more time to process the details of each note and how it relates to the notes around it. Listening to the quality of the negative space or gaps between the notes can lead to more thoughtful and expressive interpretations. I have a friend who practices very slowly with the metronome, not for rhythmic accuracy, but to keep himself in that very slow, meditative state. For him, the repeating clicks of the metronome induce a positive sort of mindful trance. For slow practice to be an effective mindfulness activity, it is important to repeat sections of music rather than entire movements or pieces. Otherwise, maintaining that degree of intense concentration can be difficult and fatiguing. If this slow technique is impractical for your instrument, you can still *think slowly*, and in larger gestures and units, while playing quickly.

Mindful Listening

Mindful listening of your own performances can be a challenging and rewarding practice. It is one thing to listen carefully when repeating passages during a practice session, but it is a very different experience to listen to a recording of yourself while exercising nonjudgment, acceptance, and beginner's mind. As you listen, you can practice observing your playing without excessive criticism, viewing unintended events as feedback for improvement. You will recall that nothing we think or do can change the immediate past, even if the immediate past is caught on a recording device. So, listening with a sense of detached compassion can help you improve your playing without getting too wrapped up in extraneous thoughts and emotions.

Mindfulness Meditation

> *When there is silence, one finds the anchor of the universe within oneself.*
> —Tao Te Ching

Meditation is, for many people, the secret to good mental health and a happy life. For decades, researchers have demonstrated the varied and extensive benefits of mindfulness meditation. These include physical health benefits (strengthened immune system, lower blood pressure, lower pulse rate, improved memory and cognitive functioning, better pain management, delay of the aging process), as well as psychological health benefits (decreased stress, anxiety, depression, and anger, improved mood, increased compassion, greater sense of well-being). A few studies have even suggested a relationship between meditation and decreased performance anxiety in musicians. Furthermore, as an integrative health practice, it is simple and free.

People often share with me their reasons for not wanting to practice meditation. Most frequently, these involve unsuccessful past experiences ("I couldn't quiet my mind," or "I was too distracted," or "I just couldn't find the time"). Other times, people communicate narrow beliefs about their abilities to be successful ("I have trouble concentrating," or "I'm just too hyper," or "I get bored"). As you read those quotes, can you sense the degree of judgment? To me, these statements reveal a misunderstanding about what meditation is. As I have mentioned, quieting the mind is not the point, but observing the mind is. After all, nonstriving is one of the attitudes of mindfulness. If you reread the excuses in this paragraph as answers to the question, "Why don't you pay attention to the world around you?" you might see what I mean.

There is an old Zen saying that goes, "You should sit in meditation for twenty minutes a day, unless you're too busy, in which case you should sit for an hour." I love the wry humor in this quote. It's a poetic way of saying: If you think you don't have time to meditate, then you need meditation more than you think! Take another look at the statements in the previous paragraph, and imagine a musician using those same excuses not to practice. Chances are that you practice even when you feel distracted, hyper, or bored. In fact, our most successful habits are those we do without thinking about them. Do you wait until you are motivated to brush your teeth in the morning or do you just brush your teeth? Consider the notion that *we make time for what we want to do*, regardless of what we say. Our behavior, rather than our words, reveals our true beliefs. We set our priorities in various ways, either consciously or unconsciously, and turn our attention to what is most important.

Preparing to Meditate

You don't need to acquire any special equipment or skills in order to meditate. I believe the traditional stereotype of proper meditation (sitting on a cushion in a cross-legged position) has deterred many Westerners from trying or sustaining the practice. Despite the many books and schools professing a correct or definitive posture or method, the truth is that meditation techniques around the world are as diverse as the meditators themselves. Furthermore, as people grow and develop in their practice, their posture or approach may change as well.

The philosophies of meditation are equally diverse. Depending on whom you ask, meditation may be a practice in mental training, relaxation, spirituality, or stress management. One time, a woman approached me after a lecture I gave to a national audience. She was upset that I had failed to explain that meditation was a spiritual practice first and foremost, meant to facilitate a higher level of consciousness. I responded that while that was true for millions of people worldwide, it was not true for everyone, and my goal is always to be as inclusive as possible. I did not convince her, and I didn't expect to. The practice of meditation can be as private and individual as any set of personal beliefs. I don't believe that any philosophy or faith tradition can hold exclusive claim to the practice of meditation. Awareness is for everyone! For that reason, this chapter describes the secular practice of mindful awareness, a practice that can be adapted to any personal philosophy, faith tradition, or life situation. In the words of David Lynch, "The thing about meditation is . . . you become more and more you."

To begin, find a relatively quiet spot where you will not be disturbed. This can be any room in your home or a peaceful outdoor area. It is helpful, although not always possible, to use the same spot every time. You might like to post a "do not disturb" sign on your door. If practical, turn off your phone and other vibrating or sound-generating devices. It is not realistic to find a completely quiet space, and that's perfectly fine. Sometimes extraneous sounds are useful for focusing the mind and bringing awareness to the present moment.

Be sure the body is comfortable. Just as musicians are often unaware of their bodies when they begin to practice, meditators sometimes forget to pay attention to the needs of their physical selves. You may feel uncomfortable and distracted if your clothes are too tight, if the temperature is too hot or too cold, if you are hungry or sore, or if you choose an uncomfortable posture. The body temperature tends to drop slightly during meditation, so you might choose to have a wrap nearby.

Meditation postures vary greatly and should be chosen with body comfort and personal preference in mind. Many people prefer to sit in a simple cross-legged position on the floor. Others sit in a half-lotus position (where one foot rests on top of the opposite thigh, with the other foot tucked under) or in a full-lotus position (with each foot resting on the opposite thigh), both of which require a considerable degree of flexibility. If you choose to sit in any of these positions on the floor, you may want to sit on a cushion or folded blanket so that your knees are slightly below your hips. To protect your ankles, particularly if you are barefoot, you may want to have some cushioning between your ankles and the floor. Sit tall but not rigid, adopting what many teachers refer to as a dignified posture. Your head should be comfortably balanced atop your spine, with your chin in a neutral position. It sometimes helps to drop your shoulders down and back, to avoid hunching forward. Your back will not be perfectly straight, because the spine is naturally curved, and you should feel balanced on your sitting bones. If you feel stiff, it may be helpful first to try some of the stretches discussed in Chapter 5. If this posture feels tight or uncomfortable in your legs or back during the first few minutes, I suggest you find another position rather than become distracted by your discomfort during meditation.

Many Westerners, particularly those who are required to sit in a chair for several hours during the day, are uncomfortable maintaining a cross-legged position for an extended period of time. An alternative floor posture is a kneeling posture, sitting back toward your heels. To make this posture more comfortable, you can place firm folded blankets, books, or yoga blocks between your ankles to have something to sit on. Kneeling meditation benches, sometimes called Seiza benches, can be very comfortable because you sit back on a low bench with your legs tucked under. The weight of your body then rests on the bench rather than on your knees or ankles. It is still helpful to have a blanket or cushion underneath you, and perhaps a rolled-up towel under your ankles to support them if they are sensitive. If you choose to experiment with different seated postures, remember that you are not in competition with anyone, not even yourself. Don't force yourself into a traditional posture if it doesn't feel natural, or if you can't maintain it for an extended period of time.

A great many people prefer to sit in a chair to meditate. One benefit is that you can easily meditate anywhere without any special props or supports. For this posture, you might first like to try a firm but comfortable chair, one without arm rests, and one in which you can sit close to the edge of the seat without back support. It is helpful to sit tall with your head and neck in a neutral position as previously described. If this is uncomfortable to do, because of back pain or weakness in the core muscles, you can sit toward the back of the chair and allow your back to be lightly supported.

Any of these seated positions are excellent for meditation. For those with pain or accessibility issues, reclining or lying down to meditate may be preferable. Lying down on the floor, usually on a towel or mat, is practiced in many traditions. Just be careful not to fall asleep! In meditation, the phrase "relaxed body, alert mind" indicates that the mind should not get drowsy, which sometimes happens when lying down. (You may have recognized an interesting parallel here between meditation and performance. Tennis champion Arthur Ashe once said, "The ideal attitude is to be physically loose and mentally tight.") If you find yourself drifting off to sleep, be sure to switch positions or wait until you feel more alert, so that you don't accidentally train your mind to believe that meditation is a trigger for nap time! A nightly meditative practice for alleviating insomnia is a completely separate activity. (I refer to this as beditation.)

What should you do with your hands during meditation? This is a personal choice, and there is truly no correct answer. You may rest your hands palms down on your thighs or knees, or palms up with your fingers gently curled in their natural position. Some people find that keeping their hands palms up feels more neutral because the sensitive fingertips aren't in contact with any solid surface. Another option is to sit with one hand gently cupping the other hand, with both palms up. If you find your mind frequently drifting off during meditation, you may find it helpful to rest your hands palms up on your thighs or knees, with the thumbs gently touching the middle fingers.

Closing your eyes during meditation is particularly helpful, because it induces the relaxing alpha brainwaves which calm the mind. If you prefer not to close your eyes, you can direct your gaze gently downward, focusing on a single spot. Some people prefer to gaze at an object, such as a candle flame, to keep the mind from wandering. Experiment and see what works best for you. Although some people like to listen to soothing music while they meditate, I have found that professional musicians frequently find this distracting. Tonal melodies, harmonies, or regular rhythmic patterns can engage the conscious, critical mind, and some people find themselves thinking about the music instead of meditating. If you prefer not to sit in silence, or if you want to mask some of the extraneous noises in your environment, nature sounds or white noise can be very helpful. You can find free white-noise apps and generators online. Turning on a fan or another device with a neutral sound can offer the same effect.

Objects of Focus

> Alice: "How long is forever?"
> White Rabbit: "Sometimes, just one second."

The brain never stops thinking, not even when we are asleep. Since the mind is never completely still, it is important to have an object of focus when meditating. That way, when our mind wanders (and it will), we can gently guide it back to our object of focus. Imagine a basketball player practicing free throws. As he makes shot after shot, his eyes and his mind concentrate fully on the rim of the basket. If someone speaks to him, or if he is momentarily distracted, he immediately returns his focus to the basket. For the meditator, an object such as a candle flame offers a concrete visual anchor. For others, these objects of focus are perceived internally.

Once you settle into a balanced position, close your eyes or direct your gaze downward. Begin to draw your attention to the breath. At first, observe your natural breathing pattern without trying to control or regulate it. See if you can detect all the places in your body that feel the sensations of your breath. These may include the tip of your nose, the back of your throat, your chest, abdomen, or countless other locations. Notice how the temperature of your breath changes between the inhale and the exhale. Natural breathing patterns are not always regular, so you might be able to detect if the breath cycle seems to speed up or slow down somewhat. Observing the breath in this way, with a sense of discovery, is one way to practice beginner's mind.

When you find your mind starting to wander, gently guide it back to a specific focal point of the breath. Focusing on a single location (tip of the nose) or detail (length of exhale) is much easier than simply focusing on "the breath," because the mind has a very specific anchor to work with. The noticeable details of the breath are endless. For example, you can focus on the subtle moment in which the exhale becomes an inhale or the inhale becomes an exhale. This is an interesting point of observation, because you may or may not find that it is a single moment in time, as the lungs expand and contract. You may prefer to practice one of the specific breathing exercises or visualizations from Chapter 5 to keep your attention focused and engaged. Or, you might listen to the quiet stillness or "gap" between each inhale and exhale. If, after a while, you become bored or tired, switch your focus to another point of awareness.

As you continue this activity, you may begin to notice that your attention is drawn to other things as well. These may include the sounds around you, sensations in your body, even scents in the air. Rather than trying to block any of these out, embrace and experience them in your practice. Notice with curiosity if any thoughts or emotions accompany these other sounds or sensations. One of my most remarkable meditation experiences occurred when a neighborhood dog started barking incessantly. At first, I noticed my own annoyance. But I was gradually able to let that go as I began to pay very close attention, as if I had never heard a dog bark before. After a few minutes, I could hear every detail of each bark: the complex timbre, volume, rhythmic patterns, and unpredictable moments of silence in between each bark. This held my full attention for a very long time; I was completely captivated. You may find that you have similar experiences with a physical discomfort or an itch. Once you guide your awareness beyond the negative thoughts, you can become fully absorbed in the experience. You may even discover that itches seem to disappear, or move, or that pain becomes milder and more diffused. Learning to observe experiences, without mentally labeling them as good or bad, can help develop skills of nonjudgment and acceptance of the present moment.

You will hopefully notice the many thoughts that accompany you as you meditate. See if you can observe each thought as it arises, with playful curiosity and nonjudgment. Chances are that you will become intimately familiar with what many meditators refer to as *monkey mind*.

Embracing Monkey Mind

Think and wonder, wonder and think.—Dr. Seuss

This humorous phrase has been used for generations to describe the natural inclination of human thought. Many people who begin a meditation practice hope to calm the mind or stop the thoughts, but the truth is that the mind is conditioned to be active, even greedy. In our modern culture, it is not uncommon for monkey mind to feel more like Tasmanian devil mind. When we remember the tenets of acceptance and nonstriving, we realize that monkey mind is natural and that it is not likely ever to go away. The challenge is to accept the activity of the mind for what it is, without evaluation.

In the previous chapter, I compared my mind to a toddler. Monkey mind and an active toddler have one thing in common: It is impossible to tame or reason with either one of them. Imagine that an enthusiastic 2-year-old charges toward a dangerous environment, such as a busy neighborhood street. What would you do? You probably wouldn't try to explain the situation or reason with the toddler, because it wouldn't do any good. Getting angry or frustrated wouldn't help, either. Chances are that you would simply guide the toddler toward a safer direction. And if you've ever spent time with a very young child, you know that you would repeat this action over and over again, several times each minute, perhaps hundreds of times in a day. In the same way, you can gently redirect the mind over and over again, with an attitude of patient acceptance. Adopting a friendly mindset also helps.

It is the nature of the mind to wander and drift. Your mind has probably wandered numerous times while reading this chapter. Since you are still reading, the assumption is that you have patiently and repeatedly guided your mind back to the object of focus, the content of this chapter. Sometimes our minds meander into what I think of as a *thought chain*. A stray thought leads to a related thought, which leads to another thought, and so on. Eventually, when you snap back into the present moment, you may find yourself wondering how it was that you came to think about whatever it was you were last thinking about. During meditation, it is interesting to distinguish thoughts that you simply observe from thoughts that carry you away, so to speak. If your mind were like a river or stream, and thoughts were like the leaves floating on the surface of the stream, there is a difference between watching a leaf float by and diving in after the leaf.

Mentally detaching from our thoughts is a helpful way to remember that we are not our thoughts. A thought is simply the activity of the brain. Most people have trouble disengaging at first and frequently find themselves lost in thought during meditation. Sometimes it is helpful to identify each thought as it occurs, perhaps by mentally labeling each one with a word such as "thinking." Remember that you will never get to the point of unthinking, so continue to enjoy acknowledging each thought as it pops up. You can give yourself permission to think about the thought later, if that helps, and temporarily set it aside.

The earlier quote by Tolle reminds us that we are not the voice in our head, but the one who observes that voice. Sometimes it helps to distinguish the self that is doing the thinking. For instance, you can imagine that you are sitting behind yourself, watching yourself meditate. In this way, you can watch the person that is you, noticing each thought as it comes into consciousness. You might even think about yourself in the third person, if that is beneficial, recognizing each time that "Vanessa is thinking," for example.

This all requires a considerable amount of concentration. For this reason, I recommend short meditation sessions at first. It is better to experience several moments of pure awareness during a 10-minute session than to become frustrated by a drifting and distracted mind during a 30-minute session.

If you are interested in exploring the concept of monkey mind in the context of music performance, you might enjoy the section on Mindfulness of Mental Chatter in Chapter 8 (pages 198–199).

Optional Visualization Techniques

Let's get a little crazy here.—Bob Ross

If you find your mind wandering more frequently than you would like, or if you prefer to have a solid mental image on which to focus, you may want to try one of the following visualizations, or create your own. These are very short, repeated mental images that can help keep the mind focused and objective.

One option is to imagine that each thought is a bubble, floating up and away, or popping in front of you. These could resemble transparent soap bubbles, or bubbles of air underwater. Once you find yourself thinking, you can visualize that thought as a single bubble. Imagine that you watch the thought bubble drift up and out of your field of vision, or softly pop into nothingness. With careful observation, you may notice that the parade of bubbles is continuous, that some thoughts are larger than others, or that some bubbles appear together in clusters.

In the previous chapter, I discussed a technique of mentally labeling thoughts and placing them in containers such as boxes, jars, or bottles. You might imagine that a label appears on the container, with a word such as "thinking," or "planning," or "judging," and then you can set that container on a shelf, out of sight. Experiment with anything that appeals to you, but is not too involved or distracting. Remember that this is a simple mental image that you will be repeating over and over again.

The earlier example of thoughts floating like leaves on the surface of a stream comes from Pema Chödrön, a well-known teacher, who learned it from her teacher. If this image appeals to you, you can imagine that you are sitting on the bank of the river or stream, looking down at the water as it flows into your field of vision and out the other side. As thoughts emerge, imagine that they are leaves (or flowers, or whatever pleases you) drifting by and eventually out of sight. If you discover that you become lost in one of these thoughts, or have metaphorically jumped into the water after it, you can gently pull yourself out of the water and back up onto the riverbank.

You may prefer to imagine a similar scenario in which your mind is a highway. Thoughts can be cars, trucks, and other vehicles that drive past you. I once had a meditation student who struggled with self-disparaging thoughts until she began to imagine that these thoughts were uttered by imaginary cartoon monsters in a dollhouse. She would relegate the monsters to different rooms in the dollhouse, depending on what they were thinking, and return her attention to the present moment. If visualizations such as these help you stay focused in the present moment, feel free to be creative, using anything that keeps you alert, engaged, and in a state of quiet awareness.

Establishing a Practice

Even if you are on the right track, you will get run over if you just sit there.
—Will Rogers

Meditation, like music, is a skill that must be practiced. Unlike music practice, however, there is never a need to take a day off because of a busy schedule, vacation, or injury. Since your mind doesn't take a day off from thinking, you might as well set aside a few short minutes to observe those thoughts. It is very helpful to choose a time of day to meditate, and try to stick to that schedule regularly. However, it would be better to meditate for short intervals at various times of the day rather than to skip a regularly scheduled time, if it helps you maintain consistency of practice. You may not always be able to make your scheduled time, or even your favorite place, but meditation can be done just about anywhere, at any time.

Ten minutes is a good amount of time for a beginning meditation, and you can set a timer so that you won't have to keep an eye on the clock. You can download free meditation timers, many with soft and pleasant-sounding bells, for your mobile device. If you find that 10 minutes is too difficult at first, try 5 minutes, or 1 minute, or simply take one conscious breath. In the spirit of nonstriving, remember that there is no goal for how many minutes you should eventually work up to. You will begin to see how long you are comfortably able to sustain the activity of meditation; long enough to be challenged and not bored, but not so long as to become too frustrated or distracted. After a while, you may notice that you naturally want to increase your meditation time. I know meditation teachers who meditate only 20 or 30 minutes a day, and others who meditate 90 minutes to 2 hours a day. You may find that you prefer two meditation sessions, one in the morning or midday, and one in the evening. But again, no one earns a gold star for meditating for an impressively long time.

Occasionally, people will tell me that they prefer to listen to guided meditations rather than meditating on their own. For many people, the verbal directions on the recording help them stay focused in the present moment. I think that is perfectly fine, especially if the guided meditation contains several moments of silence, rather than continuous talking. Since there is a difference between meditation and guided imagery, it is difficult to observe your own thoughts if someone else is continuously talking in your ear. The best recorded meditations usually begin with a guided relaxation and a few gentle suggestions, then taper off into several minutes of silence punctuated occasionally by another verbal cue or suggestion. In some traditions, a soft bell will ring periodically to bring the meditator back to the present moment in case his mind has wandered. When I am especially scattered and distracted, I will set my meditation timer to chime every couple of minutes or so, and have found that to be helpful. Since your mind and your life situation change every day, you may need to adjust the details of your meditation practice as well.

You will find two guided meditations on the companion website (⊕ items 7.1 and 7.2).

Meditation is just one of many ways to practice awareness of the present moment. If you are conscious of each moment as it happens, you have been successful. If you are aware that you have *not* been focused on each moment, you have been successful. It is virtually impossible to fail. Your ability to concentrate on stage while playing music, disregarding distractions and always guiding your awareness back to the present moment, will be greatly improved with regular mindfulness practice. The irony is that such a peaceful and compassionate practice can be used as a secret weapon for success!

8 THE MINDFUL ACHIEVER

PRACTICAL APPLICATIONS
FOR LONG-TERM SUCCESS

It always seems impossible until it's done.—Nelson Mandela

These last two chapters will provide additional opportunities for you to develop and refine the mindfulness skills discussed in this book. For ease of reading and practice, I have divided them more or less into activities that develop very focused self-awareness, organization, and evaluative skills (Chapter 8, The Mindful Achiever) and those that encourage imagination and cultivate creative visioning skills (Chapter 9, The Mindful Visionary). While I do suggest that you read through all of them, do not feel compelled to complete every exercise in these two chapters. Practice first the activities that seem immediately relevant to you. In truth, you can try any of these in any order, and your mindful performance skills will improve. You may wish to refer to your answers from the Performance Skills Self-Assessment included in Chapter 1 and on the companion website (⊕ item 1.1) in order to establish a personal context.

> If you are a music instructor interested in using some of these activities with your students, please consider this advice. It may be advantageous to collect and evaluate some of these activities from your students, especially the assignments regarding time management, organization, and goal setting. Other activities, particularly those related to habits, thoughts, emotions, and other internal processes, are considerably more personal in nature. Since students may not wish to share their private thoughts and feelings with a teacher, some of these would be best if practiced by the student, but not reviewed by the instructor except at the student's request. It is my hope that readers will be mindful of their students' privacy.

The following activities are essential for optimal planning, self-assessment, and problem solving for peak performance. They also require some documentation, organization, and mindful commitment to the formation of new habits. As you already know, thinking about what you want will not be enough to change your reality. As George Santayana once said, "Habit is stronger than reason."

Record Keeping

Fill your paper with the breathings of your heart.—William Wordsworth

Remember that the purpose of your practice journal is to document habits, goals, behaviors, and other elements related to the psychological side of music making. You will want to have this journal with you when you practice your instrument or one of these mental skills. Most of the time you will only use it once or twice a day, and your ability to track your progress will be imminently useful later on.

If you have begun to track your practice habits, you are already on your way to becoming a more confident and self-aware performer! As a reminder, Chapter 2 contains several pages of ideas about what and how to document on a daily basis. The most important thing is that you develop the habit of regular documentation, no matter how you go about doing it. Think of personal record keeping as a muscle. The more you exercise it, the stronger it gets.

Activity: Obtain a journal of your choice if you have not already done so. Begin to document each of your practice sessions in a way that is sufficiently detailed but not time consuming, in a manner that resonates with you personally. It may help for you to structure each entry in roughly the same manner, for example, beginning with the date and ending with a goal for your next practice session. If you forget to log a practice session, add it as soon as you remember so that the details are fresh in your mind. Plan to document briefly any performances, mock or practice performances, or informal gigs as well.

Goal-Setting

A goal properly set is halfway reached.—Zig Ziglar

Activity: List three specific musical goals for this month, season, semester, or year. Include the development or improvement of at least one mindfulness skill in your list of goals. Each goal should be specific, measurable, and realistic, according to the amount of time given. These should always be stated using positive language.

In learning to set robust goals, it can be helpful to consider a few weakly articulated goals. Here are some examples of goals that are too broad, general, or vague to be helpful for this activity: "To be a better musician," "To play more difficult music," "To build my repertoire," "To improve my technique." These are all wonderful ideas, but they are difficult to assess. Of course you want to be a better musician! But what does that mean and how will you get there? Instead of wanting to play more difficult music, you might choose one challenging piece to master. Rather than simply building your repertoire, you might consider a more specific goal, such as to memorize a new jazz standard every week or to learn a piece from each historical period this year. If you want to improve your technique, you will need to identify exactly what that means for you. Do you want to work on speed, articulation, legato, diction, tone, intonation, breath control, or improvisation? And even if you pick one of those, you will need to be even more specific. Will you improvise for 10 minutes every day before you practice? Will you record your improvisations and solicit feedback from others? Will you take improvisation lessons or join an informal improv group? All of those examples are specific, realistic, and measurable. Here are a few more examples of setting specific and attainable goals:

Weak:	"I will become a better musician this month."
Better:	"I will seek objective feedback on my playing this month."
Even better:	"I will play for three professional musicians for feedback this month."

Weak:	"I will improve my posture and alignment this semester."
Better:	"I will practice in front of a mirror every day this semester."
Even better:	"I will video record myself performing, once a week, and compare what I observe about my posture from week to week."

Weak:	"I will improve my coloratura technique."
Better:	"I will improve my ability to sing rapid scale passages."
Even better:	"I will master a five-note scale passage this month, and master a nine-note scale passage next month."

Positive, specific language is very important when setting goals and forming action plans. If your goal is "I want to stop being so nervous when I perform," you are emphasizing the negative or the unwanted. Remember that your mind does not process negative qualifiers such as *don't*, and you want to focus on what it is that you do want. Once you focus on a positive goal, you can determine a specific action that will help you succeed.

Negative goal:	"I want to stop being so nervous when I perform."
Positive goal:	"I will work to improve my confidence on stage . . ."
Action:	" . . . by performing once a week to friends and colleagues, and by documenting my thoughts and feelings."

Negative goal:	"I need to quit fixing my mistakes on stage."
Positive goal:	"I will improve my musical continuity . . ."
Action:	" . . . by recording my practice performances and analyzing how I handled each mistake."

Periodic evaluation of your progress is essential to success. If one of your goals is to play your scales faster, for example, that won't mean much unless you know how fast you currently play them and how fast you eventually want to play them. Without that information, you won't be able to check your improvement each week or determine if you reached your goal. Some goals are admittedly harder to assess and quantify. If you wish to perform with greater focus and composure, you will need to document your feelings and emotions in your practice journal each week, in the manner that sport psychologists recommend. You can then compare your responses from the beginning and end of the goal period. This is why daily documentation, audio and video recordings, and periodic written reflections are all invaluable tools for musicians.

Whenever possible, try to break your larger goals down into bite-sized mini goals. This can make your objectives feel very attainable. You may wish to plan daily, weekly, and monthly goals in addition to your long-term goals, to help organize your practice or rehearsal time and keep you on track. You can then reassess yourself regularly and set new goals. This sort of mindful record keeping will save you many minutes (and eventually many hours) of wasted practice time.

Check out the companion website for a goal-setting worksheet (⊕ item 2.6).

Contract With Yourself

> But I have promises to keep, and miles to go before I sleep.—Robert Frost

Activity: Take your most meaningful goal for the upcoming month, season, semester, or year, and write out a short but official contract with yourself, and sign it. In the contract, be very precise about what you intend to accomplish, and by what date. Hang it on your wall or put it someplace where you will see it often.

Interestingly, the more official looking your contract, the more likely you may be to honor it. You may prefer to type out your contract, perhaps even working in some humorous legal-sounding terms or fine print. I notice that I am more likely to honor my own official contract than accomplish goals hastily jotted on a sticky note. Once, I set a big, scary grant application goal that I was afraid I would back out of, so I had a friend "witness" my contract and sign it as well. You can have fun with this activity or not, but the point is that the contract should be very short, specific, and official. If you are a student, you may find it more motivating to write out a contract to your teacher or mentor instead.

You will find a contract template on the companion website (⊕ item 8.2).

Organized Practice

Happiness is not just a place, but also a process.—Ed Diener

Activity: Take a moment to reflect on all that you need to accomplish in your next practice session, and plan out a practice agenda for yourself. Create a timeline or checklist of what you will practice, for how long, and what progress you hope to make. When you do practice, follow your agenda, and notice if it helps keep you more focused and productive. If that is the case, do this prior to every rehearsal.

Mindfully structuring your practice ahead of time can be tremendously motivating. You can begin by asking yourself a few key questions. How much time do I have to practice right now? What do I need to accomplish today? What are my priorities? You might prefer to organize your agenda or checklist into various categories, depending on your instrument and goals. If you manage to create a template that works well for you, you can simply duplicate it and fill it in each day, to save time. One of my piano majors is a virtuoso of the color-coded practice spreadsheet.

You will find several practice organization templates on the companion website (⊕ items 2.1–2.5).

A great writer once told me, "Whatever gets done first gets done." If you have five new pieces to learn in one hour, you are guaranteed to learn the first piece, but not necessarily the fifth. If you need to accomplish tasks x, y, and z, and task z is the most important one, begin your practice with task z. Some musicians are masters of procrastination in the practice room. If you have a very challenging piece looming, something that will require a great deal of effort and concentration, perhaps something that feels scary because you're not sure you can do it . . . it is far too easy to fill your practice time with warmups, sight reading, review pieces that you can already play or sing, or ensemble parts for other events. By the time you get around to your most pressing music, your practice time is almost up! Mindfulness can help you become aware of these very natural and universal human tendencies.

Time Management

By failing to prepare, you are preparing to fail.—Benjamin Franklin

---

Activity: Create a color-coded weekly schedule using your online calendar, spreadsheet, planner, or blank paper schedule. Use one color for your most important and nonnegotiable appointments, such as your job, classes, family obligations, and other standing responsibilities. Study the remaining open slots, and use a different color to plan out your practice times. For the remaining open slots, use another color to represent meals, exercise or sports, devotion or meditation, time spent commuting, even social time with friends and family.

You will find a scheduling template on the companion website (⊕ item 8.4).

Evaluate the schedule you just created. Does it look full but relatively balanced? Were you able to find sufficient time each day to practice? What, if anything, did you have to give up in order to prioritize your most important tasks? Did you schedule in enough breaks? Tweak your schedule if you need to and follow it faithfully for 1 week. Make a note of what worked well and what you need to change. Adjust your schedule again, if necessary, and follow it conscientiously for another week.

Finding enough time to practice is the main challenge for most musicians, amateurs and professionals alike. All human beings have families, jobs, school, and/or other responsibilities, and it can feel daunting to carve out enough practice and personal time. Luckily, scheduling becomes easier each year with the proliferation of new fancy planners and organizers, digital calendars, and mobile apps. The mistake many people make, I believe, is that they schedule and keep track of their most important appointments, but they don't manage the empty "free time" that remains. Without a plan on how you will use that time, you risk disappointment or burnout.

Many authors have used the metaphor of *rocks, pebbles, and sand* when teaching time management. The idea is that you could fill a very large imaginary jar with the largest, most important rocks first. If you then added smaller pebbles to the jar, those could fill up the space around the big rocks. Finally, even if it looked like your jar was full, you could pour in a quantity of sand which would fill the spaces left around the other rocks. In real life, the large rocks would represent your most important, unmovable responsibilities. Pebbles would represent items that are also important, but that could be moved around if necessary. This would include your practice time, scheduled around your nonnegotiable rocks. Some people find it unusual to schedule in their meals, but I am struck by how often my students skip meals or scarf something down quickly because they "don't have time" to eat. These important pebble time slots could potentially be very short: 10 minutes for a meditation, 20 minutes for lunch on a busy day, and so on.

Although the sand in your jar is generally scheduled last, this does not mean these items are the least essential to your health and happiness. They can represent the most flexible parts of your schedule: recreation, favorite TV shows, even breaks for email and social media. Studies suggest that if you schedule time to play on the internet, you are less likely to let that activity take over your day. For many people, time spent on a computer or mobile device actually becomes a rock, in terms of hours spent each day. What if you used a portion of that time to practice your instrument or journal about your musical goals? A good schedule helps you better prioritize and balance your life.

Life Balance: An Editorial

Any darn fool can make something complex.
It takes a genius to make something simple.—Pete Seeger

We interrupt this series of organizational activities to bring you a short opinion piece on the concept of life balance. I love the idea of living a balanced life, but I also think our society has blown it completely out of perspective. I like that it encourages us to view our lives holistically. We can be aware of how we spend our time in many areas of our lives, not just our work. Years ago, I presented a workshop on the topic of burnout to a wonderful group of teachers in California. I had searched online for one of those balance wheels that people are supposed to fill out to assess their time spent in each of eight areas of their lives: career, finances, health, spirituality, friends, family, home, and recreation. It sounded like a great idea, but I noticed how uncomfortable I felt as I studied the worksheet.

I felt a subtle internal pressure to address and improve each of these life areas more than I already do. After more searching, I found another example of a balance wheel with 10 categories (10!), including self-esteem and life purpose. Life purpose! *Oh, the pressure!*

I understand and wholly support the underlying philosophy of these activities, which is to cultivate mindful awareness of the many dimensions of human life. I also think it is helpful to look at how we really spend our time and energy. But life is, and will always be, messy and out of balance. A grouchy toddler doesn't care if you have set aside this hour to think about your life purpose if it just so happens that now is the time to scream. The truth is that we will never "get there," to that point where our balance wheels look beautifully tidy. We will never get it all done. Nothing makes me feel worse, at the end of a mind-bogglingly busy day, than the idea that I didn't do everything that *I should have.* The pressure to try to cultivate unattainably pretty lives is simply not worth it. So I say, let it go and do what you can. A voice teacher I know has the following quote on the wall in her teaching studio: "I can only do what I can do. Any more than that is more than I can do."

In the previous activity, what if you weren't able to follow your weekly schedule completely, but you were able to do more than half of the things you had planned? This is still more than you might have done if you hadn't planned out your week at all. Success!

Mindfulness of Personal Habits

It is wisdom to know others; It is enlightenment to know one's self.—Laozi

---

Activity: Choose a personal habit to track for 1 to 4 months. I list some examples below to get you started. The goal is not necessarily to change or improve what you are doing, but simply to observe your patterns of behavior at various times during the year.

There is no need to judge or compete, here, so try to be completely honest with yourself. The priority is mindful awareness, not assessment. Each day, it will be helpful for you to include at least one phrase or sentence about how you felt, overall, throughout the day. This will help you determine if the habit is affecting your mood or health. You may choose one of the following habits, or any other.

Sleeping Habits

Track the time you go to bed each night, and the time you wake up each morning. If you take any naps, do the same for those. Record the number of hours you sleep in each 24-hour period and your average hours of sleep over the course of each week. Some people also like to keep track of the quality of their sleep, which can vary greatly from night to night. Others prefer to wear an activity tracking device or download a sleep app.

Eating Habits

Track what you eat every day. You do not need to count calories or other nutritional data, since this is mostly a practice in mindfulness. If, as you track, you realize you would like to change some of your eating habits, I suggest you work on only one small habit at a time. For example, you might eat one additional piece of fruit per day or eliminate your daily trip to the snack machine. If you try to overhaul your diet all at once, you will not get an accurate sense of your natural eating habits and trends.

Drinking Habits

Track the beverages you consume each day. You may wish to identify specific types of drinks (water, caffeine, alcohol), if there are certain trends you especially want to observe. Or, you may want to indicate what time of day you drink certain beverages.

Exercise Habits

Track the approximate number of minutes you are moving each day. This can include scheduled activities such as workouts or sports, but can also include time spent running errands, walking to and from your daily work, etc. You may prefer to use a pedometer or other fitness gadget to help you track. Try to notice daily or weekly trends and whether these affect your overall mood.

Internet, Gadget, and Social Media Habits

People can develop heathy and unhealthy relationships with, and even addictions to, mobile devices and various online platforms. Tracking these habits requires perseverance, but can reveal important information about how we use our time.

For desktop or laptop computer use: When you open your personal email, read the news online, or check social media, simply indicate the time you start. When you close these programs, indicate the time you finish. Do this each and every time, no matter how often you engage in these activities each day. If you use a computer as part of your daily work, keep your personal applications closed so that you will be aware each time you open them. Some people find that turning off notifications can regulate the number of times they open an application. Online tracking programs can help simplify this activity.

For mobile device use: You may prefer to track your gadget use in the same way, although this can be impractical if you check your device as frequently as many people do. Several apps and programs will track the number of times you unlock your device each day, daily minutes spent on your device, or daily minutes spent using various apps. The point is not to vilify the use of mobile devices, since this component of our culture is here to stay. Again, the objective is personal awareness.

Remember that our habits affect our health, well-being, and productivity. If you remember to indicate your overall mood, for each day or for certain parts of the day, this will help you develop important skills related to the next activity.

Emotional Mindfulness

How much has to be explored and discarded before reaching the naked flesh of feeling.—Claude Debussy

---

Activity: In your practice journal, document your moods and feelings before and after each practice, rehearsal, trial performance, or public concert. Try to find the perfect word or phrase to describe how you feel, or draw cartoon faces or symbols that are specific and meaningful to you. Do you notice any patterns? Do certain situations and events in your life affect your emotions during music practice? Do certain pieces of music affect your mood?

Sport psychologists often address *emotion regulation* when training elite athletes. This two-step process involves first becoming aware of your moods and emotions in certain situations, and then learning to redirect the mind to cultivate what you want to feel at a certain time, usually during a performance. This activity addresses the first step; we will explore the second step later on. Athletes learn to identify their emotions so that they can monitor, evaluate, and eventually modify their emotional reactions when needed. You can imagine how advantageous this would be in a high-pressure situation.

This skill is particularly helpful for creative artists, including performers who may already feel emotionally invested in their music. If something goes wrong during a performance, we would prefer to feel calm and objective, rather than at the mercy of our anger or embarrassment. Even if something goes extraordinarily well, we don't want to get derailed or distracted by feelings of triumph. Musicians who believe they aren't able to influence their emotions should be aware that even the most sensitive athletes, performing in the most public and competitive venues, can improve this skill. The first step, though, is becoming aware of these moods and emotions and learning to identify them at any given time.

I believe this is harder than it sounds. How do you feel right now, as you read this? If the answer is "okay, I guess," or "I don't know," or even just "fine," you might need to dig a little deeper. None of those phrases describes a true emotional state. Even musicians who experience intense reactions or pronounced mood swings can find it difficult to articulate their mood at any particular time. Of course, it is easier to describe the feelings you have right before you walk out on stage than, say, your mood while sitting quietly and reading a book. The more you practice, the easier it gets. And documenting those feelings, in writing, preferably in a private journal, is very beneficial in revealing your emotional tendencies and habits.

Language is a powerful instrument that can help define us in very vivid and specific terms. We humans tend to be lazy, though, when using language to describe how we feel. For example, what does "fine" really mean? If you are fine, does that mean you feel good? And if you feel good, does that mean agreeable, or marvelous, or empowered? Other commonplace words, such as "sad" and "happy" are also insufficient. Take a look at Table 8.1 for a few of the many synonyms associated with these words. Notice that the meaning of each word is quite distinct. It is sometimes easier to choose the perfect word from a list than try to recall one on your own.

You may wish to begin by writing down your feelings before you begin your practice. Sometimes you might feel motivated and excited to practice. Other days you might feel exhausted, distracted, or like you really

Table 8.1

Variations of *Sad*	Variations of *Happy*
Bored	Serene
Somber	Contented
Gloomy	Secure
Troubled	Grateful
Pessimistic	Optimistic
Wistful	Carefree
Sorrowful	Merry
Heavyhearted	Chirpy
Dismal	Playful
Distressed	Animated
Heartbroken	Energized
Despairing	Effervescent
Grieving	Overjoyed
Disempowered	Vivacious
Hopeless	Ecstatic

don't want to be there. Perhaps you feel nervous about an upcoming event. Or maybe something just happened in your personal life that has affected your mood. When you are finished practicing, write down your moods and emotions again. They might be the same, but they may have shifted during your practice, and that would be helpful to observe. The quality of your practice may have boosted your mood, but it's also possible that you could feel fatigued and spent. Perhaps a certain piece of music affects your mood in a very specific way. Maybe the time of day, day of the week, amount of sleep you had, or something you recently ate or drank influenced your emotions during a practice session.

If you do this activity every single time you practice, you will begin to notice interesting trends over the course of several weeks. You may discover that the quality of your practice is greatly affected by your mood. You may be surprised to discover how frequently your emotions fluctuate, or how steady you feel when you are focused. Although we are sometimes disconnected from our feelings, we can learn to get back in touch through mindful awareness.

You will also want to complete this activity before every performance. Vivid emotions are sometimes easier to identify. You may discover that the type of audience, the other musicians in your group, or the attitude or actions of a music director influences your emotions as well. Once you become proficient at identifying and documenting your moods, you can learn to identify the thoughts that trigger those emotions.

Thoughts and Emotions

To understand yourself is the beginning of wisdom.—Krishnamurti

---

Activity: Think back to a recent experience that left a negative impression on you. It could be a failed attempt, personal conflict, or bad performance. This experience most likely generated a series of thoughts that then triggered one or more negative emotion. Reflect for a moment to see if you can identify the thoughts behind the emotions. How could you reframe those thoughts in a more positive way? What different emotions might arise from those more positive thoughts? If that situation should occur again, how might you approach it differently?

In Chapter 4, we discussed the power of the mind in directing our thoughts and in constructively reevaluating irrational beliefs. In this activity, the idea is to uncover the thoughts behind each emotion, and to play around with reframing those thoughts to see if a different feeling emerges. If, for example, a conductor negatively singles you out in a rehearsal, it can generate some powerful emotions. The reaction might vary greatly from person to person. You could get angry and offer a retort, you could feel shame and slink out of the rehearsal, you could silently seethe and plot your revenge, you could ignore the remark or shrug it off, you could feel grateful for the constructive feedback, you could feel compassion for a socially insensitive music director, or any other interpretation you can imagine. The point of focus, for this activity, is the thought behind the feeling.

Other examples of negative experiences might be completely internal. For example, perhaps you drew a blank in the middle of a song and were obliged to fake some of the words. Your internal dialogue would guide your feelings about that mistake. If you thought about letting the audience down, you might feel shame or embarrassment. If you mentally chided yourself, you might feel anger or resentment. If you focused on thoughts of failure, you might feel despair. Any of those scenarios would potentially affect the rest of your performance, if you were unable to rein in those thoughts and feelings. If, on the other hand, your thoughts were more nonchalant ("oh, well!"), evasive ("nothing to see, here"), encouraging ("just keep going"), humorous ("I sound like a Teletubby"), objective ("maybe no one noticed"), complimentary ("nice recovery"), or empowering ("you can do this!"), your emotions would help you continue to perform at your best.

Planning out some of your thoughts ahead of time, as strange as that may sound, can help train your mind for success. As you work on this activity, think about the best thought you could have, realistically, depending on the situation. Although no one will ever achieve complete control of their thoughts or emotions, you can learn to be more mindful of the role of your thoughts in determining how you feel and react.

You will find a worksheet for this activity on the companion website (⊕ item 8.5).

Emotion Regulation

> *I am the master of my fate, I am the captain of my soul.*
> —William Ernest Henley

Activity: After you have documented your thoughts and feelings for a week or more, reflect mindfully on the full spectrum of emotions that you experienced during this time. Take a moment to appreciate the optimistic and uplifting thoughts you documented, noticing the contexts that encouraged those experiences. Then take an objective, compassionate look at the more negative feelings. Are you able to identify the thought or the event that triggered each emotion? Experiment with one or more of the following techniques to redirect negative emotions the next time they occur. Keep track of what you tried and whether it worked for you. I have adapted the following sport psychology strategies for musicians.

Disputing

Practice identifying unrealistic thoughts that contain qualifiers such as *should, must, always, ought,* or *never,* or that sound unreasonable or extreme in some way. Dispute and reframe these thoughts using logic and reason. You can refer back to the Chapter 4 section Hold That Thought for additional examples and strategies. This may require you to ask yourself questions such as, "Why did I just think that?" or "Is that true?" or "Is that always the case?" Here is one example of how this process might work.

Irrational thought:	I shouldn't have missed that high note.
Disputed:	• Great musicians miss notes all the time.
	• No one gives a perfect performance.
	• I was well prepared, and I did my best.
	• I can still give a commanding performance.
	• One missed note won't ruin this concert.
	• One missed note doesn't define me.
	• I can handle any surprises that come my way.
Reframed:	I missed that high note, and I will continue to improve.

You will find a worksheet for this activity on the companion website (⊕ item 4.3).

Distracting

This technique works well when your situation requires that you not react immediately or that you not disturb your flow of concentration. If someone insults you, for example, you could choose to remain neutral by mentally reciting the alphabet backward. If your performance is interrupted by a disturbance from the audience, you might imagine that you are alone on a tropical island, playing or singing to yourself. Although distraction works for only a brief period of time, it can help with short-term emotion regulation.

Reappraising

Sometimes the best course of action is to change your perspective, just as you did when disputing irrational thoughts. With reappraisal, you can reframe more than a single thought. You can reinterpret an entire situation by putting it into a larger perspective. Musicians who live for the spotlight often feel the same surge of adrenaline as anxious musicians, but they are likely to reinterpret that surge as excitement rather than fear. They tend to generate feelings from a broader perspective ("I love to perform for an audience!") rather than from a more specific viewpoint ("I don't feel ready for this concert"). Reappraising often involves looking at the overall quality and impact of a performance rather than focusing on isolated incidents. Recording yourself can help you see the bigger picture through a more objective lens. You can also use reappraisal to view mistakes as learning experiences and use them as tools to improve your next performance.

Distancing

This technique involves the same sort of healthy detachment that we discussed in the previous chapter on mindfulness. You might disengage your awareness slightly during a performance, perhaps thinking about yourself from a third-person perspective. This sometimes happens automatically to people when they are in a flow state of consciousness, but you can also use it as a tool to refocus and offer yourself a new perspective. If, for example, you get so emotionally involved in a piece that it starts to affect your ability to perform well, you can mindfully detach and imagine that you are watching yourself perform without judgment. To distance yourself from negative thoughts and experiences, you can practice some of the disidentification affirmations discussed later on in this chapter.

Refocusing

Affirmations, creative imagery, and clearly stated goals can all help you focus on your objective, while diverting your attention away from self-defeating thoughts. During a performance, you can focus on the positive goals you have written for each piece, or you can recall some of the positive imagery from your creative visualizations. Suppose you notice that you are suddenly playing too fast. Rather than urging yourself to stop doing that unwanted thing ("Don't rush!" or "Slow down!"), you could think to yourself what you do want ("Steady and secure").

You might prefer to compose a single refocusing affirmation for yourself to use when needed. It can be as simple as "I've got this!" or "Easy does it," but could also be more specific, such as "Relaxed body, alert mind." Athletes often choose a single trigger word, which can be energizing ("go!") or calming ("release"). Try using these during your practice sessions, and see what works for you. We will discuss more strategies related to mindful refocusing later on in this chapter.

Avoiding

Although this may be the least effective strategy in the long run, it can be helpful at times. This technique implies that you simply evade the thought or situation that triggers an unwanted emotion. You can't realistically avoid a performance that makes you feel nervous, but you can sometimes ignore unwanted thoughts that pop up. This is what I call the Scarlett O'Hara strategy. For readers who are unfamiliar with the classic film *Gone with the Wind* (1939), Scarlett was a southern belle who would typically brush aside unwanted conversation topics by saying, "I can't think about that right now . . . I'll think about that tomorrow." My Scarlett O'Hara strategy is simply, "I'll think about that tomorrow." This can work well when something goes wrong during a performance, because you can give yourself permission to ruminate later, and move on. The problem with avoidance is that if it is overused, musicians can end up not dealing with their problems and challenges head-on. When used judiciously, avoidance can help you refocus quickly and ignore hurtful self-talk.

Accepting

This mindfulness technique requires the most practice, but can be very healing. It is a complete paradigm shift to suspend the human tendency to seek pleasure and avoid discomfort. We always have the option of acknowledging our emotions and then accepting those without trying to change anything. I sometimes imagine that I invite these feelings to tea. In this visualization, I don't scold or criticize my negative thoughts and emotions, but simply sit with them in nonjudgment. Sometimes I imagine that I listen quietly, to see if they have any wisdom to offer me. In real life, I would treat my allies and my enemies the same if we were having tea together.

While acceptance is virtually the opposite of emotion regulation, it can allow us the opportunity to embrace what we think and feel, without evaluation, and with the knowledge that we can redirect those thoughts if we choose to. Through mindfulness, we can build resilience while retaining personal autonomy. Keep in mind that we are not limited to just one of the techniques discussed in this section; we can try them in any combination.

Emotional Triggers

Our feelings are our most genuine paths to knowledge.—Audre Lorde

You may already be able to identify some of your emotional triggers. These would include thoughts or events that seem to hit a nerve with you or that cause a quick negative reaction. Some may be very subtle, such as gloomy weather triggering feelings of melancholy. Others are more obvious, such as a personal rejection triggering feelings of abandonment or shame. Identifying emotional triggers ahead of time can allow you to handle these more readily when they occur. These are sometimes very private, personal responses. Again, I would encourage you not to judge your thoughts or emotions, but simply to become aware of them.

Activity: What triggers, if any, have you identified over the last few weeks? What was the thought or event that precipitated these, and what feelings did they generate? For every emotional trigger that you identify, plan out how you might handle it the next time it occurs. Is there an action you can take, something you can say or think, or another reminder that will help you better acknowledge and stabilize your negative emotions?

Disidentification Affirmations

I am a human being, not a human doing.—Wayne Dyer

In Chapter 4, we contemplated that creative artists often get wrapped up in the idea that their self-worth is determined by the quality of what they produce or perform. This mindset can become "I am what I do." In truth, music is something we do and love, but not something that defines who we are. If we perform a bad recital or audition, we may talk about botching the recital or failing the audition. But if we accidentally spill a glass of water, we don't talk about botching the drinking process or failing our beverage. We tend to take our musical abilities very personally, which includes all of our successes and failures. Mindful disengagement reminds us that we are not our music; we are more than our music will ever be.

Activity: Write a few disidentification affirmations that resonate with you, based on your habits of thought and your past experiences as a musician. This new perspective can feel empowering, and you may choose to refer to these expressions after a negative experience in the practice room or on stage. Here are some examples to help get you started:
  • I may perform music, but I am not my performance.
  • I am not my successes or my failures.
  • I am greater than my performances.

- I am not this audition.
- I am not this solo.
- I feel anxious, but I am not this anxiety.
- I am more than the part of myself that feels nervous right now.
- No matter how or what I do, I am okay.

Mindfulness of Mental Chatter

After giving it some thought, I've decided to name my monkey mind Ricky Bobby.—Anna White

Activity: During your next rehearsal, pay attention to the little voice in your head that sometimes creates a running commentary as you perform. At the end of your practice, make a list of some of the things you "heard," either positive or negative. How much of the mental commentary was optimistic and supportive? How much of it was critical but encouraging? How much of it was negative and unhelpful? What can you think to yourself to counteract the self-defeating thoughts?

Activity: Repeat this exercise, but this time schedule a performance in front of one or more humans. Once again, pay attention to the commentary of the mental chatter in your mind. Afterward, make a list of some of the comments you heard, both positive and negative. Did the quality or intensity of the self-talk change when you had an audience? Can you implement a mental plan to counteract the more negative thoughts next time?

We aren't always aware of what those inner judges are saying to us. If you have practiced the mindfulness technique of gently acknowledging and then setting aside your thoughts, this exercise may seem somewhat easy for you. The act of noticing stray thoughts as they sneak into your conscious-ness will feel familiar. What if you had a magical dictation machine in your head that could print out your thoughts as they occurred? What would that final printout look like? What sorts of statements would you read?

Much of this chatter would likely be critical or judgmental, because evaluation is a necessary component of good musicianship. An analytical thought such as "I need to articulate more clearly in this auditorium" is constructive because you can adjust to the venue in order to improve your performance. The thoughts to release or redirect are those which are unhelpful or distracting. Thinking, "That was stupid," after a mistake does not help you at all. Thinking, "I hope Greedo isn't in the audience, because he hates me," is equally distracting and stressful. As you become aware of your own mental chatter, you can begin to identify unhelpful thoughts and either laugh them off or let them go, focusing on the more positive and encouraging thoughts.

Handling Criticism

You can write rhymes but you can't write mine.—Hamilton

Although some musicians are able to handle negative feedback more easily than others, harsh criticism is difficult for everyone. And, of course, musicians desperately need objective assessment in order to grow. Sometimes it feels like getting a flu shot: It hurts a little, but will hopefully pay off.

Some criticisms are offered with great kindness, and with the intent of helping us improve. Unfortunately, that's not always the case. Feedback can be delivered in a thoughtless or insulting manner, sometimes directly, or sometimes couched in passive or manipulative language. Harsher criticisms can be hurled in an attempt to cut us down or make the critic seem superior. And, let's face it, some feedback is simply worthless. Straightforward criticism can sometimes surprise us or leave us at a loss for words. We sometimes think of the perfect response after the fact or wish we could take back a defensive reply. Sometimes, the most mindful reactions require a bit of advance thinking. How might our response change if we planned it out ahead of time? This sort of preparation is an excellent mental skill for gracious and appreciative musicians.

Most often, the best way to diffuse negative criticism is to thank the critic and move on. Whether you agree or disagree is often beside the point, because your own internal reaction doesn't always need to be shared. Sometimes if you protest or defend yourself, it will just inspire your critic to offer additional evidence to justify her comments. In my experience, it is rarely fruitful to argue with a critic, unless that person happens to be a close and trusted friend. Sometimes it is helpful to ask questions for further clarification. And remember, thanking someone for offering his opinion, solicited or otherwise, doesn't necessarily mean that you agree with him. It is simply a way of practicing radical acceptance.

Activity: Compile a short list of phrases that you might use to respond the next time someone criticizes you or your music. These might include at least one response to a positive, constructive criticism ("Thank you, I will give that some thought"), one response to a negative criticism ("I appreciate your feedback"), and one response to a particularly thoughtless, mean, or unsolicited negative comment ("I'm sorry you feel that way"). It may help to think about a criticism you received in the past, how you responded to it, and how you might best respond if it were to happen again. Since we are sometimes our own worst critics, you may choose to practice this activity with yourself!

For more practice in processing negative experiences, see A Letter to Your Critic in Chapter 9 (pages 227–229).

Repackaging Perfectionism

Pictures of perfection make me sick and wicked.—Jane Austen

Perfection is something that many musicians strive for and that a scarce few ever achieve. It is a double-edged sword, because on the one hand, we need to aim high in order to improve our skills and realize our greatest potential. On the other hand, if we fall short of our most ambitious goals, we can experience shame and disappointment.

Luckily, we can distinguish between two types of perfectionism. *Perfectionistic strivings* are relatively healthy, because they can keep us reaching for the best outcome possible. They may challenge us to raise performance standards, improve musical and technical skills, and maintain a keen focus on the task at hand. Perfectionistic strivings are positively oriented, focusing on the achievement of set goals or tasks, rather than on the performer. We can cultivate the ability to assess our performances honestly, realistically, and with compassion. Did you ever have a music teacher or coach who never seemed satisfied, no matter how well you played? If that person directed those elevated standards to you in an encouraging and inspiring way, always offering advice for improvement, chances are that she was working to help you develop a healthy ethic of high achievement.

Perfectionistic concerns, however, can have negative effects. In fact, the artistic pursuit of perfection can be one of the greatest psychological stressors for a high-achieving musician. With this type of perfectionism, we are never happy with our performance. We fear negative evaluation and are overly concerned with mistakes and flaws. Sometimes this involves an excessively competitive outlook, whether or not the competition is real. It is not uncommon for this sort of performer to slip into an all-or-nothing mindset: Either it was flawless (I won), or it was awful (I lost). There is a strong correlation between this negative form of perfectionism and general feelings of anxiety; musicians who identify as worrywarts might reflect to see if this describes them. With perfectionistic concerns, performers will focus intensely on themselves, rather than on the task at hand. It is easier for them to berate themselves on what they were not able to accomplish ("I *should* have been able to . . ."), than to assess their performances with mindful objectivity.

Activity: Do you experience perfectionistic tendencies? If so, try to identify if those are positively associated with striving or negatively associated with concerns. For those times when you are optimistic, acknowledge the healthy thoughts that propel you toward high achievement. For more negative mindsets, write out how you might change your perspective or your habits to be more helpful. You might refocus on your goals rather than on your talents or abilities. You may choose to identify and dispute irrational thoughts with healthier beliefs. You might see if you can mentally distance yourself from the part of you that performs, and direct your attention to the music instead. Deconstructing unhealthy forms of perfectionism does not happen overnight, but awareness of your own tendencies can be a positive step in the right direction.

Dealing With Distractions

The art of knowing is knowing what to ignore.—Jalal ad-Din Rumi

---

Activity: Think about a past or upcoming performance. List five possible distractions that have happened to you before or during a practice or performance or that could possibly happen in the future. These can include distracting situations, events, or thoughts. For each distraction, write out a strategy for how you can refocus yourself. Plan ahead. For each possible situation, what will be the best action for you to take?

Mindfulness equally embraces positive expectations and possible challenges. This exercise invites you to think realistically about minor disturbances, and imagine how you might handle each situation. Distractions may be subtle or obvious, internal or external. Audible interferences are common for musicians. You might hear a sound from the audience such as a sneeze, a child talking, or someone slowly removing a piece of candy from an impenetrable space-age wrapper. Even your fellow musicians can offer distracting sounds in the form of squeaks, missed notes, or loud page turns. Other distractions might be visible, depending on what you might see in your peripheral vision or even in your direct line of sight. Once, during a student degree recital, I watched a security guard walk *across the stage* and out the side door. The student was so focused she never even noticed him! More likely visual distractions might include a flash from a camera or a flickering stage light. Kinesthetic distractions might occur if the temperature is uncomfortable, if your clothes are tight, or if you are sore.

Small distractions can become very large mental obstacles if we don't refocus quickly. I have seen pages of music blow onto the floor, drumsticks fly out of hands, strings snap, cufflinks fall off, and choristers faint on the risers. The point is that life happens, and musicians can be so prepared that no surprise seems like a calamity. What would you do if you heard an audience member have a coughing fit in the front row? You could silently seethe with anger, you could glare at the offender with your best stink eye, you could silently laugh with compassion, or you could let it fade into the dim periphery of your awareness. (The concert pianist Alfred Brendel once stopped playing in the middle of a recital, turned to face the audience, and scolded, "Either you stop coughing or I stop playing!" But one can really get away with that only when one is Alfred Brendel.)

If you are attracted to the idea of anticipating and navigating unexpected events, you might enjoy exploring a sport psychology concept called *simulation training* or *adversity simulation*. The idea is to ask a trusted friend to distract you purposefully, yet realistically, as you practice performing. A teacher friend of mine practices this with his students when they are in the final stages of recital preparation. While they play, he will loudly crunch on an apple, turn the studio lights on and off, or "accidentally" drop a book on the floor. This game of distractions isn't for everyone, but it can be a fun way to practice various mindfulness skills.

Situational Control

> *The mind that is not baffled is not employed. The impeded stream is the one that sings.*—Wendell Berry

---

Activity: Imagine a recent recital or ensemble performance. Which parts of that experience were within your control? Which parts of that experience were not within your control? How can you best focus on those things that you can control and accept or let go of everything else?

Mindful awareness of situational control can be powerfully freeing, because you can learn to stop worrying about circumstances that are beyond your control. For example, you can't often control the temperature of the room or concert hall, the acoustics, or the etiquette of the audience. You can't control if your chair wobbles, if a firetruck passes by, or if a stage light starts to buzz. These examples may seem obvious, but what is not always so obvious is that it doesn't help if you become irritated or distracted.

One time I was obliged to perform on a piano with a ridiculously squeaky damper pedal. Every time my foot went down, it created a long, loud squeak, and every time my foot came back up, it created a shorter, softer squeak. At first I tried to shift my foot around, then I tried to adjust the speed and depth of the pedal's descent. However, nothing I did made any difference to subdue the chorus of *SQUEEEEAK squeak SQUEEEEAK squeak*. I suddenly realized that my preoccupation with the pedal had caused me not to hear the entire first page of my music.

To this day, I couldn't tell you how I played that first page. At that point, I had no choice but to let it go, because there was nothing I could do. I returned my focus to the music I was playing (later nicknamed the sonata for piano and squeak), and finished the concert. To my disbelief, I found out later that some audience members hadn't even noticed the squeak.

What situations, then, are truly within your control? Most of these involve the quality of your preparation, including your practice, organization, and time management. You can control how often, and how well, you rehearse for an upcoming event. You can control the number of times you perform in front of other people in order to work out the rough spots ahead of time. You can control how you practice mindfulness, creative imagery, or any of the other skills presented in this book. You can usually control how, when, and how long you warm up before an event. And, with practice, you can also learn to control how you react to surprises and challenges. It is easy to forget that, during a performance, memory lapses and missed notes are not usually within your control. Assuming that you have practiced well and are extremely prepared, there's no way to anticipate whether you will accidentally forget part of the lyrics to a song or turn a page early. But you have some control over how you handle mistakes, how you get back on track, and what sort of broad artistic picture you present to your audience.

You will find a worksheet for this activity on the companion website (⊕ item 8.9).

Mindful Focusing

Concentration is the secret of strength.—Ralph Waldo Emerson

Many musicians would like to improve their ability to maintain concentration. Performers are notoriously worried about their minds wandering during a concert or getting back on track quickly if something goes wrong. Often we tell ourselves to focus or pay attention, but what exactly are we focusing on? The act of practicing focus cues in advance is another form of mindful awareness.

I believe two things about musicians and focusing. The first is that we can't possibly maintain a single point of focus during a very long piece of music or for an entire concert. The mind simply doesn't work like that; it needs to relax or wander every now and then if possible. The second is that, when under pressure and without advance planning, the human mind will most frequently drift toward negative thoughts or reactions. The ability to discern danger is a biological strength that keeps us safe from harm, but that also enables us to identify flaws more easily than successes. If a focus plan emphasizes positive attributes or desired outcomes, we can learn to identify the points at which more or less focus is needed in a piece of music. Since we cannot stay focused indefinitely, a point of focus should be something that gently brings us back to the present when our minds wander. This is a musical form of meditation.

Many people use single words or short affirmations as their points of focus. I once observed that one of my students had written "Triceratops" at a point in her Prokofiev piece. When I asked her about it, she laughed and said, "Oh, that's to remind me to think of this part as very heavy and lumbering, like a clumsy dinosaur." A focus cue does not have to make sense to anyone else, because it is yours alone. Other musicians might prefer to use an imagined image, a part of the body, or an external object to focus on. If I am playing a piece of impressionistic French music, for example, I might like to direct my attention to a mental image of one of Monet's paintings. A violinist might prefer to choose a visual focal point on the fingerboard or scroll of her instrument. Another musician may prefer to feel the core of his body as a tool for centering. I once had a friend who carried a little plush frog around in her instrument case for good luck. She would hide the frog on stage, usually out of the sight of the audience, but in a place where she could look at it if she wanted to. At first I thought it was just a cute and silly idea, but when we performed chamber music together, I found myself looking forward to seeing the little frog. While I'm not suggesting that you rush out to purchase your own magical power frog, it may be that a special or meaningful object can work well as a healthy point of focus.

Activity: Create a plan of focus for a specific piece of music that you are preparing. This might take the form of an abstract visual map, or you may wish to mark in the music itself. Where are the most important parts of the piece, when you need to focus the most? Often these are right before an important solo, climax, or coda. However, they can also anticipate the most poignant or deeply expressive parts of a piece. For each spot that you identify, write a word or short phrase that describes your desired point of focus. Once you decide on these, see if you can find easier places in the music where your mind can intentionally relax a little, with the idea that you will never wander too far away. After several practice sessions of playing or singing the piece of music, notice if it helps to have those planned focus spots. Tweak them if necessary.

You will find a worksheet and an example for this activity on the companion website (⊕ item 8.10).

If the idea of planning peaks and valleys of focus doesn't appeal to you, you might consider dividing your music into sections and assigning each section an expressive phrase or reminder to capture your attention. You can still mark the most important focus points if you wish, but you can also designate a different personality, character, color, memory, or feeling to the different sections. Your focus will shift depending on where you are in the music, but the cue will always be vivid, specific, and easy to return to if your mind wanders.

Activity: Imagine the day of a big performance, and plan out general focus cues for different times of the day. What will you focus on the morning of the performance? What about when you are standing backstage? When you are performing, where will you direct your attention? What will you concentrate on when the performance is over, and you are assessing yourself? It might help to think of gradually narrowing your point of focus throughout the day. You might imagine the shape of an hourglass, with a broader focus at the top and bottom, both before and after the performance, and very narrow and specific points of focus in the middle of or during the actual event.

You will find a worksheet and an example for this activity on the companion website (⊕ items 8.11 and 8.12).

If you create specific performance cues for various points throughout the day, your mind is less likely to entertain negative or anxious thoughts about the concert. And if it does, you can gently guide it back to your positive focus cues.

Emergency Refocusing Cues

My barn having burned to the ground, I can now see the moon.
—Chinese proverb

Let's face it, not every performance will be free of problems. Smaller mistakes and distractions can be relatively easy to manage, but more serious problems can trigger mental sirens and flashing lights. At times when we are completely thrown off guard, it is helpful to have a mental arsenal of attentional cues to get back on track.

In this activity, you will create specific focusing cues to internalize and pull out like an insurance card when needed. It is always helpful to prepare a speedy course of action for getting back on track. I advocate a three-step process:

1. Acknowledge and accept the mistake or distraction.
2. Relax and return your attention to the present moment.
3. Mentally repeat a refocusing cue.

In real time, these three steps unfold within the span of 1 or 2 seconds. Some of the most powerful mindfulness concepts are represented here: acceptance, nonjudging, letting go, and ultimately reengaging with the present moment. Of course, you may prefer a slightly different method than the one I am suggesting. Just keep in mind that it should be a very quick process that includes a refocusing cue. Since time is of the essence here, an abbreviated (one-word) cue can be very beneficial. You might use "steady" for "calm and steady, back on track," or perhaps "power" for "remember that you are a powerful communicator." In the previous activity, my student might have thought "Triceratops" to direct her attention away from the mistake and back to the character of the piece. Or, you may prefer to imagine images or symbols as refocusing cues.

> *Activity:* Create a personally meaningful emergency focus cue to use when something goes awry on stage. This could be a very general cue that can be used with any music, in most performance venues, or it could be specific to one event or piece. Periodically repeat this cue to yourself as you practice, particularly when you feel your mind start to wander.

Performance Essentials Kit

Be prepared.—Tom Lehrer

> *Activity:* The week before a big performance, make a list of all the items you will need to take with you. Assemble a little performance essentials kit using whatever container is most convenient for you: music case, tote bag, or metal Scooby-Doo lunchbox. What items will you include?

You may be thinking, what is this activity doing in a book about mindfulness? Don't forget that organization and advance planning, even down to the smallest details, all lead to mindful awareness. When you are about to leave to go to the airport for an important trip, you probably don't wait to start packing until 10 minutes before the taxi arrives. Every performance requires mindful preparation, down to the details of your attire and transportation. And yet, musicians often forget to put together an essentials kit until the very last minute.

Some of the items on your list may include essential gear, printed music, reeds, amplifier, water, etc. Additionally, many professionals have their own personal performance "emergency kit" that they carry with them to concerts. Depending on your situation, this might include a pack of tissues, an emergency sewing kit, safety pins, nail clippers, buttons, bandages, cough drops, headache medication, a handkerchief, even gloves for cold hands. You can use clear nail polish to mend stocking runs, or laundry dryer sheets to combat sudden static cling in your hair or clothes. I have one gentleman friend who gleefully repairs all wardrobe malfunctions with strips of duct tape. I knew another pianist who perspired so much that he kept a stick of antiperspirant in his performance kit and would glide it over the backs of his hands to keep them dry! Perhaps you will need to have extra strings, reeds, or mallets. It is helpful to imagine what, if anything, might go wrong that you would want to be able to fix quickly. Once you assemble your little kit, you can take it to every performance.

You will find a template for this activity on the companion website (⊕ item 8.13).

Performance Game Plan

Prepare while others are daydreaming.—William Arthur Ward

Activity: Think about an upcoming recital or gig. Write out a detailed plan, in the form of a timeline, for the day before and the day of your performance. Schedule in all of your practice and warm-up times, and include errands, meals, and sleep. Be sure to include quiet time to breathe, focus, and meditate or practice mental imagery.

When musicians take the time to plan logistics in advance, it frees them up to focus on their music rather than scrambling at the last minute to get things done. Some performances require a dress rehearsal or sound check, but some do not. If you are the coordinator of an event, your errand list may be significantly longer, and you may wish to create a timeline for the week leading up to the performance. Organizing a concert may include printing programs, planning a reception, arranging for piano tunings, setting up the stage or performance area, moving instruments, adjusting lighting, and delegating responsibilities. Do you need to bring the address of the performance venue, directions, or a contact number? Do you need to plan ahead to arrange transportation or find parking? Will you need cash or any sort of identification? A good checklist is a mindful performer's best friend.

You will find a template for this activity on the companion website (⊕ item 8.14).

Closely related to your performance game plan is an effective preperformance routine that works well for you. This would outline what you do 1 or 2 hours before a performance, including the few moments before you walk out on stage. Experienced performers are often able to describe the exact details of their preperformance routine. For others, it might take a little bit of trial and error to see what works best. Some musicians prefer to keep to themselves before a concert, while others appreciate the distraction of friends or even their small children. Some people know what they prefer to eat before a performance, or they know what will upset their stomachs. You may prefer to warm up for only 10 minutes, or you may like to practice mindfully for a longer period of time.

Adhering to a consistent preperformance routine is not superstitious if you believe that you are the only one who controls your successes.

Activity: Write out a preperformance routine that works well for you or that you believe will serve you well in the near future. Don't forget to include the imagery, affirmations, or focus techniques that you like to use. After each performance, assess what worked and what didn't work, and revise your plan for the next concert.

You will find a worksheet and an example for this activity on the companion website (⊕ item 8.15).

Postperformance Assessment

If you don't know where you are going, you'll end up someplace else.
—Yogi Berra

Regular assessment is an essential yet often overlooked component of mindful performance. This is somewhat ironic, of course, since assessment assumes evaluation and mindfulness emphasizes nonjudgment. Nevertheless, we can learn to critique ourselves in an objective and compassionate manner. How you evaluate each performance will determine how you prepare for your next performance. Remember that the mental skills required for a performance are quite different from the mental skills required for a practice session or rehearsal. Likewise, a performance mindset is different from a practice mindset. When we practice, we necessarily engage in a great deal of self-critiquing and problem solving. We are usually not in the spotlight, so we are somewhat less concerned with issues of focus, confidence, and performance anxiety. Public performances demand a certain degree of courage, trust, and acceptance. Keep this in mind as you assess your performances, and make sure that you are able to prioritize your goals, weaknesses, and successes mindfully.

When assessing the musical and psychological aspects of each performance, strive to view everything objectively as feedback, without attaching a positive or negative emotion to it. For example, "I missed one entrance but was able to recover" is more impartial than "I let everyone down by bombing that entrance." I believe it is helpful to put a short buffer of time in between the end of the performance and your assessment of it; either a few hours or a few days. It might also be helpful to assess yourself before you listen to a recording of the performance, and again after listening, to see if any of your observations changed.

> *Activity:* After a rehearsal or concert, write out a short but honest assessment of your performance. Review the goals you set for this event, your contract with yourself, your focus cues, or anything else you prepared beforehand, and consider those in your self-assessment. Acknowledge all of the positive aspects of the performance, and be honest about what you need to improve. Reflect on any mistakes or distractions that may have happened and your ability to refocus or recover from these. End with a few words of encouragement for yourself, as if you were your own student, and set a realistic goal for your next performance. Be sure to keep a copy of this assessment, so that you can compare your progress from one performance to the next.

If you aren't quite sure how to begin, you may wish to complete some of these statements as part of your assessment:

> The three best aspects of my performance were . . .
> Next time, I will work to improve . . .
> The most helpful mental preparation included . . .
> The mindfulness skills I would like to work on include . . .
> These things worked for me . . .
> These things did not work for me . . .
> Today I learned . . .
> I truly believe . . . .

You will find a template for this activity on the companion website (⊕ item 8.16).

***

Oscar Wilde once wrote, "To look at a thing is very different from seeing it." The activities in this chapter, whether focused on thoughts, emotions, behaviors, or habits, all have in common the ultimate goal of self-awareness. The ability to see clearly, with compassionate objectivity, is the greatest skill any human can develop. There is another perspective, however, that involves shifting your mindful gaze from what *is* to what *can be*. The next group of activities will help you develop a clear vision of personal and professional success and well-being.

9 THE MINDFUL VISIONARY

MORE PRACTICAL APPLICATIONS FOR LONG-TERM SUCCESS

> If you want the tree to grow, it won't help to water the leaves. You have to water the roots. —Thích Nhất Hạnh

We can choose to guide our awareness to the present moment or to project it instead into the future. Without a clear and mindful vision of our dreams, it will be much harder to make progress toward those professional and personal desires. Becoming a visionary requires only quiet reflection, unrestricted imagination, and a bit of courageous mental risk-taking. This chapter will help develop mental flexibility as you practice observing the present moment, solving problems creatively, and envisioning a fulfilling future.

Some of these exercises require little more than your own attention to your aspirations. For those activities, I recommend that you stop reading, close your eyes or look out the window, and give your imagination free rein. In other words, don't feel obligated to multitask as you read. Other activities involve a written component. For those, I cannot recommend strongly enough that you write or type out your reflections and answers, rather than regarding them only superficially as you read. Study after study confirms that composing your dreams and objectives in writing will greatly enhance your chance of achieving them.

These activities were developed to be fun, imaginative, and deeply personal. You don't have to share your responses with anyone, and you may prefer to let your ideas develop quietly in your mind and heart for a period of time. I encourage you to reflect and respond to these in a way that speaks to your own personality and ambitions. Or, as the poet Billy Collins says, "Write the poem only you can write."

Passion, Purpose, and Core Values

> *A musician must make music, an artist must paint, a poet must write,*
> *if he be at peace with himself. What a man can be, he must be.*
> —Abraham Maslow

Why did you choose to be a musician? What ignites your greatest creative passion? What drives you to continue doing what you do? No matter how many years you have been making music, there must have been something that led you to it or that sustains you when things get tough.

Purpose

Activity: Write out your own statement of purpose. Why do you love what you do? Why do you *do* what you do? First identify three reasons why you are passionate about music. (If you can list more than three, great. If you find only one big reason, that is enough.) Then, use these to help you articulate your purpose as a musician. If you are having some trouble getting started, you can finish one of these sentences:

> I am a musician because . . .
> I perform music because . . .
> I am passionate about music because . . .
> What really drives and inspires me is . . .
> My calling is to . . .
> My objective as a musician is . . . .

Values

Activity: What are your most cherished values as a musician? Think of those standards or qualities that you hold in the highest regard. When you focus on these, they keep you motivated, and they direct your energy and attention toward what is most important to you. What desired qualities act as your own guiding compass? I invite you to finish any of the following sentences.

> As a musician, I treasure these things most deeply:
> The most important thing I can achieve as a performer is:
> What I value most in other musicians is:

You may choose to list four or five of the values that mean the most to you. These can be single words ("inspiration") or short phrases ("the ability to communicate expressively") if you prefer, rather than lengthy explanations.

Mission Statement

> *Activity:* Write out your own personal mission statement. This is different from a statement of purpose, because a statement of purpose is often a description of *what is,* or a reason for doing something. A mission statement is an action-oriented declaration of *what will be,* according to your personal calling. To construct a powerful mission statement, first identify a number of action verbs that describe your intent, your strengths, or your desired successes. Then think about who will benefit from your mission. Finally, select a number of nouns that represent your guiding values, perhaps distilled from the previous activity.

If you have trouble getting started, here are a few short word banks to serve as examples. Feel free to use any of these or create your own.

Verbs: inspire, educate, communicate, entertain, affirm, connect, create, discover, share, unite, heal, impact, move.

People: audience, students, friends, family, community, myself, mentors, listeners, the world, musicians, artists, humanity.

Values: insight, creativity, fun, freedom, artistry, innovation, authenticity, change, passion, justice, love, awareness, fame, pleasure, success, balance, happiness, beauty, fulfillment, faith, accomplishment, peace, adventure, self-actualization.

Once you have a strong list of words that speak to you, you can begin to construct your mission statement. You might choose to structure it in one of these ways:

> My mission is to [verbs] [people] who seek [values].
> My mission is to [verbs] [people] in order to bring about [values].
> I [verbs] for the purpose of [values].

Of course, you may construct your personal mission statement any way you like. One of the greatest values of having such a statement, for me, is that I can refer to it for guidance when I am struggling to make a decision. Reaffirming my mission can help me figure out if my choice will serve my personal vision of the future.

If your answers to any of the activities in this section helped you to feel more focused, empowered, or optimistic, you may find it helpful to post something where you will see it frequently. For example, you might paste your purpose or mission statement in the front cover of your journal, or keep them on an index card in your instrument case. You may choose to review these when you are feeling stressed out or pessimistic.

You will find worksheets for these three activities on the companion website (⊕ items 9.1 and 9.2).

Present Moment Check-Up

We have only today. Let us begin.—Mother Teresa

In Chapter 7, we explored the important role of mindfulness practice in self-awareness and music performance. This short and easy activity can help train your mind to refocus in the present moment if you become distracted during the day, or during a performance. You can also combine this activity with One Conscious Breath, described in Chapter 5.

Activity: Five to ten times a day, when you remember to do so, pause whatever you are doing and direct your awareness to the present moment for 20 seconds or more. Notice the world around you, including your internal experiences. Where are you, and what are you doing? What do you see and hear around you? What does your world smell like, right now? What were you thinking about, just before this? Was your mind focused in the past, the present, or the future? How does your body feel right now? What is your mood? Can you answer these questions without judgment, basking in the pure acceptance of right now?

The point of this activity is not to critique yourself or change any of your thoughts or behaviors. The objective is simply to come back to the present moment from wherever you happen to be. If you are able to set an app or alarm to chime softly or vibrate at random intervals throughout the day (for example, every 2 hours or so), you will not need to remind yourself to pursue this activity. The more you practice random awareness of the present moment, the easier it is to become quickly centered in that moment of consciousness.

Noticing Out Loud

There's only now, there's only here.—Mimi, *Rent*

Activity: This is a more active and audible version of the previous activity. When practical, stop whatever you are doing and take 1 minute or more to observe your present surroundings. Communicate each observation out loud, with a sentence that begins, "Right now I am noticing . . . " or "Right now I feel . . . . " These may include things that you are seeing, hearing, smelling, thinking, or feeling.

This activity works best when you are by yourself, obviously, but can also be fun with a group of like-minded friends who are willing to play along. If you prefer to try this as a group activity, you may choose to take turns as each person offers an observation. When we speak our thoughts aloud, we are obliged to articulate them with greater specificity and clarity. We choose precise words to describe our perceptions, and we are compelled to offer them in a linear fashion, one thought after another. This is very different from the experience of mentally noticing the present moment and can help develop our skills of awareness.

Musical Bucket List

The highest and most beautiful things in life are not to be heard about, nor read about, nor seen but, if one will, are to be lived.—Søren Kierkegaard

Activity: Create a musical bucket list for yourself. Write freely, and without too much critical thought. A bucket list might include future repertoire, performances, venues, collaborations, creative projects, inventions, or other achievements. Include easy, short-term items as well as bigger dreams that might take many years to fulfill. Try not to restrict your own imagination. The list can be as long as you want! Once you have finished, you may wish to edit and organize your list in a different way. For example, you might separate some of your items into different categories or you might arrange them in order of how important they are to you.

A personal bucket list is beneficial in many ways. It can help you articulate your dreams and desires, it can encourage you to discover and prioritize what is most important to you, and it can act as a sort of guiding compass for your subconscious mind. I possess several bucket lists, most of them hastily scribbled in the back of old notebooks. Several times in my life, when I have come across an old list that I completely forgot about, I have been surprised at how many of the items I managed to complete. Of course, I don't personally recommend this haphazard strategy. It would be much more advantageous to have a fun, official bucket list that you refer to every few months or so. You will find it enjoyable to add items to the list, and to shuffle others around, as your experiences and preferences change.

After you spend a period of time dreaming about your future projects, it is helpful to return your attention to the present moment. We can easily become lost in our tantalizing futures that, as you will recall, don't exist. The practice of setting future goals and then returning to the present with patience and acceptance can feel disconcerting at first, but can ultimately be very healing. If, for example, I have envisioned my dream job but am currently unemployed, I can learn to witness my present situation with compassion and nonjudgment. I can practice entertaining my dreams while sitting in a place where I'm not yet there, and I can choose to acknowledge and set aside any unwanted thoughts about my current situation. I can appreciate my own life process as it slowly unfolds.

Best Performance Memory

Be a first rate version of yourself, not a second rate version of someone else.
—Judy Garland

Activity: Think back to one of your very best performances. Write a paragraph about how you felt and how well you played or sang. What made this performance so great? Can you remember the specific thoughts and feelings that you experienced before, during, and after this event? Keep this reflective paragraph in a place where you can easily review it before your next performance.

Top athletes strive to keep their peak performances in recent memory. They will often review video recordings of some of their greatest public achievements or triumphs. When it comes to building or maintaining self-confidence, this process is more advantageous than ruminating about disappointing performances or other bad experiences. By remembering and reliving their best efforts, these athletes stay mindfully focused on how well they know they can do. Why don't more musicians utilize their best memories for energy and motivation?

I suggest you write out this memory using either past or present tense, whichever you prefer. Try to recall all of the little details that made this performance special. These might be related to your personal habits that day ("I took a nap earlier, and I felt refreshed and energized"), the details of your preperformance experience ("Laughing with my friends backstage really settled me down"), or moments of the performance itself ("I was surprised to realize how much I was enjoying myself"). Be sure to include the details of your best internal dialogue. Maybe the critical little voice inside your head was unusually subdued. Or maybe you felt more prepared than usual. Perhaps the reaction of the audience or a compliment from a respected musician triggered even more positive thoughts and feelings. As you review this reflection periodically, you may begin to remember even more details as the memory becomes clearer.

Sometimes a musician will ask me, "What if I don't have (or can't remember) a peak performance?" or "What if I experienced negative thoughts or feelings even during my best performance?" My suggestion would be to focus on the most satisfying aspects of a past performance. As you continue to strengthen your mental skills, this sort of exercise will become easier and easier. If you honestly can't think of a great performance that inspired you, fear not. The best course of action will be to imagine a possible future performance, as in the next activity.

Best Performance Imagery

Imagination is not an empirical or superadded power of consciousness, it is the whole of consciousness as it realizes its freedom.—Jean-Paul Sartre

This is an abbreviated version of the Imagery for Peak Performance process described in Chapter 6. You can try this unguided, spontaneous visualization activity at any time, without much advance preparation.

You may find that you want to tweak your imagery practice as you get closer to a performance event. You may wish to imagine some elements in even greater detail, or you might choose to be more specific about your personal goals. Feel free to experiment, so that you can learn what works best for your mind. If this activity interests you, but you find it difficult to stay focused or to visualize what you want, I suggest you review some of the preparatory activities discussed in Chapter 6. If you can daydream or fantasize, you can become very successful with creative imagery.

Activity: Find a quiet place where you will not be bothered. You may choose to sit or recline comfortably. If you are worried that you will fall asleep or miss an appointment, set a quiet alarm for 10, 15, or 20 minutes, depending on how long you wish to practice this activity. Close your eyes or direct your gaze downward, and allow your mind and body to settle. You may wish to focus your attention on your breathing for a minute or two as you gradually relax. Begin to imagine the best-possible scenario for an upcoming performance. Include as many details as possible, and as many of your imagined senses as you wish. Remember to affirm all of the positive thoughts and feelings you want to experience before, during, and after this performance. Be realistic but optimistic!

Mental Performance Script

Until you make the unconscious conscious, it will direct your life and you will call it fate.—Carl Jung

---

Activity: Using Chapter 6 as a guideline, compose a detailed performance imagery script for a single piece of repertoire. This would ideally be a piece of music that you plan to perform in the future, but it can be anything. Include the positive thoughts and feelings you want to experience before, during, and after the performance. Using affirmations or first-person statements, be specific about the best-possible internal dialogue you want to experience.

Writing an account of your visualization is a very different sort of exercise than simply closing your eyes and imagining a peak performance, because it requires you to choose your words and phrases very deliberately. Begin your narrative with your location right before the upcoming performance. Describe how you want to feel and what sorts of encouraging thoughts would be drifting through your mind. Write a detailed plan for your performance itself, including your experiences at the beginning, in the middle, and at the end of the piece. Remember to incorporate the situations that you will experience immediately after the performance, such as a social event. Conclude with a few sentences that reflect your feelings toward the entire experience, including some positive affirmations about yourself and your performance ability. This does not have to be a formal writing project; your writing style can reflect your personality and the way you normally speak. It can be inspirational, humorous, or quietly reflective.

When you have finished writing out your imagery script, read it out loud. See if it sounds natural to you, as if it were coming from your own mind and heart. Edit or rewrite certain passages as needed. Keep this narrative in a convenient place, where you can access it and read it anytime you want to feel motivated or inspired. You can tweak this narrative or compose a new one for any upcoming event or performance.

Activity: If you are having a hard time getting started, you may wish to begin your script by using this template, filling in the blanks with your own words of positive expectation.

I am ready to perform. As I look around at my surroundings where I am waiting, I can see ____. I am also aware of ____. The temperature feels ____, and I can hear ____. I may even be able to smell the familiar scent of ____ where I happen to be standing. I am wearing ____, and I acknowledge that I look very nice. I am pleased to observe that my body feels ____, and my thoughts are ____. I notice that my hands feel ____, my shoulders feel ____, and my breathing is ____. In the past, I may have felt a little bit of ____, but now I realize that I also feel ____ about my upcoming performance. I know that I am well prepared, and I'm confident that I will be able to ____, and that everything is going to be just fine. As I walk out to perform, I feel ____. When I look out at the audience, I can see ____ and I feel ____. Before I begin my music, I take a short moment to focus on ____. As I begin to play, I am pleased to observe that my body feels ____ and my thoughts are ____. This is an enjoyable and exciting experience, because I know that my greatest strengths are ____. When I finish my performance, I can see and hear ____. I feel very positive about my ability to ____. As I assess my performance, I realize that I successfully ____. I am thankful to have had this experience, and I feel a sense of deep satisfaction and peace.

You will find this template on the companion website (⊕ item 9.3).

Guided Imagery Recording

If one is lucky, a solitary fantasy can transform one million realities.
—Maya Angelou

Some musicians enjoy engaging in a new imagery activity each day, while others prefer to relax and listen to a recording. A prerecorded script is especially helpful if your mind wanders frequently during your mental practice. In a guided visualization, you have the opportunity to listen to an external voice rather than to your own internal mind. You can also drift into a more deeply relaxed state of consciousness if you wish. As you listen to the recordings included on the companion website (⊕ items 6.1–6.4), you can experience the difference between a guided visualization and a spontaneous self-directed visualization.

One benefit of making your own recording is that you can create a very individual experience, but you can also listen without worrying about controlling the activity as you practice. A personalized recording, downloaded to a portable listening device, can be a very convenient tool to have on hand. If you don't care to hear the sound of your own voice, you can always bribe a silky-voiced friend to read and record your script.

Activity: Using the performance imagery script you composed in the previous activity, record yourself reading it out loud. This does not need to be a professional-quality recording; a smartphone or handheld recorder often works just fine. Read slowly, pausing more often than you normally would and longer than you normally would, between sentences. Wait slightly longer after important affirmations to give them time to sink in. Practice listening to your recording when you are very relaxed, and allow your own voice to guide you in the imagery exercise.

Multiple-Perspective Imagery

Don't only practice your art, but force your way into its secrets.
—Ludwig van Beethoven

When we visualize ourselves performing at a particular venue, we can imagine ourselves from a number of different perspectives. When we think from a first-person perspective, we might imagine ourselves performing, looking at the music or out at the audience through our own eyes. If we imagine ourselves from a third-person perspective, we might shift our awareness to the audience, as if we were watching ourselves perform from a distance.

From a first-person perspective, you can include the most positive and constructive thoughts, feelings, and sensations that you have when you are performing music. A third-person perspective allows you the opportunity to "observe" outstanding form, technique, poise, and stage presence as if from the viewpoint of another person. This perspective can take many visual angles. You can imagine that you see yourself from the front or side, as an audience member might see you. You can imagine watching the back of yourself as you perform. You can even imagine gazing down on yourself from the top, as if from a bird's-eye view.

Some people are quite adept at this type of visualization, while others find it difficult to switch from one perspective to another. The most important thing is that you practice "seeing" yourself from different angles or points of view, even if you don't feel very proficient at this technique. If it helps, you can imagine that you are a tiny insect, able to fly around and observe the stage from a variety of perspectives. Or, you can imagine a series of television cameras, placed around the stage, zooming in and out from a number of different angles.

Activity: Find a quiet, comfortable place, and allow your mind and body to become relaxed. Begin to imagine a positive scenario for an upcoming performance. Consider what it will feel like to be inside your body as you perform: what you will see, how your mind will be focused, and all the exhilarating feelings associated with performing well in front of other people. After a while, shift your focus to imagine that you are in the audience, sitting in the very back of the room. Focus on the details of what it would be like to watch the musician, you, give an outstanding performance. Perhaps notice the confidence, poise, and technical mastery that you might observe as an audience member. What positive thoughts and reactions might this audience member experience? Then, shift your awareness to imagine that you are sitting in the first row, much closer to the performer, or perhaps from another side of the room. What do you observe from this angle? Have fun switching your imagined perspective any way you like, perceiving your outstanding performance through the eyes of another, and occasionally coming back to being yourself on stage.

Spotlight Imagery and Practice

The more boundless your vision, the more real you are.—Deepak Chopra

This guided imagery activity requires less visualizing and more hands-on practicing with your music. I find it helpful to imagine the experience first, however, before practicing it in real life.

Coaches and sport psychologists frequently use the metaphor of a spotlight or flashlight to describe methods of focusing. Imagine that you are shining a flashlight in a darkened room. Although you might be vaguely aware of all of your surroundings, you can see clearly only those objects that fall within the beam of the flashlight. It is easy to pay more attention to objects inside the beam, while more or less disregarding everything else. At any time, you can direct the flashlight elsewhere, shifting your awareness to something else. To continue this metaphor, you can hold a flashlight very close to an object, and the circle of light becomes small and intensely bright. Or, if you stand back and shine a flashlight on an object farther away, the circle of light will be much larger and more diffused. A spotlight on stage can work in the same way.

If we imagined that we possessed a similar attentional beam, we could choose to hold it steady or direct it elsewhere. This would be the opposite of allowing our focus to jump around randomly, depending on our own distractions or current state of mind. A metaphorical spotlight can follow a single item of focus, such as a line of music on a page. Or, it can shift from one object to another, as if to different faces in the audience, to other band members, internal affirmations, or reminders. Some theorists believe that our attention acts like a beam of light because it is always shining on something. In other words, we never really lose our focus; we simply allow our focus to shift to something else. The greatest benefit of the spotlight metaphor, in my opinion, is that we can learn to redirect our focus with more conscious control.

Attentional focus can be internal or external. Internal focus involves directing your attention to yourself, just as if you had shined a spotlight on your own thoughts, feelings, hopes, or fears. External focus might include paying attention to elements of the music, audience, or performance venue, as if you were shining the spotlight outward to various objects around you. Performing chamber music is a good example of positive external focus, because it is necessary to pay attention to your fellow musicians for effective visual cues and transitions. Internal focus would be most advantageous when you are about to express a very personal emotion in your music or when you need to pay attention to a specific movement of your body.

In addition to being internal or external, the quality of our focus can be broad or narrow, just as the metaphorical flashlight beam can shine on an object at close range or farther away. When you look out at your audience during a concert, you can see the general audience as a whole (broad), or you can zoom in on one particular person's face (narrow). It is possible, then, to categorize focus as being broad internal, broad external, narrow internal, or narrow external. Of course, this is a considerable oversimplification of how the mind works. In fact, the most important thing is not to obsess or fixate on how you are thinking, because one danger of the spotlight metaphor is that it can potentially lead to unhelpful overthinking or overanalyzing. It is best to think about the following activities as fun and informal experiments in mindful awareness.

> *Activity:* Imagine that you are performing one specific song or piece of music in the performance venue of your choice. See if you can casually shift your attention to the various modes of focus, from broad to narrow and back again, and from internal to external and back again. This will require conscious control of what you imagine you are thinking about, and where you imagine you are looking as you perform.

If you are performing from music, for example, see if you can envision the entire page of music (broad external focus) and then one specific note or beat (narrow external focus). If you are playing from memory at an instrument that requires your visual attention, such as a piano, imagine seeing the keyboard or instrument as a whole (broad external focus) and then the keys under or around one hand (narrow external focus). If you are singing or playing and looking out at the audience, congregation, or nightclub patrons, imagine the various ways you could pay attention to larger and smaller points of focus. Imagine, too, that you are able to shift your attention between broad and narrow *internal* objects of attention, depending on your thoughts and feelings. These examples might include perceiving the music or your feelings as a whole (broad internal focus), or focusing in on one specific thought or moment in the music (narrow internal focus).

Although this can be a challenge, see if you can discern when it might be beneficial to shift your attentional focus with conscious intent. If you struggle with performance anxiety, for example, focusing on a single neutral point on the wall above the audience (narrow external focus) might be helpful. Many nervous performers find that external focusing techniques can reduce self-critical thoughts when necessary. If you are struggling with a memory slip because your eyes became too fixated on your instrument or something else, it may help if you shift your focus away from the music and onto your own projected feelings of confidence or musical expression (broad internal focus) or look away in the distance for a brief time (broad external focus). If you become distracted by a noise in the audience, silently repeating a positive affirmation (narrow internal focus) may have a centering effect. Because every performer is different, it is impossible to anticipate or prescribe attentional techniques for every situation. Nevertheless, you can become more mindful of how best to direct your focus when needed.

Activity: When you are engaged in a routine activity that has nothing to do with music performance, practice this activity in a similar way. You might try it, for example, when you are driving your car. You could notice when your attention shifts from a gauge on the dashboard (narrow external), to the rearview mirror (also narrow external), to the view of the road or landscape in the distance (broad external), to remembering to take an upcoming exit (narrow internal). If you are cooking dinner, watching a football game, or taking a walk, you can easily practice this technique for a few short minutes.

Activity: The next time you run through a piece of music in the practice room, periodically become aware of the naturally changing quality of your focus. If you are able to, either during your practice or afterward, see if you can identify various moments of attention as being internal, external, broad, or narrow. Human attention is difficult to comprehend and categorize, but it can be helpful simply to become aware of how and when you prefer to focus at various times. Think about this for only a few moments, before eventually letting go of the activity.

A Letter to Your Critic

Behind every beautiful thing, there's been some kind of pain.—Bob Dylan

The practice of focusing on positive expectations can be tremendously beneficial. This is not always realistic, however, because the human condition is more like an emotional roller coaster. Learning to manage negative experiences mindfully is another important component of self-awareness.

The negative words of a critic, even when well intended, can echo in our minds for many years afterward. When we were children, these thoughtless words might have come from a guardian, a teacher, or another clueless or even mean-spirited person. As adults, we need and expect criticism in order to become better musicians, but the words can still sting. I try to live by the advice of Anne Lamott, who wrote, "You don't always have to chop with the sword of truth. You can point with it, too." In other words, you can offer even the harshest critique with kindness and compassion, if you choose your words wisely and constructively.

Unfortunately, many people (master teachers, adjudicators, newspaper critics, even family members) can be thoughtless, unkind, or just plain cruel in how they judge others. Sometimes they are mean in order to make themselves look more competent or respectable. Sometimes, instead of a specific truth ("That wasn't your best performance"), they offer an inaccurate or more personal generalization ("You aren't good enough" or "You'll never make it"). We are not always in a position to respond, so we bury their sharp words deep within us and try to move on as best we can. When we are having a bad day, however, those negative words can bubble up like poison in our minds.

Our critics come from all stages of our lives. Some of our critics are ghosts from the past, or imagined or assumed critics. Sometimes *we* are our worst critics, and that little ornery voice in our head is the main culprit. If you were to write a letter to one of your critics, to whom would you address it?

Activity: Write a letter in response to someone who has criticized you unfairly or unkindly. This can be someone who hurt you many, many years ago, or just yesterday. You may address it to a single person ("Dear Mrs. Muzgash"), to a group of people ("Dear Crappy and Disrespectful Audience Members from Last Night"), or to yourself ("Dear Mean Little Chatterbox Inside My Head"). In this letter, tell the recipient exactly what he or she said that was hurtful and how it made you feel. Describe and justify your anger, if it helps. Explain the impact that their negative words can have on other human beings. Perhaps offer a different way they could have expressed themselves toward you. Most important, stand up for yourself and offer a few empowering words about your hard work, talent, or determination. The closing part of your letter can be reconciliatory or not, whatever feels right to you.

It is important to remember that this is a letter you will *never* send, because the activity is for you alone. After you write it, you may choose to keep it, tear it up, or fold it into an origami turtle, but it is not to share. I should mention that although this activity is designed to address judgments related to your competence as a musician or creative artist, you could also write a letter to anyone else who criticized you unfairly. You might choose to respond to the stranger who made an offhand comment to you or to a politician or civic leader who offended you. It can be a great way to articulate your thoughts and assuage pain and anger. Afterward, just be sure to do something that returns your focus to the present moment: Play with your hamster, go out with some friends, or listen to some great music. The point is to validate the anger and let it go, not stew in it.

A colleague of mine decided to write a letter to her mother-in-law, a woman who would endlessly judge and correct my friend's parenting skills when she came to visit. Although my friend thankfully never sent the letter, she said the process of writing it really helped her sort out her feelings. She also came to realize that her mother-in-law was reacting out of fear and jealousy, because she lived in another country and did not feel like regular member of the family. In this example, rather than ending the letter in anger, it was best for my friend to end it with compassion and resolve ("I understand why you act this way, but I will also insist that you respect my boundaries").

Healthy Burn

Sorrow like rain makes roses and mud.—Austin O'Malley

Activity: Write out some hurtful thoughts and irrational beliefs that no longer serve you, and that you would like to let go. These can be past thoughts of your own worth as a person or musician, a mean-spirited criticism, or any other self-defeating ideas from your past.

When you are finished, read what you have written, and allow your-self to sit with these thoughts and feelings for several moments. See if you can acknowledge them with mindful compassion, per-haps sensing how they may have helped you develop self-awareness. Then, offer an affirmation to yourself that you are ready to let these ideas go, and fold or crumple the paper up. Light it on fire in a safe place, and allow it to completely incinerate. As you watch the paper burn, imagine that you are releasing these old thoughts and beliefs into the atmosphere, along with the smoke and flames.

A few years ago, a friend and I organized a similar activity for a group of music majors who were struggling with performance anxiety and self-confidence. After we wrote out our negative thoughts, we headed out-side to the picnic area near our music building. The sun was setting as we gathered around the charcoal grill and piled all of our papers in the middle. We took a moment of silence together before one of the students ignited the papers with a lighter. I was struck by how profound and pow-erfully meditative this activity was, for everyone involved. Even though it was chilly out, the students stood in meditative silence for a very long time, softly gazing at the pile of ashes in the grill long after the fire had extinguished itself. Afterward, one student said she felt as if a weight had been lifted from her shoulders.

This is one of my favorite New Year's Eve rituals, by the way. If you like, you can gather all of the thoughts, feelings, and events that you are ready to release in the new year, and burn these as a meditative activity. You can imagine that letting them go creates more room for healthy, self-empowering thoughts and behaviors, and you can write those down on a fresh sheet of paper if you wish.

Achievement Log

The little things? The little moments? They aren't little.—Jon Kabat-Zinn

The good thing about most musicians is that they are intensely self-critical and quick to identify and improve their own faults. The bad thing about most musicians is that they are intensely self-critical and quick to identify and improve their own faults. Creative artists do not often stop to pat them-selves on the back unless they win a big competition or earn a rave review.

Small accomplishments are often overlooked, and daily achievements are sometimes brushed aside as if they don't really matter in the large scheme of things. But they really do matter!

The world's top competitive athletes keep track of every achievement, every obstacle conquered, and every personal best record, in order to keep them inspired and focused on an upcoming goal. You can imagine that when you feel unmotivated, or when you're really having an off day in the practice room, reflecting on your past achievements can guide you back into a more optimistic mindset. Mindful awareness includes acknowledging and accepting the whole human experience, including the tiny accomplishments along the way.

Activity: In a separate section of your practice journal, or in a different computer file or app, begin a running achievement log. You may call it whatever you like: My Accomplishments, Victories, Random Awesomesauce, anything. For each entry, put the date and a short description of what you achieved. I would encourage you to think in terms of these three categories:
- Significant accomplishments
- Mini-victories
- Nonmusical achievements

Significant accomplishments will be the largest and most noticeable musical achievements for you. These might include conquering a difficult piece of music, mastering a particular skill, or accomplishing a performance goal such as a recital, audition, or studio recording. You might list challenging repertoire that you mastered, positive feedback that you received from someone you respect, or any personal musical breakthrough.

Mini-victories are the smaller achievements that you might overlook if you weren't mindfully documenting them. Some of these may seem small on the outside, but might symbolize part of a much larger accomplishment or an important mental shift. For example, one mini-victory might be remembering to take breaks during a long rehearsal to avoid fatigue and injury. Another might be expertly disguising a mistake or memory slip from your audience. If there is a behavior or mindset you have been working to improve, documenting your baby steps can be a valuable motivator, even if the little victory might be invisible to others. Years ago a good friend of mine, a professional jazz trombonist, aspired to memorize one new tune every week. The ability to play the melody and know the chord changes of one standard song might not seem like a massive accomplishment for someone in the music industry. Try to imagine, however, the *hundreds* of songs he can now play at the drop of a hat, at any time for any gig, 15 years later. (How do you build a castle? Brick by brick.)

Nonmusical achievements are important to document as well, especially if they affect your musicianship or overall happiness. What we do offstage affects how well we perform onstage. Some of these nonmusical achievements might be personal changes in behavior: Perhaps you got an extra hour of sleep last night, ordered a side salad instead of French fries, or made time for a yoga class. Some of these might be subtle but important psychological shifts: Perhaps you handled an annoying, inappropriate person with professionalism and grace, rather than losing your temper as usual. Maybe you finally worked up the courage to ask you-know-who out on a date. Maybe your plan of setting three alarm clocks finally got you to an early meeting on time. Perhaps you didn't look at your mobile device during a family gathering. Perhaps you practiced a guided imagery that you have been putting off for several days. Or maybe you tried something new, baked a baguette, fixed a squeaky door, finally beat your dad at poker, or didn't kill your favorite plant. Including even the silly-sounding victories in your achievement log can help create a mindful and balanced self-image.

You will find two templates for this activity on the companion website (⊕ items 9.4 and 9.5).

Mental Breaks and Mini-Rewards

All the colors I am inside have not been invented yet.—Shel Silverstein

---

Activity: Write out a list of personal mental breaks and mini-rewards. You may create two separate lists, if you prefer, although some of the items may overlap. Creative mental breaks would include a number of short, easy activities that you enjoy doing and that take your mind off your daily stresses. Small rewards are helpful to keep on hand for when you accomplish something large or small, or to help you avoid procrastination. Try to include a number of activities that are inexpensive, fun, and positive. You will never be too old for treats.

Here are some examples of mental breaks or mini-rewards:

- A few rounds of a favorite electronic game or puzzle
- A soothing hobby, such as knitting, woodworking, or gardening
- A guilty-pleasure magazine
- A cup or glass of your favorite beverage
- An activity originally intended for children, such as coloring books or Legos
- Puppy videos

It can be tricky to distinguish a break from a reward, since many of the items on your list can function either way. Sometimes, if I have been practicing for a long time, I will get distracted just before I am about to finish. For example, if I have just one task left to do, I will hear a message pop up on the phone that I forgot to turn off. Often, it is little more than a juicy bit of personal news or a cute cat video. My sudden desire to watch fluffy kitten shenanigans might be, at this point, far stronger than my desire to practice Bach for another 20 minutes. So, I need to make a choice. I can fool myself into thinking that opening that message might be a nice mental break, but the truth is that it would just be another distraction or means to procrastinate. Instead, I decide to make it a mini-reward. After I practice for 20 more minutes, I then congratulate myself by watching portly felines try to fit themselves into small cardboard boxes.

Most of the time, because I keep a list on my phone, I am not at a loss for a fantastic reward idea. My impressive collection of wine has already gotten out of hand, so I keep a wine wish list with me at all times. If my break or reward is a trip to the neighborhood wine store, I choose one favorite bottle from my list, and no more. If I were to buy them all at once, I would have no more wine rewards left to collect! (I would also have no more space left in my house.) It helps me to remember that one of the characteristics of good mental health, according to influential psychologist Albert Ellis, is a commitment to long-range hedonism.

We are much more likely to remain productive and focused if we have planned out a few engaging breaks and rewards, and if we use them judiciously. This component of mindfulness helps us practice conscious, deliberate control of our thoughts, impulses, and time.

Affirmations

> *People are like stained-glass windows. They sparkle and shine when the sun is out, but when the darkness sets in their true beauty is revealed only if there is light from within.*—Elisabeth Kübler-Ross

Unlike professional athletes, most musicians do not have skilled coaches to supervise their practice sessions or keep them inspired and focused. Good musicians are obliged to become their own qualified trainers. Establishing goal statements and affirmations can help with mindfulness training because it can teach us to redirect negative ideas into more constructive, helpful, and motivating thoughts when necessary.

In Chapter 6 we discussed the power of thought and the importance of focusing on what we desire, as opposed to fixating on what we do not want. Because the human mind very naturally gravitates toward the negative, positive goal-oriented thinking often requires more deliberate conscious intent. Meaningful affirmations are important because language is such a powerful tool, and we never really stop talking to ourselves.

Activity: Think of an upcoming performance, formal or informal, and write two or three short sentences of affirmation that express what you want to think, feel, or do. Be sure these sentences are optimistic but realistic, and construct them using first-person present tense. Try to avoid comparative statements in favor of those that foster personal satisfaction.

The following are some affirmations that have worked well for people I know, both amateur and professional musicians alike:

· My body feels the energy of positive anticipation.
· I am in control of my music, but free enough to let go.
· I feel comfortable and secure on stage.
· I am a powerful and genuine musician.
· I have nothing to prove.
· I am greater than this performance.
· I am eager to communicate something special.

- I love a new adventure.
- I embrace the unknown with positive expectation.

Once you compose an affirmation that really seems to resonate with you, write it on a card and tuck it into your music or instrument case. Or, post it on the wall where you often practice. The more you read the words or repeat them to yourself, the more they will find their way into your powerful subconscious mind.

Attitude of Gratitude

> *But tonight, the lion of contentment has placed a warm heavy paw on my chest.*
> —Billy Collins

What the heck does gratitude have to do with being a better performer? As it turns out, quite a lot. Psychologists have known for decades that cultivating an optimistic mindset creates stronger, more motivated, more resilient human beings. When we express appreciation for what we have in the present moment, we focus on abundance instead of lack. This can lead to increased energy, empathy, and well-being. In earlier chapters we discussed that mindset is a habit, and that habits can be reinforced or broken. Focusing on what we are grateful for, even the small things, can help retrain negative habits of thought. This type of mindful awareness also facilitates acceptance and self-compassion.

Activity: Plan to document one thing that you are thankful for, every day. You might choose to keep a separate gratitude journal, or you may prefer to use one of many mobile apps. Or, you might consider keeping a gratitude notebook by your bedside, writing down one entry each night before you go to sleep, or each morning before you hop out of bed. Either way, you will start or end your day mindfully, and on a positive note. One of my sport psychologist friends has his clients end each training session by finishing the sentence, "I'm thankful for ___." This is a great idea, because no matter how your practice or rehearsal goes, you can end on an appreciative note.

Sometimes, when we are going through a particularly difficult time, it may feel tiresome or pointless to try to think of things to be grateful for. There's nothing wrong with this, and I don't think it's very helpful to force any observations that don't feel natural. For me, the most beneficial solution in this case is to play the "pay it forward" game. Rather than focusing inward, you can direct your attention to other people, and do or say something that will give *them* the opportunity to feel gratitude. You might compliment a friend's appearance, double a restaurant server's tip, leave a piece of chocolate on someone's desk, or send an email of appreciation. I find that alternating moments of gratitude with random acts of kindness helps to keep my own life outlook in balance.

A Letter to Young You

The real you is still a little child that never grew up.—Don Miguel Ruiz

I mentioned in Chapter 7 that I sometimes pretend I am interacting with a 4-year-old version of myself, because it helps me to be mindful of my own self-talk. Although our bodies get older and our life experiences accumulate over the years, our inner consciousness is exactly the same as when we were children. It can be therapeutic to imagine that you reconnect with your younger self, creating a healing bridge between past and present. If this idea appeals to you, you can imagine the sort of conversation that might take place between younger you and older you.

Activity: Write a letter to your younger self, as if you were a voice from the future. You can write to your child self or your teenaged self. Try to recall, as specifically as you can, what your life was like back then. If you can remember your age, your grade in school or your teachers, your friends and neighbors, or your favorite activities, you can almost transport yourself back to that time. As you write your letter, remind your younger self about all of your wonderful strengths and characteristics. You might like to offer yourself some advice on how to handle some of the challenges that lie ahead. Be soft-hearted and reassuring toward your younger self, focusing on positive and affirming phrases. What did you need to hear, at that age?

Surprise Opportunity

Live out of your imagination, not your history.—Stephen Covey

This fun activity can help you envision an exciting and unusual future turn of events.

Activity: Imagine that your phone rings 5 years from now. You answer it, and the voice on the other end is someone who is very well known and respected in your field. Perhaps it is someone you greatly admire, or a spokesperson for a specific organization or institution. He or she makes you a fantastic offer related to your music: a new job, a performance opportunity, an award, or some kind of new initiative for which you have been hand-selected based on your reputation and achievements. Write out exactly what the offer is, including as many imagined details as possible. (When will this occur? Where will you be? What will be involved? Why did they choose you?) Feel free to dream big, with no limits or restrictions!

Lifetime Achievement Award

Life's like a movie. Write your own ending.—Kermit the Frog

Imagine a future in which you are still sprightly and healthy at the age of 90. You have been retired for many years, but you have been invited back to an important institution or organization to be granted a lifetime achievement award. This is one of the greatest honors that someone in your field could receive. The people in the audience, those who nominated you, are the people whom you mentored or inspired. They feel great affection for you and will soon give you a standing ovation when you accept your award.

But first, imagine that you are sitting backstage, waiting to walk out and accept the award. An important person is standing at a podium under the stage lights, introducing you. He or she is summarizing, for the audience, all that you achieved during your long and prosperous life. As you listen, you are struck by how much you have accomplished over the years. The announcer mentions your many musical achievements, describes your strengths, explains how you influenced others, perhaps even mentions your family, favorite pastime activities, and what you did to make the world a better place.

> *Activity:* Write out a transcript of this introduction, one that you imagine is being read aloud at the podium. It doesn't have to be lengthy, but should include everything that you would want to hear when you are nearing the end of your life. I have subsequently included some sample prompts in case you have a hard time getting started. You may also choose to think about the people you most admire, if that helps inspire you. In this activity, you should aim as high as possible. This exercise should be uplifting and true to your dreams at this point in your life.

When you are finished, you may choose to reflect on the extent to which you are working toward or away from some of these achievements. Sometimes, thinking in the extreme long term can affect what you do this week to bring yourself closer to that reality. Here are a few examples of sentence starters:

> [*Your name*] was best known for . . .
> [*Your name*] inspired everyone with these musical strengths . . .
> [*Your name*] surprised us all by . . .
> We all learned the following from [*your name*] . . .
> [*Your name*] overcame these obstacles with optimism and grace . . .
> The people whom [*your name*] touched the most include . . .
> The most amazing thing about the life of [*your name*] is that . . . .

Self-Compassion Meditation

The privilege of a lifetime is being who you are.—Joseph Campbell

Self-compassion might be the most challenging habit to pursue, but it can also be the one of the most healing mindfulness practices of a lifetime. Our universal desire is to be free from suffering. Some people believe that compassion is our true nature, and we can return to that state of awareness with regular practice. In a self-compassion meditation, you interact with the part of yourself that cherishes, feels tenderness, and extends loving kindness. It calls for an open mind and heart and a willingness to accept yourself completely as you are. At times, this degree of vulnerability requires great courage and trust. You may find it simplest at first to practice this meditation when you are in a relatively good mood and good health. It will then be easier to practice when you are in pain, unhappy, or going through a difficult time; in other words, those times when you most need to experience self-compassion.

Activity: Relax and prepare yourself to practice mindfulness meditation as discussed in Chapter 7. Focus first on the breath, and on the sensations of the body as you release any excess tension. Observe your thoughts with patience and nonjudgment. As you settle into the natural rhythm of your breath, begin to direct your awareness to yourself as a sentient being. Open to your natural capacity to extend kindness toward yourself. If it helps, you can remember a time when you were exceptionally caring, generous, or tender toward someone else. Or, you may imagine seeing yourself through the eyes of someone who adores you, such as a child or a beloved pet.

As you begin to generate thoughts of compassion and affection, notice how this feels in your body. You might feel a sense of warmth in your core, or a faint tingling sensation, or a subtle calmness of mind. Repeat the following sequence of phrases silently to yourself, as many times as you wish:

> *May I be well.*
> *May I be whole.*
> *May I be at peace.*

You may choose to continue this activity until your meditation ends. If you wish to vary the phrases you repeat to yourself, or if you prefer to contemplate a new statement each time, feel free to create your own. Here are some of my favorites:

> *May I be happy.*
> *May I be safe, protected, and free from harm.*

May I be healthy and contented.
May I live with ease.
May I accept myself wholly.
May I experience the peace of well-being.
May I know my basic goodness.
May I be held in loving kindness.
May I know the joy of being alive.

Activity: Another version of this meditation encourages the practice of compassion on a broader scale. Many people find it easier to extend loving kindness to others, and this meditation can help facilitate genuine awareness and acceptance. In this meditation, as previously, you may repeat a series of phrases to yourself.

First direct your awareness toward yourself, as you repeat the following sequence of phrases in your mind as many times as you like:

May I be well.
May I be whole.
May I be at peace.

Then, bring to mind someone you care deeply about, perhaps a family member or dear friend. As you hold this person in your awareness, repeat the following phrases:

May you be well.
May you be whole.
May you be at peace.

If you like, you may wish to think about someone who plays a more difficult role in your life. This may be someone with whom you've had a recent conflict, or someone who has made you angry or unhappy. If you choose to bring this person into your awareness, you may practice setting your negative feelings aside as you repeat the same phrases several times:

May you be well.
May you be whole.
May you be at peace.

Finally, direct your awareness to a much larger group of people in your environment. This could be your extended family, your neighborhood or town, the country in which you live, or the inhabitants of the world.

> *May we all be well.*
> *May we all be whole.*
> *May we all be at peace.*

***

Congratulations! If you have made it all the way through this book, and even if you have completed only a few of the activities in these last chapters, you have already learned about some of the most important mental skills of performing musicians. Simply reading about these strategies will offer new perspectives that you may not have considered before. The most important thing, however, is to put these skills into practice. Just as you cannot learn to play the hammered dulcimer by reading a book about it, you cannot learn effective mental skills without practicing them as regularly as you practice your music.

The practice of mindfulness—pure, deliberate, nonjudgmental awareness of the present moment—is the journey of a lifetime. Your consciousness will continue to expand as long as you attend to it. There is no limit. If you are open to this awareness, you will continue to become a more conscious musician and human being. I believe the poet Rumi must have been a master of mindfulness, or at the very least, of nonjudgment. He wrote, "Out beyond ideas of wrongdoing and rightdoing there is a field. I'll meet you there. When the soul lies down in that grass the world is too full to talk about." I hope that you and I have met in that field, every now and then, throughout the course of this book. No matter what your musical journey may bring, I honor you.

Don't adventures ever have an end? I suppose not.
Someone else always has to carry on the story.—Bilbo Baggins

REFERENCES

Barbezat, D. P., & Bush, M. (2014). *Contemplative practices in higher education: Powerful methods to transform teaching and learning.* Jossey-Bass.

Benson, H. (2000). *The relaxation response.* New York: William Morrow.

Berenson, G. (2011). Preparation for performance: Ensuring student success. In J. Lyke (Ed.), *Creative piano teaching* (4th ed., pp. 441–464). Champaign, IL: Stipes Publishing.

Berenson, G. et al. (2002). *A symposium for pianists and teachers: Strategies to develop the mind and body for optimal performance.* Dayton, OH: Heritage Music Press.

Bertollo, M., Saltarelli, B., & Robazza, C. (2009). Mental preparation strategies of elite modern pentathletes. *Psychology of Sport and Exercise, 10,* 244–254.

Bishop, S. et al. (2004). Mindfulness: A proposed operational definition. *Clinical Psychology: Science and Practice, 11*(3), 230–241.

Boyd, R. D., & Myers, J. G. (1988). Transformative education. *International Journal of Lifelong Education, 7*(4), 261–284.

Brach, T. (2004). *Radical acceptance: Embracing your life with the heart of a Buddha.* New York: Bantam.

Brown, K. W., & Ryan, R. M. (2003). The benefits of being present: Mindfulness and its role in psychological well-being. *Journal of Personality and Social Psychology, 84*(4), 822–848.

Brown, K. W., & Cordon, S. L. (2009). Toward a phenomenology of mindfulness: Subjective experience and emotional correlates. In F. Didonna (Ed.), *Clinical handbook of mindfulness* (pp. 59–81). New York: Springer.

Carson, R. (2003). *Taming your gremlin: A surprisingly simple method for getting out of your own way.* New York: Quill.

Casals, P. with A. Hahn. (1970). *Joys and sorrows: Reflections by Pablo Casals.* New York: Simon & Schuster.

Chang, J. C., Midlarsky, E., & Lin, P. (2003). The effects of meditation on music performance anxiety. *Medical Problems of Performing Artists, 18*(3), 126–130.

Chödrön, P. (2016). *When things fall apart: Heart advice for difficult times.* Boulder, CO: Shambhala.

Clark, D. B., & Agras, W. S. (1991). The assessment and treatment of performance anxiety in musicians. *American Journal of Psychiatry, 148*(5), 598–605.

Clark, T., & Williamon, A. (2011). Evaluation of a mental skills training program for musicians. *Journal of Applied Sport Psychology, 23*(3), 342–359.

Cornett, V. (2015). Mental skills and music performance: The teacher's role. *American Music Teacher, 64*(4), 28–30.

Cornett, V. (2012 Sept). Nurturing the whole musician: mindfulness, wellness, and the mind-body connection. *MTNA e-Journal,* 15–28.

Cornett, V. (2011). Performance anxiety management. In J. Lyke (Ed.), *Creative piano teaching* (4th ed., pp. 491–509). Champaign, IL: Stipes Publishing.

Cornett, V. (2011). From beta to theta: Human consciousness, hypnotherapy, and music performance. *College Music Symposium,* 49–50, 265–270.

Cox, R. (2007). *Sport psychology: Concepts and applications* (6th ed.). New York: McGraw-Hill.

Csikszentmihalyi, M. (1990). *Flow: The psychology of optimal experience.* New York: Harper & Row.

Cumming, J., & Williams, S. E. (2012). The role of imagery in performance. In S. M. Murphy (Ed.), *The Oxford handbook of sport and performance psychology* (pp. 213–232). New York: Oxford University Press.

De Felice, M. G. (2004). *Mindfulness meditation: A new tool for understanding and regulating musical performance anxiety—An affective neuroscientific perspective.* Unpublished doctoral dissertation, University of Miami.

Driskell, J. E., Copper, C., & Moran, A. (1994). Does mental practice enhance performance? *Journal of Applied Psychology, 79*(4), 481–492.

Dryden, W., David, D., & Ellis, A. (2010). Rational emotive behavior therapy. In K. Dobson (ed.), *Handbook of cognitive-behavioral therapies* (3rd ed., pp. 241–276). New York: Guilford Press.

Emmons, H. (2010). *The chemistry of calm: A powerful, drug-free plan to quiet your fears and overcome your anxiety.* New York: Touchstone.

Forsyth, J., & Eifert, G. (2007). *The mindfulness & acceptance workbook for anxiety.* Oakland, CA: New Harbinger.

Frankl, V. E. (2006). *Man's search for meaning.* Boston: Beacon Press.

Gardner, H. (1993). *Multiple intelligences: The theory in practice.* New York: Basic.

Gawain, S. (2016). *Creative visualization: Use the power of your imagination to create what you want in your life* (anniversary ed). Novato, CA: New World Library.

Germer, C. K. (2009). *The mindful path to self-compassion: Freeing yourself from destructive thoughts and emotions.* New York: Guilford Press.

Gould, D. et al. (2013). Imagery training for peak performance. In J. L. Van Raalte & B. W. Brewer (Eds.), *Exploring sport and exercise psychology* (3rd ed., pp. 52–82). Washington, DC: American Psychological Association.

Gravios, J. (2005). Meditate on it: Can adding contemplation to the classroom lead students to more Eureka moments? *Chronicle of Higher Education, 9,* A10–A12.

Green, B. with W. T. Gallwey. (1986). *The inner game of music.* New York: Doubleday.

Gunaratana, B. (2011). *Mindfulness in plain English.* Somerville, MA: Wisdom Publications.

Gunnlaugson, O., Sarath, E., Scott, C., & Bai, H. (Eds.). (2014). *Contemplative learning and inquiry across disciplines.* Albany, NY: SUNY Press.

Hiroto, D., & Seligman, M. (1975). Generality of learned helplessness in man. *Journal of Personality and Social Psychology, 31*(2), 311–327.

Horan, R. (2009). The neuropsychological connection between creativity and meditation. *Creativity Research Journal, 21*(2), 199–222.

Kabat-Zinn, J. (2005). *Full catastrophe living; Using the wisdom of your own body and mind to face stress, pain and illness.* New York: Cambridge University Press.

Kabat-Zinn, J. (2003). Mindfulness-based interventions in context: Past, present, and future. *Clinical Psychology: Science and Practice, 10*(2), 144–156.

Kee, Y., & Wang, C. (2008). Relationships between mindfulness, flow dispositions and mental skills adoption: A cluster analytic approach. *Psychology of Sport and Exercise, 9*(4), 393–411.

Kirchner, J. M. et al. (2008). The relationship between performance anxiety and flow. *Medical Problems of Performing Artists, 23*(2), 59–65.

Klickstein, G. (2009). *The musician's way: A guide to practice, performance, and wellness.* New York: Oxford University Press.

Knaus, W. J. (2008). *The cognitive behavioral workbook for anxiety.* Oakland, CA: New Harbinger Publications.

Kornfield, J. (2008). *The art of forgiveness, lovingkindness, and peace.* New York: Bantam.

Lehmann., A., Sloboda, J., & Woody, R. (2007). *Psychology for musicians: Understanding and acquiring the skills.* New York: Oxford University Press.

Lin, P. et al. (2008). Silent illumination: A study on Chan (Zen) meditation, anxiety, and musical performance quality. *Psychology of Music, 36*(2), 139–155.

Mah y Busch, J. D. (2014). A pedagogical heartbeat: The integration of critical and contemplative pedagogies for transformative education. *Journal of Contemplative Inquiry, 1,* 113–133.

Maisel, E. (2005). *Performance anxiety: A workbook for actors, singers, dancers, and anyone else who performs in public.* New York: Back Stage Books.

Maltz, M. (2015). *Psycho-cybernetics: Updated and expanded.* New York: TarcherPerigee.

Martin, M. M., & Rubin, R. B. (1995). A new measure of cognitive flexibility. *Psychological Reports, 76*(2), 623–626.

McAllister, L. S. (2012). *The balanced musician: Integrating mind and body for peak performance.* Lanham, MD: Scarecrow Press.

Moore, A., & Malinowski, P. (2009). Meditation, mindfulness and cognitive flexibility. *Consciousness and Cognition, 18*(1), 176–186.

Moore, B. (2011). *Playing your best when it counts (mental skills for musicians)*. Norman, OK: Moore Performance Consulting.

Moran, A. (2012). Concentration: Attention and performance. In S. M. Murphy (Ed.), *The Oxford handbook of sport and performance psychology* (pp. 117–130). New York: Oxford University Press.

Nagel, J. J. (2010). Treatment of music performance anxiety via psychological approaches (a review of selected CBT and psychodynamic approaches). *Medical Problems of Performing Artists, 25*(4), 141–148.

Neff, K. (2015). *Self-compassion: The proven power of being kind to yourself.* New York: William Morrow.

O'Donnell, A. (2015). Contemplative pedagogy and mindfulness: Developing creative attention in an age of distraction. *Journal of Philosophy of Education, 49*(2), 187–202.

Orsillo, S. M., & Roemer, L. (2011). *The mindful way through anxiety.* New York: Guilford Press.

Oyan, S. (2006). *Mindfulness meditation: Creative musical performance through awareness.* Unpublished doctoral dissertation, Louisiana State University and Agricultural and Mechanical College.

Paskin, G. (2005). Interview with Wayne Dyer. Seven secrets of a joyful life. *Family Circle,* June 2005.

Salmon, P. G. (1990). A psychological perspective on musical performance anxiety: A review of the literature. *Medical Problems of Performing Artists, 5*(1), 2–11.

Salmon, P., & Meyer, R. (1992). *Notes from the green room: Coping with stress and anxiety in musical performance.* San Francisco: Jossey-Bass.

Sarath, E. (2006). Meditation, creativity, and consciousness: Charting future terrain within higher education. *Teachers College Record, 108*(9), 1816–1841.

Schoeberlein David, D. (2009). *Mindful teaching and teaching mindfulness: A guide for anyone who teaches anything.* Somerville, MA: Wisdom Publications.

Schons, S. (2011). An introduction to brain research and learning for the piano teacher. In J. Lyke (Ed.), *Creative piano teaching* (4th ed., pp. 477–490). Champaign, IL: Stipes Publishing.

Seligman, M., Maier, S., & Geer, G. (1968). Alleviation of learned helplessness in the dog. *Journal of Abnormal Psychology, 73*(3), 256–262.

Steptoe, A. (1989). Stress, coping and stage fright in professional musicians. *Psychology of Music, 17*(1), 3–11.

Suzuki, S. (2011). *Zen mind, beginner's mind.* Boulder, CO: Shambhala.

Tolle, E. (2008). *A new earth: Awakening to your life's purpose.* New York: Penguin.

Tolle, E. (2004). *The power of now: A guide to spiritual enlightenment.* Novato, CA: New World Library and Vancouver, BC: Namaste Publishing.

Toneatto, T. T., & Nguyen, L. L. (2007). Does mindfulness meditation improve anxiety and mood symptoms? A review of the controlled research. *Canadian Journal of Psychiatry, 52,* 260–266.

Weil, A. (2001). *Breathing: The master key to self-healing.* Louisville, CO: Sounds True.

Werner, K. (1996). *Effortless mastery: Liberating the master musician within.* New Albany, IN: Jamey Aebersold Jazz.

Westney, W. (2003). *The perfect wrong note: Learning to trust your musical self.* Pompton Plains, NJ: Amadeus Press.

Wilson, G. D. (2002). *Psychology for performing artists* (2nd ed.). London: Whurr.

Wristen, B., & Fountain, S. (2013). Relationships between depression, anxiety, and pain in a group of university music students. *Medical Problems of Performing Artists, 28*(3), 152–158.

Wristen, B. (2013). Depression and anxiety in university music students. *Update: Applications of Research in Music Education, 31*(2), 20–27.

Zajonc, A. (2013). Contemplative pedagogy: A quiet revolution in higher education. *New Directions for Teaching and Learning, 134,* 83–94.

INDEX

Note: Boxes are indicated by an italic b following page number

CPSIA information can be obtained
at www.ICGtesting.com
Printed in the USA
BVHW030438260321
603296BV00004B/10